The Angel

from home, to Vietnam, to forgiveness

Jim Stewart

D1738380

BookLocker

BookLocker, St. Petersburg, Florida

Published by BookLocker.com, Inc., St. Petersburg, Florida.

Printed on acid-free paper.

BookLocker.com, Inc.
2020

First Edition

Do not remember the sins of my youth, nor my transgressions; for Your name's sake, O LORD, pardon my iniquity, for it is great. Look on my affliction and my pain and forgive all my sins.

The Angel

Foreword

Many books have been written about this most misunderstood of wars. It seems the men who have come out of this war have all been narrowly stereotyped.

Vietnam was more than just a place that most of us were sent to for a year, and while there, prayed with renewed reverence that we would be returned to "The World" as soon as possible. Most veterans look back at Vietnam, and don't regret their tours of duty and wouldn't change any of it. Good or bad. They also feel they are undeserving of the false stereotypes heaped on them for many years after the end of the war.

Vietnam was the beginning of real-life experiences for many of us. Most of us, from humble beginnings, would experience things that could only strengthen us as human beings. This was true of soldiers from all wars and resulted in a bond and understanding that would reach across time. Did we make mistakes? Sure, we were young. Did we regret some of the things we did? Of course, we did. Men carry guilt with them today because of this.

Some of us spent more than our mandatory one-year tour in country. It was not uncommon to see men extend their tours for another year. The war aside, the country had many things to offer young men whose life experiences were rather modest, and one-dimensional. I went to Vietnam on the largest troop carrier in the world, the U.S.S. Buckner. It was September of 1966. I would return stateside for visits, but called Vietnam my home until July of 1970, and to this day hold the country near to my heart.

This book is not about blood and guts, nor is it a clichéd look at the war. To me there were no "gooks." It was a nation at war, and although I may not have understood it much then, I have come to realize that it was a country fighting for its future. We were part of their struggle whether we accepted that fact, or not. Individually we had a tremendous impact on the country and its people. After all, we were there a long time, and were going to be there forever. Weren't we? We wouldn't turn tail and run. We wouldn't be pushed out and defeated by the communists like the French. We would stay and build. We would always be in Vietnam. Of course, we didn't stay. We left. We looked over our shoulders and hoped it would all just quietly go away and be behind us like a bad dream that never really happened. But it has never gone away. It will always be with us far beyond the dying breath of the last Vietnam vet. The legacy will remain.

For every combat soldier fighting in the jungle and rice paddies there were many more of us in the background, relatively safe from danger supporting their efforts. Although it was a war where there were no front lines, it was also a country where there weren't always guns waiting around every corner to do us harm. During that time soldiers were able to forge relationships and go about their lives in an almost normal fashion.

There were eternal friendships made, relationships built on love, and decisions made that would impact us forever. I have drawn from my own personal experiences, many of them humorous, some of them painful.

Vietnam was a place that changed me forever. Today I'm still not sure how I handled everything that I experienced. I've sat down to write this hoping it will help me, and with the hope that you will understand a little bit more about the other side of Vietnam.

Names have escaped me at times, but characters such as John Prahl, Doug Dragert, Mike Ramirez, Jim Troupe Jim Peterson, Tom Likely and Per A.W. Christiansen are real. I have been able to come in contact with them in recent times, and it has been like talking to long lost brothers.

When we left Vietnam, we all took our own pieces of this country and carried our own individual experiences with us. Some reluctantly chased in the dark by nightmares, others gladly remembering even the toughest of times as the best of times.

There are ghosts that chase us. This is a book of my ghost. My ghost was a little girl. A little girl whose image would cling to me for over 30 years.

Chapter 1

There was a little girl from Saigon She lived far, far away
I wanted to see her one day, But I went far, far astray

I've been fortunate to have traveled many parts of this great country, and the world. But as I think of all the places, I've been I can honestly say to myself that the place where I grew up was nothing short of paradise. Like in the Bible it was a peaceful, beautiful place. An innocent place of good. That's where I grew up. I grew up in paradise.

My little paradise was called Fair Hill. Fair Hill was located about seven miles west of Newark, Delaware on route 273, and about seven miles north of Elkton, Maryland. The famous Mason-Dixon Line was just a few miles north as the crow flies, separating us from Pennsylvania.

Neighbors? Had a few, but only a few back then. The Wilkinson family lived up the road, the Kells across the road, and the Clays right next door. I was lucky enough to be able to share this paradise with my boyhood friend Dee Clay. He was a year younger than me, different in so many ways, yet so alike in our boyish exuberance for adventure.

We even shared a two-car garage with the Clays. It stood between our homes at the end of a gravel driveway. Strangely enough, we also shared the same water and telephone lines. If my dad could hear the water pump running for too long, he would pick up the phone and call over to Mr. Clay, a gentle and soft-spoken man, and tell him to shake the darned handle on their toilet. Half the time Mr. Clay would tell him it must be our toilet that was running, and my dad would apologize, and pass the scorn onto whichever son was within reach.

"Somebody get upstairs and shake the handle, now!"

The telephone situation was the strangest of all. The party line was part of the life of the '50s and early '60s. One ring of the telephone belonged to the Clays. Two rings was our phone, and three rings was for the Kells across the street. If it rang four times it was for the Wilkinson family up the road a bit. Patience was required before picking up a ringing telephone. Snooping on other people's conversations was a great, risky adventure. Fun, too.

When I bought a new *Duane Eddy and the Rebels* record, I would call Dee and hold the phone up to the record player speaker letting him hear a cut. Now, it would have been easier just to walk across the driveway, knock on his door and play it on his record player. But, hey, we had a phone. If we tied up the phone too long Mrs. Kell would come on the line and begin yelling for us to get the hell off. Well, Mrs. Kell never said hell, but you know what I mean. People just didn't cuss in paradise. Well, when I think hard, my dad did sometimes. But I always took his "Jesus H. Christ" more in a biblical sense, than one of anger at me for what sin I may have committed to get his belt snapped at my backside.

Fair Hill was painted with slow rolling hills of wheat and corn surrounded by mile after mile of lush forest. It was country, real country. Most of the land was property of the very rich Dupont family. No housing developments to be seen, but instead, planted fields. It was just acre after acre of virgin wilderness. We had moved there just before my sixth birthday after my dad had landed a good job at the Chrysler parts plant in Newark. My parents moved from Scranton, Pennsylvania in 1950. Dad had escaped the coal mines, but had trouble finding other work in Delaware until he landed this job.

Both my parents dropped out of school when they were in the seventh grade to work and help bring money to their families. Dad was working where he could find it, but there was nothing steady for him. We had been living in a rather run-down house in Iron Hill, Delaware. Dad was struggling trying to land a better paying job, and the job at Chrysler turned out to be a blessing. It had been a real effort for the family at Iron Hill.

The move to Maryland would be a little farther for him to drive, but there would be no more outhouse adventures for us. We had no toilet in the house, and in the winter, it was so cold to venture out that it made you want to just hold it until the spring thaw came.

In those days Chrysler and General Motors employed a lot of men. Fortunately, my dad would be able to carpool with four other workers who drove to work across the state line every day.

Our nicer home was an old two-story house with a massive front and back lawn. It sat atop a huge cellar that housed a large coal furnace. Each winter a coal truck would dump a load of coal into the cement duct abutting the front of the house. It was scary, the amount of flames and heat that furnace put out. To save money in the winter my mom would hang a blanket at the top of the upstairs hall to keep the heat downstairs. We'd just have to cover up when we went to bed. Getting up in the middle of the night was still an experience, but we didn't have that outhouse anymore. The throbbing bladder that I slept with at Iron Hill could now be relieved by tiptoeing on the cold wooden floor to a toilet just down the hall. Ah, indoor plumbing. I could be back in bed under the warm blankets in no time, no time at all.

The cellar was also where dad would breed his beagles. Dad loved his rabbit hunting, and this was another way to make money. I was not allowed to watch. Any image of sex, even animals breeding, was something children were made to turn away from. Often his brother, Uncle Fred, would come and help. Not sure why it took two full grown men to breed two dogs, but I guess that was the wonder of sex. I certainly wondered about it. Till this day I haven't figured it out.

Down there my mom would wring the necks of live chickens and cut their heads off. I could never watch her do it. I didn't think any the worse of my mom for it, as I never looked at it as violence towards animals. Some animals were raised to kill and eat, and we did just that. Mom would make me pluck the feathers. I hated plucking a chicken I had just playfully chased around the yard minutes ago, but I sure didn't mind eating it. Fresh baked chicken was just part of living in paradise.

This cellar was a dark and musty place. Half the time the only light we had dangling over the stairway didn't work, making it an even scarier place for a kid to visit. Whenever I had to go down the stairs I would always whistle nonchalantly. I'm sure this sent the scary things living there scurrying for a darkened corner. During the day mom would wash our clothes in a tub, and I would help carry what she couldn't fit into the clothes hamper out to the backyard. From there we'd hang the clothes on the clothesl i n e for drying. I don't know why, but I used to like watching the clothes flap in the warm summer breeze. It wouldn't take any time for the clothes to dry in the summer. We'd fold them, put them in the hamper, and carry them inside where my mom would do the ironing. During the cold month's things were different. Clothes would be hung inside the house somewhere near a heater vent. Mom would always try to have all the clothes down and ironed before my dad walked through the front door after work.

There was, however, true danger in the house...the attic. It had a small narrow stairway leading up to it from the upstairs hallway. I would carefully, and quietly, push the hatch up and peer wide-eyed in anticipation. I was always waiting anxiously for something to jump out at me. I would never venture any farther than the edge. It just looked too spooky to go any deeper into the darkness than was necessary. Who knows what lived amongst all the cobwebs, and that musty odor? If I was told to store something in the attic it usually wound up along with everything else, close to the edge. I was not about to extend my arms and push a box out of fear of being grabbed by whatever demon surely lurked there.

Danger also lurked menacingly outside intertwined on the wooden fences amidst the honeysuckle and blueberry vines. We were always careful not to touch one rich yellowish/green leaf that gave birth in the spring, and branched out tranquilly, yet menacingly, on the wooden fence posts. A baseball hit into the poison ivy was considered lost, except for one invincible man. Our only saving grace was waiting for my father to get home. He was completely immune to poison ivy and pulled many a baseball from underneath this thicket. The man could have slept on top of the stuff and not have suffered one itch, or rash. When I would try to imitate his bravery and retrieve a ball on my own, I would wind up with poison ivy all over my hands, and up my arms.

If my mom caught me scratching the hives, which would spread it, she would daub my arms, and hands with calamine lotion, place white socks over each hand, and tape them at the wrist. I couldn't get them off. I was unable to dig my nails into the rash, or claw at the agony caused by this poisonous predator. I guess even paradise wasn't completely safe all the time.

The back porch faced directly south toward the cornfields, and beyond the green meadows where Mr. Dupont's Brahma bulls would graze the fertile land nestled against the thick forests. From our back porch we could stand and yell into the woods, and hear our voices echo back at us over, and over again. If my friend Dee was gone for the day I could always play with my echo. But when Dee and I were together (which was almost always) the back woods were our immense playground.

Dee and I would spend many a day in these woods catching frogs, playing army, or cowboys and Indians. We'd always have brown bagged lunches of peanut butter and jelly sandwiches, and apples. In paradise you could drink water from the cool running streams hidden in the forests. We built a fort of sticks and hay, known only to us. For padding we would scavenge pieces of wood by foraging through the corn and wheat fields. We chose a rise in the ground just off an old dirt road. It flattened out up against a chain link fence, and under a humungous oak tree. Nobody could see us. We saw all who approached. No one would have any idea where we hid. I'm sure this fort, our Alamo, is still there after all these years. Unless, of course, Santa Ana found it.

There was nothing like bringing home a jar of tadpoles and presenting them to our mothers as gifts. My mom would smile, act pleased, thank me, but make me take the tadpoles back and release them the next day. That was okay with me though, as tadpoles didn't make very good pets anyhow. Now frogs...

When Dee and I knew our moms weren't pleased with us we'd pick a bouquet of wildflowers, instead of a jar of tadpoles. This would always get us a special treat. Mrs. Clay, Rose as she was called, always had homemade pie cooling on a windowsill . It had never dawned on us that we would have been much better off always bringing them flowers every time. I guess it was the magic that tadpoles held over little boys.

It was tough to get us out of those woods. We could either hear Rose, or my mom, Katie, yelling out for us when it was time to come home for dinner.

"Jimmy, Dee Dee, time to come home!"

We would always hear them the first time but would usually make them yell it out a few more times, especially if we were in a good battle. It was difficult for Davy Crocket, with his Tennessee volunteers, and Texans, to defend the Alamo against the hordes of Santa Ana's charging Mexican army when your mother was yelling for you to come for dinner. However, one booming voice would always get our attention.

"Jimmy!" it was my dad. "You two got five minutes to get your butts up here! Do you hear me?"

Dad was home from work and was ready to eat. We always sat at the dinner table together, but I was still busy on a slope trying to massacre Texans.

"Yipes!" I threw down my musket. "Okay dad, we're coming!" I yelled out.

Dee and I retreated towards the house like a hive of bees was chasing us.

My dad always seemed to be the enforcer, and the protector. Seldom did I hear Mr. Clay yell out, or Dee's mom. When my dad spoke to the both of us, we listened. My dad was not beyond letting Dee know exactly who Jesus H. Christ was.

Food shopping was done on Friday night - every Friday night. If we were down to our last nickel and happened to run out of meat during the week my mom would make us mayonnaise and pepper sandwiches. I still have a fondness for them. If we were really bad off, my dad and I would go to Cochran's General Store down at the crossroads. In those days there were no credit cards. I could see my dad talking to Mr. Cochran while he placed a gallon of milk, some bread, and lunch meat on the counter. Mr. Cochran would write these items down in a book, and my dad would simply go in on payday, and pay him. Paradise.

If dad, or I needed a haircut he would drop mom off at the grocery store. We boys would stop in at Culley's Barbershop in Newark.

Seemed like all the dads hung out there while the moms shopped for food, and each dad knew the other by first name. It was the friendliest of atmospheres, with sports talk ruling the day.

Mr. Culley was an expert with the straight razor. He would wave it about animatedly as he discussed his beloved Baltimore Orioles, pausing to shave fuzz off the back of my dad's neck. I was thrilled when Mr. Culley asked me who my favorite player was.

"Robin Roberts, Mr. Culley. He's the best."

"Ah," waving the straight razor dangerously close to my dad's ear. "You're a Phillies fan? Maybe they'll play my Orioles someday in the World Series?"

Sometimes when only my dad needed a haircut, I would go into the National Five and Dime store. A quarter would buy me five packs of baseball cards. Once inside I would nervously look through all the packs, pinching at each one before buying it, trying to see through the wrapper. If done carefully I could distinguish which baseball players card was on top without opening the pack. If I could recognize the player, and already had a card of him I would pass and go on to the next pack. I loved baseball. The lowly Philadelphia Phillies had been my team. They had been horrid over the years, but they were *my* Phillies.

I would hurriedly buy the packs of cards, run outside, and sit on the bench next to the barber pole. Each pack was slowly, and carefully peeled open. This could lead to glee, or total disappointment. How many duplicate Granny Hamner cards did I need when I didn't have one single Robin Roberts card? Now, I loved Granny Hamner, but already had five of his cards back home in a shoe box. I also prayed there were no other player cards in the pack that I already at home. I'd slowly remove each card in the pack, with great anticipation about the next card in line.

It was a great day when most of the cards were ones that I didn't already have. It was an even greater day when I got my first Robin Roberts card.

After dad's haircut we'd pick up mom and head home with the groceries. I'd spend the entire ride home looking at each card, front and back, putting my face on the card. I would close my eyes and throw an inside fastball to Duke Snider, striking out that hated Brooklyn Dodger. It was a good ride home.

We didn't need to go away to go camping. We had our backyards.

Many a hot and humid Saturday night was spent lying in the backyard on a blanket, looking up at a clear star-spangled sky. Of course, this was after catching a jar full of fireflies, and putting them next to us to light up the darkness. Sometimes the moon would be so full and bright we wouldn't need the fireflies. Our sleeping bags were blankets thrown on the grass. If we were hungry, the refrigerators were just a stone's throw away.

If we were lucky, we could arrange a good game of hide and seek with the Kell brothers, Matt and Mike, and the Wilkinson kids, Jay and Erin. Erin was probably twelve years old, tall and thin with her hair always in a ponytail. Having Erin with us was a treat because she had 'boobies', as we called them. We weren't quite sure what they were for, but they were always a good topic of conversation when she wasn't around. The only drawback to having her sit around with us was that we couldn't have fart contests.

It was perfect. We kids were not burdened with the problems of our parents.

I do know that mom and dad were not always able to keep up with the $50.00 a month rent, but my concern over hearing this was always soothed with, "Jimmy, go out and play." And go out and play I did.

My mother's favorite saying was "In, or out? Which is it?"

I knew what she meant. She meant 'out'. Out of the house, and that's where Dee and I spent our time. Out in paradise.

Dee and I would be around each other from the first grade until I went into the Army in 1966. Good buddies as we were, Dee and I weren't without early challenges to our friendship. The first year together we had our share of fights and wrestling matches. Usually one good bite on the arm from Dee would send me home screaming in tears to my mother. One day my mother told me that I would never be allowed back in the house again with a bite mark unless I punched Dee in the nose after he bit me.

Now what kind of a predicament was that for a six-year-old? Fight, or be homeless. I could live with the bites and the bite marks because

Dee and I would make up within a few days, but could I live with my mother and her whacking me in the back of the head if I didn't mind her? I guess I'd have to wait until the time came, which was about once a week. Hey, boys fought.

"You stink!" Dee picked up one of my plastic army men and threw it at me.

It missed me and bounced off the tree I was leaning against. "No, no, you stink, and you have big cooties too!"

Dee, walking on his knees, moved in closer to my face. "You have bigger cooties, and your breath stinks this much!" Dee held his hands far apart.

That was it for me. I grabbed Dee around the neck, and he grabbed me around the waist. We rolled over on the ground, let go, and got to our feet. Dee ran in and grabbed me around the waist again as I pulled on his ears. Who could throw who to the ground?

"You better let go!"

"No, you! You smell like farts!"

"Farts? I'm gonna wring your neck, Dee Clay!"

We looked like two leprechauns slow dancing for the first time as we tripped over one another and fell to the ground. Then it happened. Dee opened his mouth wide and began searching with it. Where was something to bite? Where, where? Finally, like Dracula he found his mark on my shoulder and bit down. I screamed and let go of him.

"You asshole!" I screamed out. This shocked him as much as the fight, and he recoiled with a surprised look on his face.

"Oh, I'm gonna tell your mom you just cussed!"

I reached up and felt my shoulder for blood. Then I thought back to what my mother had said. I looked Dee in the face.

"Sorry." I said.

He looked at me quizzically. "Sorry for what?"

"This!" I balled up my fist and whacked him right in the nose. I'm sure Joe Louis would *not* have been proud of me, but it was the best I could do. After all, I was punching my best friend because my mom told me, not because I really wanted to.

Dee grabbed his nose and his eyes began to water. A little drop of blood came out of a nostril. Dee brought his fingers down and looked at the drops of blood. He didn't seem to know what to do. I'm not sure he had ever seen his own blood before.

I looked at him, waiting. We were in trouble now. Dee was still exploring the red on his fingertips. He gave me a puzzled look, his eyes filling with tears.

Simultaneously both of us began bawling, got up and ran screaming toward our houses. I ran up the back porch and into the kitchen. My mother heard me and came running into the kitchen.

"What in God's name happened, what happened?"

"I punched Dee in the nose."

"Did he bite you?"

"Yes, look at my shoulder." Dee had not drawn blood but left only a few 'fang' marks.

"How hard did you hit him?"

"I made his nose bleed."

I saw my mom trying to hide her smile. "Well, I'd better call Mrs. Clay. You go upstairs, wash your shoulder, and I'll fix you a sandwich."

"A sandwich? You're not going to spank me?"

"No, you did what I told you."

"Then why was I crying when I came in here? I was crying so you'd feel sorry for me getting Dee's nose bloody."

"Here, take the fly swatter and go out on the porch and kill some flies. You can wash up later. I don't think Dee has rabies."

"Rabies, what are rabies?"

"Never mind. Out! Out! Kill flies."

"Okay but make sure you ask Mrs. Clay for sure about that rabies thing."

I would spend the next half hour swatting flies. Our screen door was always covered with them. It was a punishment of sorts by my mom, but I didn't mind. I would make a game out of it. I was the fighter pilot attacking enemy soldiers. The swatter was my machine gun.

This wouldn't be Dee's last bite and it wouldn't be his last bloody nose. But the good far outweighed the bad in paradise. By tomorrow we'd be arm-in-arm heading out to the fort we had built, and I would be back trying to slaughter those Texans. He'd be Davy Crockett in his coonskin cap, and I'd have to settle for the Mexican army, but that was good too.

Ours was a childhood of play. Forts, tadpoles, fart contests and paradise.

Chapter 2

We never strayed far from home in those days. There were no superh i g h w a y s , and no 70 mph speed limits. As a matter of fact, 55 mph was downright foolish on many of the twisting, windy back roads that we traveled getting from point A to point B. Those roadways, and the lack of money, were the major reasons we didn't wander far from home. It just took way too long, and cost too much. It was money that we just didn't have.

Most of dad and mom's relatives still lived in Scranton, Pennsylvania.

Scranton was about 175 miles from our house, as the crow flies, but it might as well have been like traveling to Mars, with all the back roads we had to take. As much as possible though we'd try to have a yearly visit with one another.

One year our family would make the trek, the next Uncle Halley and Aunt Helen, my mom's sister and her husband, would put as many cousins as they could in their station wagon, and make the trip down to our place.

Now, Aunt Helen had 11 kids. (She had given birth to 12 but one died at birth). Needless to say, it was harder for them to come see us than it was for us to go up and see them.

Dad usually had mercy on them as someone in their gaggle would have to be left behind. I had a mad crush on my cousin Beth, and certainly was supportive of my dad when he said that we should go up and see them instead. I couldn't stand the thought of having them visiting us and finding out that Beth was one of the ones left behind. That was unacceptable. Plus, Scranton was a big city, and there was much more to do to keep the kids busy while the adults visited.

We'd have the station wagon packed and leave early, usually around 7:00 in the morning. Our trip took us north through the back roads to Lancaster, Pennsylvania. I would sit in the back seat of the car, play with my baseball cards, and marvel at the beauty of the Amish countryside, with their immaculate handsome wooden framed houses, on perfectly manicured fields.

We'd always stop and eat at dad's favorite diner. We'd arrive early enough that breakfast was still being served. Each table in the diner had a small jukebox on it, and I would leaf through the selections looking for a favorite tune. I was usually given a nickel to choose three songs as we waited for our food. Mom always wanted me to waste one of my three selections on a Pat Boone song. Ugh! Well, it *was* her money. She'd usually have to settle for Elvis, who she loved anyways, plus two other selections of my choice. One was usually 'Rebel Rouser' by Duane Eddy and The Rebels, and 'Raunchy' by Bill Justis. Dad usually read the paper while mom ordered food and I lost myself in the music.

After breakfast, we were back on the road for the longest part of the journey.

Slow winding roads north to Allentown, and then Redding. We knew we were almost there when we'd hit the Joe Palooka Mountains and dropped down into the town of Wilkes Barre. We'd usually arrive in the late afternoon around three o'clock, or so. Once at my Aunt Helen's house it was time to be spoiled with love and hugs. I would follow cousin Beth around as if she were the most famous of movie stars. My plan was to marry Beth. What did I know?

As I got older, I started playing Little League baseball. My dad was my manager and coach. He'd spend time in the front yard squatting down and catching my pitches. He really wanted me to be a pitcher like himself. Dad had played minor league ball for a team in Scranton and had been offered a contract with the Boston Red Sox. At that time his choice was baseball, or my mother. He chose my mom. The result was me. Good choice.

After throwing way too many pitches out of his reach, or over his head, he decided that pitching was not the answer. I knew he didn't want me to be a pitcher because he kept saying, "Jesus wept, Jimmy!" I guess I also made Jesus cry.

I wound up at shortstop and hit sixteen home runs in fourteen Little League games. I *was* growing at an alarming rate and dwarfed many of my teammates. I continued with Little League and then gave up playing in the Babe Ruth league when I saw my first good curveball. Suddenly, a baseball career was looking quite dim.

Dee was never an athlete. I admired how smart he was, as he always did well in school. Dee's parents put him in a Catholic school, while I went to public school. One day he was given a fine Gretsch guitar by his parents. He brought it over as soon as he got it and played the only chord he knew. Was the guitar going to separate us the way my baseball playing had separated us? I hadn't thought about it, but now was concerned and a little jealous.

"Jimmy, you got to get one, too. I don't want to play by myself. We could help each other learn."

"My mom and dad don't have any money. I'll never be able to have one." Dad and mom walked in my room, and watched Dee clumsily play his chord, fiddling with different strings, trying to put together a melody.

"We heard somebody playing a guitar. Can you play something?"

"Well, not yet, Mrs. Stewart. I've got a book and all. I'm going to have to start practicing a lot. Maybe Jimmy can get one too? Maybe him and me can practice together and teach each other." Dee looked up at my mom pleadingly. Dee was begging for me the only way he knew.

Mom and dad just turned and walked out of the room. I turned to Dee quickly.

"Dee Dee, you've got to practice here all the time. You've got to come here so, they'll hear you playing. Maybe they'll hear how good you are getting, and I'll get one too?"

For one solid week Dee came to my room, sat down, and we practiced. At first, I just listened, and then Dee taught me a few chords. I even called my parents in and let them hear how I was doing. My dad would always stand silently, hands on hips, listen for a moment and then walk away without a word. Mom was encouraging, but I could see sadness in both their eyes. I knew they couldn't afford a guitar for me. Dee continued to practice at my house, and we got better every day.

Dad and mom watched and listened as we progressed. Most of the time I sat and watched hopelessly when Dee played. I knew this was going to break up our friendship. Dee was totally into his guitar playing now, and I was just a sad sack cheerleader. My life was ruined. A few weeks passed and suddenly Dee stopped coming to the house to practice. I was crushed.

"Jimmy, time to get up! Time for breakfast!" My mom was yelling from downstairs in the kitchen. I rubbed my eyes and went into the bathroom to pee.

"Jimmy, hurry up now!" It was Saturday. What was the big deal about breakfast?

I washed my hands, and stumbled off towards the top of the stairway, still half asleep. As I looked down the flight of stairs my eyes burst open like old fashioned flash bulbs exploding at the academy awards. There it was! At the bottom of the stairway, propped up against the wall, was a guitar.

A beautiful sunburst color leaning up against the wall in *my* house. *My* guitar! My legs shook as I grabbed onto the banister to keep from falling down the stairs. It was beautiful. Cousin Beth was not as beautiful as this thing before me. Nope, no, no way. My dream of marrying my cousin was dwarfed by the thought of picking up this beauty before me.

On wobbly knees I poured down the stairs like melting ice cream, unable to catch my breath. My mouth was agape, and I was speechless. Surely my heart would pound its way out of my chest. I could feel the buttons on my shirt jumping and straining against the thread. I got to the bottom of the stairs and dropped to both knees as if worshipping some ancient god.

My mom and dad stood in the dining room looking in at me smiling that smile that only parents can when they've made their kids happy. My dad had his hands on his hips, my mom had her arms folded in front of her. My mouth was still wide open, but words were still not coming forth. Drool poured down my chin from my mouth being open for too long and not swallowing. I looked at my guitar in awe, looked at my parents and back at the guitar. I was gonna pass out. This was impossible. I had to be dreaming.

"Well, it ain't gonna play itself." mom said.

My hand shaking, I grabbed the guitar by its neck and looked at the name engraved on the head....Fender. I turned again and looked at my parents, still speechless.

My dad looked at me quizzically. "Are you retarded?"

"Well, Jimmy, if you stay down on the floor long enough with it, I guess you're gonna have to name it. You gotta name for it?" I looked at my mom.

"Beth."

Dad started to smile as he turned to mom and said, "I told you he liked her."

"Jimmy, you need to get that over to Dee Dee's and start practicing. Don't you think?" Mom unfolded her arms.

I grabbed Beth by the neck and streaked out the front door leaving mom and dad in my wake. Like a woman being chased by a robber I frantically banged on Dee's front door. Mrs. Clay opened the door and glared at me.

"Jimmy Stewart, whatever are you doing pounding on our door like that?" Then she saw the guitar. "Oh, my! Oh, my! Dee Dee! Dee Dee, come quick, Jimmy's got a guitar!"

I could hear Dee rumbling toward the door. He took one look at me and let out a holler.

"Yahoo! We're gonna be famous! We're gonna be rock and roll stars!"

I spent the rest of the day and night with Dee. He taught me how to tune it, strum it and play a couple more chords. We would spend every spare moment after school strumming, inventing, and listening to the radio trying to imitate the sounds we heard.

My love affair with cousin Beth was now officially over. I had a new girl in my life. Her name was also Beth. Beth, the Fender guitar. There was no room for any real girl in my life now. Who needed girls? Dee and I were in love with our guitars, and that was all that mattered. We listened mostly to Duane Eddy and the Rebels in the beginning. Dee was hooked on Chet Atkins and picked up finger picking just like Chet. Our first gig was as a duo at a wedding on a farm. Our first pay was a free chicken dinner. Well, even famous people had to start somewhere.

How I became Honey.

I was terrible in school. I don't know if I had a learning disorder, was just too lazy, or a combination of the both, but probably more the latter. Playing my guitar didn't pique my interest in scholarly things, that's for sure. So, I got the brilliant idea in the 9th grade that I would take algebra. Yep, convoluted form of math that I'm not sure anyone would ever understand, or even use after graduation. But……. I chose to give it a try. The algebra teacher was Mr. Blankenship. He was of a feminine persuasion, especially in his manner of speech.

After writing a long, long, long unsolved equation on the blackboard (had to have stretched ten feet). He turned, and with a smile and his demure tone, with somewhat of a southern draw he asked:

"Who wants to come up here and solve this?"

Foreheads slammed into their desks. All except one. Believe me I was just late in doing so. He must have thought I was actually interested in the challenge. Pointing his chalk at me.

"Come up here, you can do it."

This man was nuts if he thought I was the answer. I struggled out of my desk and meandered to the board. This was going to be brutal. I stood with hands on hips, scrolling left to right wondering who the hell invented this crap. He handed me the chalk and I took it without even looking at him, still transfixed at the gibberish on the board.

I could have stood there until the bell rung, but we had at least another half hour of time left in this class. Left, right, left, right my head turned. I even let out a fake "hmmm" feigning that I might have an answer.

Mr. Blankenship cleared his throat. My classmates had to have known what was coming. I think I even heard a fart, but that might have just been imagination, or maybe it was me.

I wrote on the board………'3/4'.

17

He shook his head, startled that I even knew how to write that and said it. Yes, he said it. It would stick with me from 9th grade through my senior year and many reunions afterwards.

"Now, **honey**, you know that's not right."

The room exploded. I didn't want to turn around. I'm sure the Principal heard the laughter 50 yards down the hall. I expected him to arrive at the door at any moment wondering what the heck had just happened. It seemed like the laughter lasted the rest of the class as I sheepishly turned, red-faced, and walked back to my chair, but.......it became a term of endearment, not meant as an insult, and I was no longer Jim. I was Honey. It would be in my yearbook and it would just be, well, natural. I sort of liked it. I guess if the rest of the kids didn't like me that would have bullied me, but that wasn't the case.

Honey Stewart………. yeah!

In 1963 we moved away from Fair Hill to a house on Cowentown Road a few miles away. Dee and I continued to live, eat and drink rock 'n' roll. From our earliest group, The Mark IV Trio, The Checkmates, The Roy Cantler Combo, and finally The Sabres, with the *sharpest sound around*. There wasn't a Roy Orbison, Beatles, or Rolling Stones song that we couldn't match perfectly. All was well, all was well. We played every military club, bar and night club from Newark to Aberdeen, Maryland.

I could hardly drag myself out of bed some mornings to go to school after finishing a gig that got me home at two in the morning. As a matter of fact, I mostly didn't. School was getting in the way. All I wanted to do was play my guitar.

I didn't know it, but my *Life of Reilly* was about to be turned upside down. Like a thief in the night, all the peace and satisfaction were going to be stolen from me. Tragedy was going to enter stage left, and paradise was about to become a horrible nightmare of events.

Chapter 3

In 1963 my dad fell off his bike at work and got a nasty bump on his leg. The injury turned his calf all black and blue. He wound up going to the doctor when the bump wasn't healing right and was diagnosed with leukemia. Dad was told that he might have a year to live.

Now I had two brothers. One, John, graduated from Elkton High when I started first grade, so I don't have much recollection of him at the time. He was a stud, worshipped by my father. I guess a chip-off-the-old-block. He went into the Air Force and off into the world, returning only rarely to visit. Bob was only three years older than me, quiet, and into cars, girls, and dancing at the hop. He had joined the Air Force right after graduating in 1961 and was stationed in Bangor, Maine.

It left my mom and me to care for dad. Dad worked a few months but got weaker and wound up back in the hospital then released to back home. Mom found a job and went to work while I attended school and played in the band. My love for music helped me deal with the pressure of knowing my dad was dying. As often as he could, health allowing, he would come and hear the band play. He would even dance with mom to her favorite song, *Mona Lisa.*

Dad had always been an outdoorsman, fisherman, and hunter. His favorite had to be deer hunting. I can still smell the venison that my mom used to cook for hours over an open flame to get the meat just tender, and juicy enough.

As ill as he was, he was still able to maintain his dignity. He didn't ask for help if he was having problems getting out of his favorite chair. When his legs were a little wobbly, or he was a little dizzy, he merely grabbed onto something near him until the feeling passed. He was determined to get in his deer hunting, and he swore that he would never go back to the hospital…never.

We had the luxury of hunting on DuPont's land. I had spent some time trying to eradicate the ground hogs that called the rolling hillsides home. The holes they dug were a menace to his cattle, and the beautiful horses that he rode when fox hunting. If I kept the ground hog population down, we would have carte blanche rights to hunting when deer season came about.

Much of his land was isolated from the public behind tall chain link fences.

The roads were mostly just dirt, not many paved. We would travel the same isolated roads to a perfect spot where dad knew the deer migrated. At daybreak they would come out of the shelter of the woods to forage the corn and wheat fields, nibbling on any berries that clung to the wooden fences.

Dad always chose the early morning hours to hunt. We'd leave at five a.m., situate ourselves in one spot, and just wait for daybreak. My brother Bob, on leave from the Air Force, had driven us there. Bob got out of the car, teeth chattering with a coffee mug in his hand, and opened the tail gate of the station wagon. I got out, helping to take out the guns. Dad would get himself out of the car.

"Jimmy, one of us has to stay with dad." Bob whispered. "What for?"

"Don't be stupid. He needs to be watched. You can do it. Just take him to a spot and pretend to leave, but don't go too far. Keep him in your sight. Got it?" My brother looked petrified.

"Yeah, just watch him, right?"

"Right. If there's a real problem fire three rapid shots in the air, and I'll come runnin'."

Dad slowly got out of the passenger side of the car and stood upright. He looked stiff and sore. He pulled the earflaps of his hunting cap down over his ears to ward off the morning chill, as a jet of frost came from his mouth. His skin was pale and his cheeks sunken.

"You boys ready to go?" He had a childish look of excitement about him. He was, after all, going hunting. Something he loved to do.

"Dad, Jim is going to go with you over towards the wood line to the north there. I'm going to go farther south and plant myself there.

Jim can then scoot into the woods south of you, come around, and maybe scare them out of the woods towards us."

Dad looked at me. "You don't have to make a bunch of noise. Just walk. They'll hear you. You want to keep track of where you are. There's a stream in there. Follow it for a way, turn left and then slowly make your way back. They'll hear you and hopefully walk out towards us. Don't spook 'em, just walk slowly."

"Yes, sir." Dad picked up his Remington 308, threw it over his shoulder and looked at me.

"Ready?"

"Sure, pop."

We walked off silently. I looked worriedly over my shoulder at Bob. I could see the concern on his face. Dad had called him up at Bangor telling him he wanted to go deer hunting. Bob had taken leave. I could see no happiness in Bob's eyes as he watched dad walking away from him. He would be home for one week, and it would be the last time he would see his father alive. The man who had taught him everything he knew about his hot rod '56 Chevy, would not be there when he came home the next time.

Dad walked slowly, very slowly, and I could see he was ever alert to his surroundings. I could tell he was plotting the hunt.

"Jimmy, there it is." Dad stopped like a finely trained pointer looking off in the distance. I looked around confused thinking he had spotted some deer.

"Where?" I felt foolish that I couldn't see what he was seeing. Whispering, "There's where I want to go. That's the spot."

He pointed to an area of woods where several trees had fallen. There were no overhanging branches to get in the way and it would give him just enough cover so that the deer wouldn't spot him. He could get off a clear shot from this spot.

He picked up his pace just a bit. He was an excited kid for the moment, but he struggled. Struggled like the aging baseball player who stuck around and played a few extra years when he should have hung up his cleats. How much did I really know about this man? Did grandpa take him hunting? As a little boy did, he run home, grab his bb gun and then head off to shoot at things real or imaginary? Did he

21

have a buddy and an Alamo? I had never asked. Would I have the time to? Would I have the courage to?

"Yep, that's it."

It was still dark, and I could see his labored breath in the cold air as he walked ahead of me. Dad picked out a large tree stump that was hidden partially from view from the open field in front of him. There was enough foliage around him that he blended in perfectly.

"Okay, Jimmy, go back to that spot in the tree line and bring 'em to me."

"Okay, but yell if you need anything." Dad didn't respond. The last thing he would do is yell out for help.

I slowly walked back toward the thick tree line. The stream he talked about snaked from the open field and disappeared into the thick shrubbery, tall oaks, and maples. I walked a few yards into the tree line and found a spot where I could watch dad through the opening in the trees. He had his back to me and was sitting quietly. What was going through his mind? The sun would be rising shortly, and I would just hope that something came along. I wasn't about to leave him to himself.

Sunrise was coming. I could see a brilliant orange glow highlight the horizon over dad's head. The orange rays looked like thousands of grains of sand filtering through the morning mist. As the sun got closer to fully rising the temperature began to change dramatically. The chill air started to lift, and a heavy cloud of mist rose from the damp grass.

Dad hadn't moved much, except for an occasional glance from right to left.

He was still quite disciplined. He knew he had to stay quiet, very, very quiet.

The first rays of sunlight began to caress the landscape. I could smell the freshness in the air. If there was a rebirth, it was happening now under God's control. He seemed to be giving dad a perfect morning for his last hunt.

Sleep was trying to overtake me. I rubbed my eyes with both hands and looked out again towards the tree line to the north. My eyes opened wide at the wonder of a big gray buck silhouetted against the green backdrop of the forest, standing all alone, majestic, and proud looking. He was so still he looked like a statue that had been purposely placed there a few feet from the safety of the tree line. The sun reflected brightly off his huge antlers.

The buck snorted and pushed his nose upward to the sky. He was looking, smelling for anything. Just a hint of anything that would be a threat to his family, who was surely hiding out of sight in the trees just a few feet from him. I glanced toward my father. His head was now turned to the right, and he was eyeing the deer, perfectly still. I could hear my own heart pounding inside my chest.

The five-pointer took a few more cautious steps out into the open field. I could see steam rising from his damp back. Then out they came. At first, one cautious doe, then another several feet behind her. I tried to control my breathing and glanced quickly at my father who was motionless, his head still facing the buck. One, two, three, four, five does. Another young spike walked onto the field followed by a sixth and seventh doe. All alert, all trusting the head of their family to keep a sharp eye, to keep them safe.

They began grazing, except for the big buck. He was still cautious, still vigilant, but I could tell that they were feeling safer, much safer. The buck kept alert and as the others grazed, he started walking towards my father, stopping every few feet to survey his surroundings. Dad was rigidly still, careful not to move a muscle. Now it was my dad who looked like a statue had been placed in the field.

Nothing else was happening in the world for him right now. This was so surreal to me at that moment. It wasn't real life, but some slow-motion vision, some dream I was having. It was so beautiful and peaceful. It was perfect.

The buck snorted again and continued walking slowly towards my dad. It was the perfect time for him. The buck couldn't have been any farther than 20 yards away. This was a shot my dad could have made with his eyes shut. What was he waiting for?

I heard a deer call. It was that clicking sound my dad had tried to teach me but had never been able to duplicate. It made the deer stop and take notice. The big buck looked inquisitively in the direction of my father. His eyes were searching in front of him. The other deer looked up casually but continued to forage for food. Dad made the sounds again. The buck walked about five more yards straight towards my father and stopped. The perfect shot, so easy. What was he doing?

Dad certainly would not have buck fever. He was a seasoned hunter. Buck fever was a mixture of pure awe, fear, and confusion when seeing your first buck out in the open. I had gotten it on my first hunt and my nervousness, indecision, and stumbling had cost me a shot. By the time I had noisily raised my rifle to my shoulder the buck had disappeared.

The defensive buck continued to inch his way toward my father's position.

He finally stopped about 10 yards in front of my father, snorted, and tossed his head up in the air. He hadn't yet seen the danger that was sitting in front of him but sensed something.

My dad stood up from the stump he was sitting on. The deer's front shoulders quaked, and his knees buckled in fright, but he righted himself and stood defiantly before my father. I couldn't be seeing this. They stood there motionless before one another. I could hear my father's voice, but he was talking softly. I couldn't hear what he was saying. Then all got very quiet.

"Hyah!" shouted my dad, weakly flailing his arms in the air.

The big buck turned tail and ran back to his herd, and just as quickly they all disappeared into the woods. The whole world fell still and perfectly silent. As I looked back my dad was again sitting on the stump. His chin was now down on his chest. I began to move toward him, worried, but then his head came back up. I stopped and watched as he looked upward to the fading moon that was still overhead.

I then knew that my dad was making peace. Peace with this great animal that had stood before him, and peace with his world. I thought how much he and the buck were alike; strong, proud, protector of their family. Maybe he was apologizing. If only I could have heard his words. I would never be able to express to my dad that I had been watching. This was his private moment that he wanted, and I needed to let him have it in confidence. I began to sob and had to put my hand over my mouth in fear that he would hear me.

I stood up straight and tried to compose myself. I couldn't go to him now. It was too soon. Better to just let this pass and let him do what he needed to do. I needed to let him decide when this was over.

After a few moments' dad got up, turned, and started to walk slowly back to the car. He would kill no deer today. I saw him stumble and right himself. I wouldn't go yet. He mustn't have any idea that I knew what had just happened. I would wait around a few minutes, or so, and catch up to him.

When I got back to the car dad was already leaning up against the hood sipping on coffee from his thermos cup, smoking a cigarette.

"Hey, what happened? I walked back out toward you, and you were gone? I wasn't having much luck herding those deer. Did you see any?"

He looked at me and gave a weak smile. "Oh, you did well. A big five-pointer walked out toward me. He looked at me, I looked at him, and I'll be god darned if he didn't just turn and high tail it into the woods before I could get off a shot. That buck was pretty smart today, I gotta say. And, you know, I think I've somewhat lost my appetite for deer meat anyway. Let him go make some more babies, and the hunting will be ripe for us next year." Dad sat down on the passenger side seat of the car and took another sip of coffee.

"We need to get your brother back here. Think you can find him?"

"Oh, yeah." I stepped away from the car and fired three rapid rounds into the air.

Dad made a startled attempt to rise but sat back down in discomfort.

"Jimmy, Jesus H. Christ, what the hell are you doing?"

"Well, Bob and I have a signal. This is it. This will get him here."

My dad didn't say anything else but took another sip of his coffee. I could see Bob frantically running up the dirt road. I knew that he thought something awful had happened to dad. I started waving both arms in the air.

"Everything's okay," I shouted to him. "Everything's okay." I started jogging toward him so dad wouldn't hear.

Bob was totally winded. "What the hell!"

"Hey, let's just get dad home and I'll explain it all later. Everything's all right."

Bob shook his head and we walked back to the car. He acted casual and looked at dad as he opened the tail gate of the car. "You wanna' head on out?"

"Yeah, that sounds good. I'm tired. Let's go home." Dad threw his cigarette to the ground, put it out with his boot, slowly placed his legs inside the car, and closed the passenger side door.

Bob whispered as he closed the tail gate, "What's gotten into him?"

"Peace. You're not going to believe what I'll tell you later, but I think he just made peace."

Bob looked more confused, patted me on my left shoulder. "Let's take him home."

At the end of the week Bob reported back to his duty station in Bangor, Maine. This would also be dad's last hunting trip. The buck would go on to make more babies, as my dad had said, and some of them would grow up to be five-pointers. Some would live out long lives, some would be hunted, but none of them would wind up in mom's pot. We had savored our last sweet taste of venison.

During the early months of 1964 my dad's leukemia got worse. As he got weaker, he could not even get out of bed to go to the bathroom. We had moved a single bed of my brother's down into the dining room, as he was unable to walk up the stairs. We had to clean him up if he messed himself. Being a proud man, I knew this really bothered him. This was his lowest point.

"Jimmy, you have to help me."

He would pull back the sheets and show me how he had messed himself. I wouldn't say anything or try to show any disgust. I didn't know what to say. I knew it was better for him if I didn't speak. Just get the soap, cloth, pan of water, and clean him up. There was no 'thank you' from him. I knew he was hurting. He just looked away and rolled on his side when I was finished. He knew he was dying. As he laid facing away from me, I could see his spine trying to protrude through his back. He was so thin. His hair was so thin, dirty and unkempt, so unlike him.

He was always a big impressive sturdy fellow. He would have normally carried about 190 pounds on his 6' 2" inch athletic frame. He was the stereotype of a 'man's man' in those days. Always strict, reserved and quiet, but a quick wit when he did choose to joke around. Under that manly, often gruff demeanor, was a kind soul.

My mind drifted as I sat next to him. I thought back to when I was a kid getting into typical kid mischief around the house that my mom considered bad enough to hand the discipline over to him.

I could see my mom standing in the dining room with her finger in my face, shouting, "Wait until your father gets home! You just wait!"

My mother would threaten me, wagging that finger of hers. Most of my crimes around the house were simple infractions, with an occasional misdemeanor thrown in by me. The spanking type discipline would be taken care of by my father. I would have to sit in the living room and wait for him. Arriving home from work he'd walk through the front door with his lunch pail and large thermos, smell what was cooking, nod a greeting to me, and walk into the kitchen where mom was making dinner.

I could hear my mom chattering unremittingly as she laid out my crimes to him. I knew it would only be a matter of seconds for him to come around the corner, belt in hand. My timing was always perfect. I would hear the rushed footsteps, and when I saw the first leg appear around the corner, I'd up and flee, up the stairs on all fours with the snap of the belt behind me. He was lucky if he got in a good one, most of them hitting the bottom of my pant legs. Having escaped mostly unscathed, but scared, I knew I was upstairs and restricted for the rest of the evening. I'd better not make a peep.

In the evening as I lay in bed, I could hear my door creak open slowly, as the light from the hall filtered in slightly. I never saw the intruder, but I could hear the slow shuffling of someone crawling on hands and knees. Closer and closer, until I was attacked with his tickling hands. I would laugh until I cried, I was so ticklish, and then without out a word, the intruder would be gone. I was probably too young at the time to appreciate it but looking back his love for me was obvious. I'm also sure that those misses with his belt were more by his design than my swiftness.

Now he lay before me, an empty shell. His body racked by a disease that would have no compassion for him. The mercy he had shown to the five-pointer would not be given to him. It would kill him and kill him in the most unmerciful of ways.

As my dad grew worse our beagle, Duke, got run over by a car out in front of our house. He was our only dog now, descendent from dogs bred by my dad when we lived at Fair Hill. I remember we had Gypsy, and after she died, we had Betty. They produced a lot of good hunting dogs. Duke was the heir of Betty. Duke had been taught to hunt by my dad.

In the spring we'd tie a long string around a dead rabbit to teach the pups scent. We'd drag the rabbit around the yard with them happily barking, as they clumsily chased after it. It was just a game to the pups, but it turned them all into good rabbit dogs. When dad got sick, he could no longer look after the mating and upkeep of the dogs, so he had sold all except his favorite, Duke.

I went outside to the backyard to see our neighbor, Mr. Mench, who was watching over the dog. Duke didn't look in pain but was sitting funny off to one side. I could see his breathing was labored and there were drops of blood coming out of his penis.

"Jimmy, I think he's probably got a broken leg, and with that bleeding he's probably got internal injuries as well."

I reached down and gently stroked Duke on his head. He was a good dog, with a broad forehead, and those perfect beagle ears. A typical beagle that was rambunctious, craved attention, and most importantly, a good chase.

Duke became more the family pet than a hunter. He spent his days being lazy and begging us, with his bark, to take him into the fields so that he could explore. There was no hedgerow he wouldn't poke his nose into looking for rabbits. I swore I could hear him laughing when he flushed a rabbit out for a quick chase.

"You'd better go tell your dad."

With dad not working I knew we didn't have money to take Duke to a vet.

Mr. Mench, our neighbor, was also our landlord, and I'm sure he had also let months skip by without my mom paying rent. I went in the house and dad was lying on his back with his eyes closed, hands clasped across his chest.

"Dad, Duke was hit by a car and he's hurt bad. He's bleeding out his thing and Mr. Mench thinks his leg is broken too." He opened his eyes slowly and stared straight up at the ceiling. Dad didn't hesitate.

"Carry him back to the field and tie him to the back fence. Come back when you're done." He still lay there, hands clasped across his chest staring blankly at the ceiling.

I went outside and picked up Duke as gently as I could. He let out a loud yelp and whimpered as we walked back to the fence. Duke felt like a helpless child in my arms. He was on his back and his big doleful eyes never left mine. Mr. Mench walked by my side.

"Jimmy, can I do something?"

"Yes, sir, could you get me Duke's rope there on his doghouse?"

"Sure." Mr. Mench gave me the rope and stood and watched as we walked back to the fence. I'm sure he knew what was happening.

The fence was just beyond the garden that Mr. Mench tended to, and beyond this fence were the cornfields that covered much of the land around our house. I sat Duke down gently and tied him with a rope to the fence and walked back to the house. I couldn't look back at him.

When I went inside my dad was sitting up in the bed. He was sweating profusely. I don't think he weighed any more than 120 pounds. He had his shotgun across his lap. I have no idea how he got out of bed to retrieve the gun from the closet. He was so thin, his skin so pale. Where there were once muscles in his arms there were now just spindles of narrow flesh and bone. It was difficult for him to raise his head.

"Jimmy, I can't do this. You're going to have to."

He didn't look up at me. He didn't have the strength remaining to do so.

This was dad's beloved hunting dog. Duke was suffering, and he didn't want his beloved dog to suffer. Dad would never have expected me to do this, but he was completely incapable. I reached down and took the shotgun without saying a word.

Duke was my dog, too. To me he wasn't a hunting dog, but just a floppy-eared friend who never asked anything of me, but to scratch his favorite spot in the middle of his tummy. My hands shook at the thought of what I was expected to do. Where was my big brother Bob?

At this moment I hated my dad. I turned and walked into the kitchen, just stood at the window looking out, unable to look back at him. I didn't want to speak to him or hear his voice. I wanted all this to go away. I wanted Duke to break away from the fence and run up to the window waging his tail at me. I wanted Duke to let me know everything was all right. That he was fine.

"Shells are in the cabinet by the sink."

With a labored groan dad fell back against the pillows. I knew this was killing him more than it was me. This same man who wouldn't hurt me with the belt, and would later tickle me, was suffering the greatest of agonies. I knew if he had the choice, I wouldn't be the one to do this.

"Jimmy, you hear me?"

"Okay."

I opened the cabinet and took one shotgun shell out of the ammo box.

Looking out the back window I could see Duke sitting with his back to me. I walked on wobbly knees out onto the back porch and down the stairs grabbing the railing to right myself to keep from falling. I just stared straight ahead unable to put a single thought into my mind, except the image of Duke in front of me. As I walked, Duke's fuzzy image seemed to sway from side to side.

I got to Duke, and he tried turning around to greet me, but fell on his side. What was I to do? I sat Duke up on his back legs and he fell to his side again. I wanted my brother Bob there.

"Come on Duke, please." My shaking hands reached down to right him.

Tears were streaming down my cheeks. I sat him up and commanded, "Sit!"

He knew what the command was, and he bravely complied, fighting to keep his balance. Turning, I walked away, loading the single shell into the shotgun. I closed the breach and faced Duke. Duke was still sitting up and looking at me. My God, obedient to the end. With my eyes full of tears, I raised my gun and fired. The blast caught Duke full in the chest and he collapsed violently backward.

I threw the shotgun aside and collapsed on my knees in front of Duke. I began to cry hysterically at the sight of what I had done. I know my dad heard the shot, and I know a little more of him had just died as well. What had I done? Why was this happening? I collapsed onto my right side and lay with my head on my outstretched arm staring at Duke. I hated life, I hated everything.

My dad died the day I was to graduate from high school after an awful, agonizing battle with the disease. I was 17. Mom would never date or marry again. She would die at the age of 81, never having loved anyone since he left her side.

Chapter 4

My band broke up in 1965, and I floated around with a couple other groups, but I knew that at 18 I needed to do something more with my life. People I graduated with were working full time, some even married. Thanks to my love of music, and hatred of school, I had graduated from high school with a D- scholastic average. Needless to say, college was out of the question, and employers would not be pounding on my door for me to come and work for them. The truth is, I found myself afraid to look for work. I was that insecure about my worth.

My childhood friend Dee was gone. He continued playing music and while I struggled trying to decide my fate, he traveled with his new band. Dee would later tour with The Box Tops, The Bill Black Combo, and never stray from being a full-time musician.

During high school I had become good friends with Chip Hurlock and Terry Cullum. Terry was actually Chip's best friend and neighbor, much like Dee Clay and me. Chip was a tall athletic type, popular, and involved in after school activities. Terry was taller, athletic, but on the quiet side. Terry had a grand sense of humor.

Chip and Terry both went to work at the E. I. DuPont de Nemours building near Newark, Delaware. I followed them and worked there for a while, but wasn't happy, and quit. I continued to catch on with local bands here and there but found myself becoming disillusioned with music. Without Dee it just wasn't the same anymore. Many of the guys in other local bands like The Furies, The Emeralds, and The Cyclones had also gotten older, gotten married, joined the service, or gotten full time jobs. They had moved onto better things. They were making the step from adolescence to adulthood. I seemed to be trapped, struggling to continue with something that may have been passing me by.

I don't remember when, or why, but one day I walked into the Army Recruitment Center in Newark and signed up for the Army. All it would take was a simple physical and I would be shipped off to basic training. I must admit I never even knew what Vietnam was, hadn't followed it on the news, and barely picked up a newspaper to read. When I did it was only to check the box scores of my beloved Phillies. So, I wasn't joining to go off to a war I knew nothing about. I was simply joining to do something with my life.

I was a physical wreck. Although always athletic, and 6'2" tall, I was very heavy, weighing in at around 260 pounds. There wasn't much muscle, if any, in those pounds. I had looked at all the career opportunities with the recruiter and decided that photography would be a good field for me. I was artistic, and there were artistic qualities involved in any good photo shoot. I flunked the written test for this field. My failure to make an effort in senior high school, thanks to my music endeavors, was now telling the tale. I flunked almost every test that involved a career with some sort of real academic skills involved. For example, communications, intelligence, and mechanics. Yes, even mechanics. I knew as much about cars as I did math. I couldn't even qualify for the military band. Guitars were not made for marching, and I couldn't read music. I was feeling disheartened. The recruiter sat across from me staring incredulously at my test results.

"Well, son, there's got to be something for you."

He looked through all my tests and asked me if I was interested in the Military Police Corps. Now I didn't know if MPs were just dumb, or what, but I knew my grandfather was a sergeant with the Scranton, Pennsylvania Police Department decades ago. This sounded interesting. It had to be in my blood.

"Sure, sergeant, that sounds good." I had no real idea.

"Okay then. We'll set you up for your physical, and then you'll be underway. Congratulations." He stuck out his big hand.

The physical took place in a small hall full of a couple dozen recruits. Tables were set up as individual test stations, and lines were formed behind each. One line was for checking your blood pressure, one for your height and weight, another for your eyesight, etcetera. I slowly passed through all of these and then took a seat for my last test, hearing.

I was placed in a booth and put on the headphones that were handed to me. A bespectacled man in a green smock bent over and looked me in the eyes. He had the name tag Johnson above his right shirt pocket. I was to sit in a soundproof booth.

"Okay, you'll hear a series of beeps. Every time you hear the beep, I want you to push on this plunger here and hold it until you don't hear the sound anymore." He handed me a small device with a plunger on top, turned and sat behind the hearing test machine a few feet in front of me.

"Any questions before we begin?" I shook my head in the negative.

"Okay, I'll give you a thumbs up when I start the test."

Johnson looked down and appeared to adjust some control knobs. He looked up at me and stuck his right thumb in the air, accompanied with a reserved smile, and a wink. I gave him thumbs up in return with a confident smile.

I waited for a sound. I stared at the man as he kept his head down, and eyes on the machine. I waited a few more seconds for a sound...nothing. Johnson looked up at me uncertainly and shrugged his shoulders. I waited a few more seconds and still nothing. Maybe the machine was broken. Then I heard it. A slight ascending high-pitched beep. I pushed the plunger and held it. It continued to pulse and get louder, and then faded away. I released the plunger. This was more like it. I looked up to see Johnson staring at me doubtfully. I smiled, nodded, and gave him another thumbs up. He gave me a puzzled smile and looked back down at the machine.

The test continued for a couple more minutes, and I was able to discern two more blocks of rhythmic beeps. Then it was over. Johnson peered at me scratching his head as he looked down at the printout.

"You flunked your hearing test." I sat up alarmed, "What?"

In a louder voice, and leaning forward, "You flunked your hearing test!" Shaking my head in confusion, "No, no, I heard you, I just can't believe it."

"Well, here it is. You need to take this print out, and the rest of your physical papers over to the sergeant at that desk." Johnson handed me the printout and pointed to a uniformed man sitting near the entrance to the examination room.

Years of playing a high pitched, screeching guitar in front of a large set of drums must had really damaged my hearing. All the amplified sounds had taken a big chunk of my hearing from me. I didn't even know it until I took this test. I had flunked. I flunked out of music, flunked out at DuPont's, and now this. I was flunking out at life. I walked dejectedly to the desk with my head down and placed the printout in front of the sergeant.

He put his glasses on and looked at it. "Whoa! You flunked big time." I had my head down and didn't respond.

He leaned forward and spoke louder. "You hear me?"

"Oh, yes, sergeant. I'm sorry, I'm just disappointed. I really wanted to be in the Army. It was important to me."

Louder than normal. "What career field were you looking at going into, son?"

"Well, the MPs, sergeant."

"MPs, huh? You must have flunked the rest of the career field tests."

"What?" Not being able to concentrate.

The sergeant leaned forward, "The career field tests! You flunk 'em?"

"Oh, sorry sergeant, I heard you. Well I was told I qualified for the Military Police and was looking forward to it. My grandfather was a police sergeant and I thought I could follow in his footsteps."

"No kiddin'? Where?"

"Scranton?" The sergeant leaned forward.

"Scranton, I'll be darned. I'm from Wilkes Barre myself, son." He took the rest of my paperwork and examined each result. Reaching to his left he took a rubber stamp in his large hand, slammed it down on the cover sheet and handed it back to me.

PASSED.

My eyes lit up. A smile came to my face as I looked to the sergeant with gratitude.

"That one's for your grandpa. Go and make him proud."

"Am I hearing you right, sergeant?"

"Probably not, now get out of here." He pointed towards the exit, and yelled, "Next!"

All that was left was signing on the dotted line. I was given two weeks to report for basic training.

Chapter 5

The wind was blowing the snow sideways. It was sticking to the evergreens in front of my friend's house, and quickly blanketing the black topped road. I looked out the window and knew I wouldn't be able to make it back home tonight. Tomorrow I was on my way to Wilmington, Delaware to catch a train to Fort Jackson, South Carolina, for Army basic training. Chip had invited me over to his place several miles from my house for a celebration of my last night of freedom before the Army got its hands on me. Terry would be there too. We referred to ourselves as 'The Big Three', or so we thought. No one else knew us by that. We were pretty square, typical of the times. We didn't drink or smoke back then, which may be hard to believe. We would sit around in the basement banging away on two guitars and Chip's drum set.

Chip was a novice on his drums. and Terry would give us reason to harass him as we always did over his dreadful guitar playing. Terry's singing was also akin to the sound of cats fighting. Chip and I were convinced we saw flies fall dead out of the air when he rendered his vocal version of The Beatles, "Twist and Shout."

Even though Terry was a beginner we had no mercy on him, because that was Terry. He was our fall guy, fully self-deprecating, and carried the title well. The one who always brought us comic relief, but we loved each other as only best friends could. Chip would play the same trick on Terry repeatedly, and Terry always willingly obliged. Well, looking back, it had to be willingly, as no one would subject himself to the penalties Chip put on him for just being around us.

Cruisin' Newark on a Friday or Saturday night, when my band wasn't playing, was our way of having fun. After all, there was a new fast food restaurant called McDonalds, and Burger King was just down the street. Terry paid the price for ordering strawberry milkshakes, over, and over, and over again.

"May I have your order, sir?"

"Uh, strawberry milkshake, an order of fries, and a cheeseburger." Terry rifled through his pants pocket for the money as Chip's eyes lit up. The time was near.

Chip would slowly drive back onto Main Street, always careful of the dip when entering the roadway. Every time, and I'm telling you every time, Terry would slowly place the strawberry milkshake to his mouth to take a swig, and Chip would gun the engine and speed up. Terry's head would lurch backward along with the cup, and he would wind up with milk shake up his nose, in his eyes, and down the front of his shirt.

Every time, without fail. It was like a religious thing. You could count on it. Pavlov's dog learned quicker than Terry.

Chip's dad had yelled down to us in the basement that it was snowing harder outside, and to come have a look. We jogged up the wooden stairs and went to the large window in the living room.

"Man, it's really comin' down now Freddie." Chip always called me Freddie, short for my middle name of Frederick.

"I don't see how I'm making it home, Chip. Even if we'd leave now, it's such a blizzard out there."

"Yep, you're stuck here for the night. Wanna call your mom and tell her?"

"Yeah, I better."

I called my mom and let her know that I would get by to see her tomorrow before Chip dropped me off at the train station. With the way the snow was falling I really didn't expect us to make it to the train station either. How was I going to explain being late to the Army if the snow didn't let up?

"Well, Freddie, we gotta get up early, so we'd better hit the sack."

I said goodbye to Terry. He pulled the strings of the hood on his sweater so that his large nose was the only thing showing, gave me a quick salute, and headed out the front door. Terry only lived about a quarter mile down the road and he would walk home. As he got out near the road he turned and gave another salute and began to jog towards his house. He was quite a character.

I was scared and there were a billion things going through my head. It still hadn't set in, but tomorrow I would be United States government issued property. I plodded upstairs to get some restless sleep. In the early morning hours Chip would drive me over to my house, I'd say goodbye to my mom, and off I'd go into the grip of the Army.

The next morning, we headed out. The snowplows had done their job and cleared off the foot of snow that had covered the roadway. The plows had also dropped salt on the road to help melt the ice, so there was no need for Chip to put snow chains on the car's tires. As we got to the turnoff for my house it was obvious that the snowplows had not yet gotten onto the secondary roads. I looked down Cowentown Road and saw that the snow had drifted completely across the road. It must have been several feet deep in some areas and was impossible to tell where the fields stopped on either side, and the roadway began.

We trudged the mile and a half to my house, not appreciating the sheer beauty and brightness of it all. Mom had always cautioned me to never stare to long at the snow, as it would cause blindness. Not sure if that was true, but I never did. Parts of the road were bordered by drift fences on both sides that would keep the snow from drifting too deep over the roadway. In places it became extremely deep and difficult. Raise your foot, take a step, and sink your foot into two feet of snow.

Chip and I arrived at the house shivering and exhausted. I knew we didn't have much time, as we had not counted on the road being covered with snow, and having to walk in. I also knew that my mother was going to be very emotional. I never liked tearful goodbyes. This would be one of those typical *mothers losing her son forever goodbyes,* and it made me very uneasy.

Mom wanted me to drink hot chocolate, and sit, but I told her the Army wouldn't want to hear that I had missed my train because I was drinking cocoa with my mother. I gave her a quick uncomfortable hug and waited for the tears that I hated. They came, and with them the guilt. I didn't like the feeling that I was causing my mother pain, but here it was. Mom thought the harder she cried the more she was showing her love, but I never understood it. She stood at the opened door crying as Chip and I headed back to the car. As I got farther from the house, I gave one final turn to see her still in the opened doorway. I waved one more time, turned and headed out toward the car.

As we trekked out to the main road ominous clouds appeared from the west, and the temperature dropped dramatically, but I was too deep in thought to think much about more snow that was coming. Unknown to me life was going to become an adventure not many 19-year olds could ever imagine.

That's how it started. It was simple. A kid in need of something, but not sure of what. I would join the Army, and not knowing it, would be saying goodbye to my home for years to come. All my friends, and my music, would have to take a serious back seat. I would only come back home a few times, and unlike many of my high school buddies, would not go to work in the Chrysler plant, the General Motors plant, or DuPont Chemicals.

I wouldn't marry my high school sweetheart, raise a family, or look forward to the upcoming high school reunions. I wouldn't stay in Elkton, Maryland, a great little town in a beautiful area with wonderfully traditional people. I would wander off. Off to war in a foreign land thousands of miles away. Even though it would always be home I would lose Elkton forever. It would never be the same…nor would I.

After our hike back to the car Chip wondered if his car would even start after sitting in the freezing cold. I blew on my hands, fighting off the cold of the long walk.

"Ready?" He said with a serious look of someone losing a friend. "Nope."

The engine turned over and Chip pulled back on the roadway, headed towards the train station in Wilmington.

I don't remember Chip and I saying goodbye. I wouldn't see Chip for a few months and would miss him. I only recall turning my back, and on unsteady legs, getting on the train. We would have a friendship that would last to this day.

I can remember sleeping on the train. Well, slipping in and out of sleep. I was cold, lonely and scared, and had only been away from my best friend for a few minutes. The snow and the dark skies made it all the more miserable for me. I was in coach, and the weather outside continued to storm. Shades of depressing gray engulfed everything. It certainly didn't help my mood. What was I doing? Where in the heck was I going? What was I getting myself in to?

Could anyone feel as insecure as I was at this moment? Certainly, there were hundreds of young men on trains everywhere heading off to basic training feeling just like me. I had gone from the warmness of my own bed, to a cold dark stale smelling bunk on a train that was rumbling south to a completely foreign place, miles and miles from home. I could have been going to Mars for all I knew. Where was this Fort Jackson?

Where was South Carolina for that matter?

Trying to force myself to sleep only made me more awake. I could hear the train slow and stop, slow and stop. It was endless. Sleep would help me so much. I needed to just concentrate, fall asleep, and when I woke up, I'd be back in Fair Hill. It would all just be a dream. If only. God, I was scared.

Chapter 6

I was awake, but I didn't want to be. I was staring out the window at the most terrifying day of my life. The snow had stopped, but it was colder, much colder. I wished I could just bury my head in the pillow and sleep forever. Maybe the train would take me home. I could ask. I had a feeling this was a bad, bad mistake.

The train was rolling to a stop. Lifeless winter trees stood drearily on the dead brown grassland of winter. The barren trees looked like I felt. Would I ever feel the warmth of the sun again, or was South Carolina always this gloomy? I managed to stand up and grab my suitcase, and head down the aisle to where other passengers were getting off the train.

As I stepped down, I saw a young man dressed in an olive drab uniform standing next to a green bus clearly marked *U.S. Army*. on the side. There were no stripes on his uniform, and he didn't look much older than me. Was this really an Army guy?

Was this what I was so worried about? He looked so nondescript. Then he spoke.

"All right, I want all you guys to assemble over here in front of the bus. All you guys who are going into this beloved Army. Move it, move it, move it!" He was no longer nondescript and had everyone's absolute attention.

It was then that I noticed that I wasn't alone. Other young men with a variety of suitcases, some dressed in disheveled looking sport coats, and ties, were stumbling out of the train. They looked confused, half asleep, scared. Phew, I really wasn't alone.

"Everyone listen up and keep your traps shut! I don't wanna hear a word out of any of you! I want you all in two lines! Let's go, let's go, let's go! We haven't got all day! We have a bus to catch gentlemen! Are you in two lines? Put your bags down on your right side and stand at attention! Do you know what attention is? Hell, do you know what right is? If you don't, then fake it for now. You're going to learn it soon enough! All of you look straight ahead, straight ahead, not at me!"

You never saw more panic. There must have been 30 of us all trying to figure out what two lines were. Some had put their luggage down on their left side, some on their right, some just held onto it, frozen in fear. This is not what we had experienced yesterday. Our mothers didn't talk to us this way.

The soldier stood in front of us, hand on hips, with a disbelieving smirk on his face. He shook his head back and forth and let out a sigh.

"Oh, we're all stupid, are we? Well, you guys must be from New York Shitty or some other queer place! You will pay! You will pay for your ignorance! You will all learn, and you will all pay dearly! Just you wait and see." A satisfied smile overtook his scowl.

The thing is, he wasn't yelling at us. It was all sort of under his breath. He looked uncomfortable and would casually nod affirmations at civilians who were passing by on the way to their cars. He wasn't too bad, really. He hadn't really raised his voice, not as bad as I thought it would be. He stood with his hands behind his back, a harmless look on his face. Minutes passed as we nervously waited for what was to come. Another nod to a passing civilian, and then it appeared we were alone. He looked right, then left. Satisfied he nonchalantly walked over and opened the door to the bus.

"Front row first! When you go into my bus you will fill the first seat on the left near that window, and all the way across to that window on the right side. You will then repeat this in the next row of seats, and so on, and so forth. Do you girls all understand this? This ain't grade school. I don't care if you don't like the fat girl that sits next to you, fill 'er up, front to back! This bus should look like one tight can of unhappy sardines when you're all on. Do you understand!" He looked around again and saw the coast was clear.

"GET ON THE FUCKING BUS, NOW!"

There were mumbles of confusion. Some said "yes", some blurted out "yes, sir!" Some just made unintelligible sounds that came from mouths that were surely sewn shut in terror. I'm sure the only thing coming from my mouth was drool, as I was panic stricken. It grew quiet for a moment. We realized we hadn't moved.

"Pick up your shit, and MOVE IT, MOVE IT, MOVE IT!"

It was a comedy of assholes and elbows stumbling over one another. Every man clumsily, without a word, made his way onto the bus. I thought we did a distinguished job, but what did I know? We were able to get in the bus and sit in the seats from left to right, front to back. We had done it. That accomplishment aside, everyone looked like they were ready to cry, after having just messed their young adult pants.

Pissing and moaning under his breath, our new friend got into the bus, pulled on the handle, shutting the door. We were t-r-a-p-p-e-d. Again, he put his hands on his hips and surveyed us left to right, front to back. If possible, even louder this time.

"All right you assholes! You are in the Army now! You're a sorry bunch of losers, and you're all going to die slow deaths! None of you jackasses are going to make it through boot camp! Not one fuckin' one of ya! You'll all wind up runnin' home to mommy and crawling right back in bed on top of her, right where your sorry asses belong! I know you were there yesterday, and you'll all be there tomorrow!"

It was official. We knew we were headed to a death camp. There was no reason not to believe him. Nobody would joke about this shit to a bunch of people he didn't even know. My god, it was written. We could do nothing but stare straight ahead. What else would this man be doing to us once we arrived at Fort Jackson? I'm sure sleeping on the bus ride was out of the question. Why couldn't the bus driver simply come and just drive us to the death camp. Why was this necessary?

Turning quickly, he squeezed himself behind the wheel of the bus, started it up, and pulled hard on the stick shift, slamming it into gear. The bus jerked forward and pulled from the curb.

Holy mother of God.....we had just been read the riot act by an Army bus driver. A stinking bus driver. If this was how *he* treated us, what could we expect when we got *off* the bus? The guy next to me began to shake. I could hear one guy sobbing. I had to check to make sure it wasn't me.

We all sat stunned, looking straight forward. No one said a word. How long was the ride into Fort Jackson? Five minutes, one hour, two weeks? I didn't know and didn't care, but two weeks would have been okay. I was too busy trying to telekinesis by body home. I was going to a death camp, not an American fort. I began to hallucinate. I saw that white light of a near death experience that I had heard of. It was funneled down to me out of the gray sky through the top of the bus. I got up and slowly, cautiously, followed the light upward. There was a faint distant figure draped in white. Closer and closer it got. I stretched out both arms to embrace it. The figure became clearer as white turned to green and a hand came reaching out to me.

"Get off the fucking bus! Now! Move it, move it, move it!"

It was our bus driver returning to snap us out of our trances. I hadn't noticed, but the bus had stopped, and he was now standing stooped over in the aisle glaring at us. Hands on hips, venting the rage onto us he must have felt for being just a bus driver. With one hand he pulled the lever opening the door and pointed with his other hand towards the exit.

"Ladies, you are about to meet your new mothers. Get the off my bus! Get the hell off my bus! Get the hell off my bus!"

Men scurried past him with their suitcases in their hands or held to their chests. If you hesitated, he pushed you along. A cattle prod could not have gotten us off the bus fast enough. Every man frantically clawed his way forward to get out of his presence. We needed to just get away from this menace.

As I fought my way off the bus, I glanced out the window and saw what looked like three identical mannequins positioned about ten yards away. They were standing rigid, tanned faced, looking straight forward. Their uniforms were perfectly fitted and starched. Stripes adorned their sleeves with shiny medals on their chests. Cool. I liked their hats, too. As the first recruit hit the ground these three mannequins started yelling. They weren't mannequins at all. They were our drill sergeants.

"Form one line on me! One line! Hurry, hurry, hurry!"

They were screaming in unison, pointing at no one in particular. Their movements were almost identical. All three were pointing to an imaginary line on the ground. They could see the line, we couldn't. How could we see a line that wasn't there, especially with all the yelling going on?

"Stand at attention when you ladies get in line! Look straight ahead! I don't want to see one eyeball looking up, down, or around! You maggots better get it right! Hurry, hurry, hurry!"

We were awful. Lines were supposed to be straight. How in the hell could we wind up in what looked like a semi-circle? They screamed until we got it right. No one dared look anywhere but straight ahead. We stood like a petrified forest. No one moved a muscle, or made eye contact, but there was always one guy who would mess it up. I reached up to brush my hair off an eyebrow.

"Who's moving? Who the hell is moving? You were told to get in line and stand at attention! Do you all understand, or are you all deaf?"

I raised my hand and said, "Sorry sergeant, I have hearing problems."

"Who the fuck is talking? You? Hearing problem? Snakes are deaf! You're a fat cow!"

The older looking sergeant stood in front of us with one eyebrow raised. His hands were on his hips, his head leaning slightly forward, jaw jutted out in a determined fashion. Methodically he cupped his right hand and brought it up to the side of his right ear. He kept that pose as if listening to some far-off noise that he couldn't quite make sense of. We waited. He stood still and expressionless. We waited some more...still nothing. He put his hand to his side and took one step forward. He then screamed letting us know that the bus driver was just a novice. "Did I just ask you jackasses a question?" This man had to be the one who was going to sign our death warrants. We answered in mixed bleating agonized tones of, "Yes, sir!"

"Sir? Sir? Do I look like an officer to you? I work for a living. My name is Sergeant Jones, and everything out of your sissy claptraps will be 'yes, Sergeant Jones'! Is that understood?"

We managed weak responses, remaining frozen before this man. He would kill us, and those of us who were virgins would sadly die virgins. Death would have certainly been better than this. We were marched to our barracks, ridiculed all the way. As we shuffled in it

46

became quite apparent that these unadorned two-story buildings were not anything like home. Bunk beds, olive drab blankets, dimly lit cold rooms. The bathrooms would now be called latrines. There were stalls with toilets, but the doors had been removed from them. There would be no crapping in private.

"The real fun starts tomorrow, girls. Get yourselves into your racks. It's the last rest you'll get. You will also note that it will not be easy for you to jack-off in my beloved latrine. The doors have been removed for your safety, and the safety of the lady next to you. Keep it in your pants and at ease gentlemen. If I find one hard-on facing me at reveille, I'll break it off with a trash can lid!"

This got a few nervous laughs.

"Who the hell thinks I'm funny? Drop all your asses where you are and give me twenty, now!" All the drill sergeants were now chewing on any recruit within reach.

So, we all hit the deck and gave Sergeant Jones his twenty. He was not our friend, and we learned a lesson about thinking he was funny. Jerry Lewis was funny. This man, no. We were nothing but meat, and he was going to be the grinder. Note to self, no laughing at what the sergeants say.

"Now grab a bunk girlies, 0600 comes pretty quick." With that Sergeant Jones and the other drill sergeants gave a brisk turn and walked out. We were alone at last. The train ride now seemed like it was last week, not an hour ago. 0600 hours? How was I going to drag my exhausted butt out of bed at 0600 hours? They'd have to throw a bucket of water on me. How was I even going to fall asleep after all of this?

Each man quietly picked out a bunk, climbed in, and covered up. None of us took our clothes off. There was nothing but wall to wall silence. What would tomorrow bring except screaming? We all knew that after tonight's sleep we were facing a day of terror. Before, I just wanted to go home. Now, I wanted to be taken in my sleep. We really had no idea of what was ahead. This unfamiliar stress started to take its toll on all of us. In a barracks full of silence and fear, sleep came within seconds.

Chapter 7

CLANG! CLANG! CLANG! CLANG!

"I better not see one cock looking at me when you get out of bed!"

Sergeant Jones was banging two trash can lids together, and all three drill sergeants were marching down the center aisle of the barracks shouting out insults and commands, pulling off blankets, shaking bunk beds. They had picked up where they had left off the previous evening.

"Up, up! Drop your cocks and grab your socks! Get out of bed, you worthless sleepy heads! This ain't momma talkin', and this ain't yesterday!"

We were awake and on our feet at attention. The sun wasn't even up. How could this be? It was freezing, and the smell of burning coal permeated the air.

"You all got five minutes to fall out for chow! Anybody need a reminder as to how quickly five minutes passes?" The drill sergeants disappeared out the front door of the barracks.

We marched off to chow, sort of, insulted and degraded all the way. One image I still have on the march to the chow hall was the smoke in the air from the coal burning stoves. I can still smell the aroma of the soot as if it was yesterday.

Basic training eating is assembly line eating. You stood at attention outside waiting to be ordered in, in groups of three, and then stood in a line with a metal tray waiting to be served by disinterested looking men standing behind the food counter.

There was no lounging.

The soldiers assigned to the mess hall all wore white t-shirts and white paper caps. Dirty white aprons adorned their chests, and each was armed with a wooden ladle to dish out the flop.

I made another in a long line of Stewart blunders. I had believed that the wooden bowl that I picked up, and placed on my tray, was a bowl of peaches. I loved peaches. The cook behind the counter smiled and gave me a mischievous nod when I carefully placed it on my tray, careful not to spill any of the sweet syrupy juice. I made my way tentatively along the line. Next the scrambled eggs, some sausage, and some toast. That would be enough for me. The peaches would fulfill the sweet tooth I had always had. This wasn't a bad breakfast.

While the sergeants stalked quietly, but alertly, throughout the mess hall, I nervously began to eat. You could tell they were looking for violators. I seemed safe so far. Then I heard a refrain I had heard a million times when my dad had gotten mad at me for something.

"Jesus H. Christ! What the…!" I could hear the thumping of combat boots bearing down behind me. Obviously, a wrongdoer had been spotted. I was praying it was someone else.

"Holy sisters of mercy!" I could feel Sergeant Jones's cigarette breath over my shoulder and next to my cheek, his Smokey Bear hat just touching my ear. He tilted his head in front of my face.

"Were you raised by a bunch of retards?"

My head was straight forward, but my eyes locked on his nose. I noticed a hair coming from his nostril moving back and forth with each angry breath he took.

"I asked you a question. Were you raised by a bunch of retards?"

"I'm sorry Sergeant Jones, but I don't understand."

"Of course, you don't. What would I expect from a boy who just left his mother's milk yesterday?" He picked up the bowl of egg whites and yolks and poured them onto my plate.

"I wouldn't doubt a retard like you thought these were peaches."

Now, how would he know that? Obviously, I wasn't the first to make a fool of myself in this way, or he was just a lucky guesser. I knew why the cook had just smiled so devilishly at me.

I was absolutely stuck in my seat. I couldn't breathe, I couldn't feel my toes, but I could feel my heart beating, slowly, slowly, slowly, until it stopped...silence. I waited, waited...waited for death. It didn't come.

As quickly as the beast had come, he was gone. I looked down at the slimy egg white that now covered my scrambled eggs, sausage and toast. Two of the raw yolks sat on top of one of the pieces of toast reminding me of a clown that I saw at the fair back home. Sadly, I had not died. Sadly, my life had been spared.

Sergeant Jones was bellowing again. "You all got FIVE minutes to eat and get your asses back out in formation! FIVE minutes!"

I would never crave peaches again.

The rest of the morning would be spent being fitted for our uniforms, boots, and haircuts. The haircuts would come first.

Now you must know that the haircuts weren't personal. Individual preferences and styles were out. Run the shears one way as close to the scalp as possible and repeat as needed. The haircuts were quick and harmless. At least to the barbers who gave them to us. To us, we instantly lost all our identities. It had the same effect as if they had cut off an arm.

After each recruit gotten his hair cut he was allowed to go to an area outside where there were payphones, and call home. This was done for a purpose. If you've ever looked at yourself in a mirror after having been completely scalped, you will know what I mean. This drastic haircut, and the pent-up emotions and stress of our first twenty-four hours, were about to be released onto our mothers.

When my chair was turned around facing the mirror, I was horror stricken. How did I get this fat? My face looked like the Hindenburg sitting on a flagpole. My god, all the cookies and milk I had eaten had certainly paid off. Why, dear God, did I feed myself like a barn yard pig? What was I going to do with this fat face? How could I face anyone looking like this? I quickly walked out of the barbershop with my head down to mill around with the other recruits. Everyone looked more the same now. Completely embarrassed and bald.

"Does my face look fat?" I said to no one in particular.

It wasn't a question as much as it was a statement. I was going to die with no hair and a fat face. Would the embalmer have enough embalming fluid to make sure my fat face didn't collapse?

Some of the recruits were joking nervously and making fun of each other about their new look. It was a way to break the tension and was the first real bonding that took place. Friendships started to form as the jokes turned to questions of hometowns and girlfriends. Perhaps the haircuts were serving a purpose after all.

I could see recruits with their heads down talking on the phones. Lines were forming, so I walked over and got in line. I could hear the faint sounds of indistinguishable chatter. But mostly I just saw other young men, like me, with phones pressed tight to their ears listening speechlessly. Listening reverently to their mother's voices. Not saying a word but being reassured as we had been yesterday when we left for boot camp. Phones were hung up with faint goodbyes. With stooped shoulders recruits walked away inconsolable, most with tears in their eyes. Far from home, no hair, no mother, no way of living through the 10 weeks we were about to face.

I was no different. I broke down when hearing my mom's voice. Who was doing the crying now? I didn't say more than a handful of words and hung up with a faded goodbye. I went and found a buddy. Someone I could talk to. The greetings were typically tentative of men who had never met, but they were icebreakers. We would be spending all our days, nights, and weeks together, so we needed to start talking. As the last man walked out of the barber shop our brief respite was ended by the bellowing of Sergeant Jones.

"Fall in, fall in, fall in! That means line up! Hope ya all like your new military haircuts. I'm kind of partial to the look myself." Would he ever take his hands off his hips?

We no sooner got in formation when a sudden stillness came over Sergeant Jones. I could see him out of the corner of my eye. I managed to peek over at him without moving my bald head and saw that he was staring straight at me. He still had his hand on his hips and had that skinny head of his poked forward. This time though it looked as if his eyeballs were popping out of their sockets.

"Jesus, Joseph and Mary." His tone was whispered, and he still hadn't moved. "Holy shit!" This is...this is unbelievable."

Looking stunned, he hurriedly walked over to me and stopped at my left side. His eyes still bulged, and his head was still peaked forward. He was silent, deadly silent. His head began to tilt slowly from left to right as he surveyed what was in front of him. His face blushed, and the veins in his neck filled with blood, throbbing to burst out through the skin.

Incredulous he asked, "What is that?" I was horrified and said nothing.

He raised his right hand, and with his shaking index finger rubbed it along the bottom of my double chin.

"That's my chin Sergeant Jones."

"That's not your chin," tapping the point of my chin with his index finger,

"That's your fuckin' chin, Einstein."

His voice was calm now, still tapping on my double chin. He ran his eyeballs along the length of fat.

"What is that? Do you have a name for it?"

His finger still toyed with it, gently pushing it so that it jiggled, being careful not to damage what he must have thought was a new life form.

"No, Sergeant Jones." The tapping noise I heard had to be my knees.

"What is your name, fatso?" I couldn't believe how calm his voice remained. Perhaps his new discovery would be his ticket to riches. He was certainly being inquisitive.

"Stewart, Sergeant Jones."

"Stewart? Is it Mr. Stewart, Miss Stewart, Fatso Stewart?"

"James Stewart, Sergeant Jones."

"James. That's a pretty name, such a good name for a fat person." I could see his face turning scarlet. I sensed an outbreak.

"How 'bout Private Stewart, you ignoramus?"

Sergeant Jones stepped back, his head turning quickly right and left, surveying the worthless globs of meat in front of him. He was, to say the least, a tad bit upset.

"All you ignorant sissies listen! I ask you what your name is you will respond first with **private,** and then with your last name! If your last name is queer bait you will respond, 'private queer bait, Sergeant Jones'! Your civilian days are over! You are government issued now! Is that understood?"

In unison, "Yes, Sergeant Jones!" The sergeant's attention turned quickly back to me, his prey.

"Tell me, Private Stewart, when the east wind blows, and hits that sail under your chin, does it push your head to the west?"

I knew I had to hurt this man. I would rally the rest of the recruits and we would jump him right here and now. We would pummel him, and I would bend the brim of his Smokey Bear hat, turn in my gear, and go home. I would free the rest of the slaves along the way. I came to my senses and answered.

"No, Sergeant Jones."

"Sergeant Edwards, Sergeant Willits, come over here on the double. I got something I want you all to see!"

The two younger drill sergeants joined him, and stood at each shoulder, inches from my face. Both looked at my double chin in disbelief. Six bulging eyeballs were now examining Sergeant Jones's new discovery.

Sergeant Edwards asked Sergeant Jones if it had a name.

"Private Stewart says not Sergeant Edwards. It's the damnedest thing I ever saw. Sergeant Willits, you ever see anything like this before in all your years in the Army?"

"No, Sergeant Jones can't say that I have. You think we can make a tent out of it? Would we have to get a patent for it?"

Sergeant Edwards chimed in. "How about I make a tobacco pouch out of it, or a marble bag for my son? Hell, we could cut it off, punch holes in it, and make a coffee filter out of it."

I needed a grenade, just one grenade. If I pulled the pin and just stood still for a few seconds, it would explode and get us all. I would not die a slow horrible death from these men. I fought back the tears and continued to stare straight ahead. I knew that they did not have to put their hands on me to kill me. I would die of embarrassment. I could just see the graduation ceremony now. Sergeant Jones would be at the podium in front of friends and family. I could hear the eulogy:

"We are gathered here today to honor these fine men who worked so hard to earn the honor of being called an Army soldier. However, before we go on, let us bow our heads for a moment of silence. Private James Stewart, son of Catherine and the late Frank Stewart, died of embarrassment on the first day of training. He will be missed. His

double chin and he were buried together. A moment of silence, if you will."

"I'm gonna have to write this one up. The C.O. ain't gonna believe it otherwise. Hell, if we could get it all in one photo the Stars and Stripes would love to have it. It'd be on the front page." Sergeant Jones and his two assassins turned and walked to the front of the formation.

If my mom ever got her hands on this man............

Chapter 8

That afternoon we assembled in a large theater. It would be a brief indoctrination given by the battalion commander letting us know what was expected of us the next twelve weeks.

There were hundreds of us. You could hear the coughing starting already.

Men brought their nasty germs from Texas, New York, Florida, all over. Upper respiratory illness hit quite a few of us, but we just had to shrug it off. No time to get sick now. No mothers to baby us, so why delay the inevitable over a little cough? To get sick meant to be rephased, and no one would want to start this all over again.

Lights were out religiously at ten p.m. We would have to learn military time now. Ten p.m. would be 2200 hours. Lights off at 2200 hours, sharp! Reveille would be 0600 hours, sharp! Nobody would stay up late, no small talk after 2200 hours. Exhaustion was the greatest sleep inducer. No one was allowed to have a watch. Time was not for us to worry about. There were no clocks on the walls. Our time, our sleep, was all in the hands of our captors.

It was always the same early in our training. The crashing of trash can lids, and the screams of the drill sergeants as they made their way through the barracks to shock us from our deep sleep. The sergeants always looked so fresh, no sleep in their eyes, not a wrinkle in their uniforms. These men never sweat. Never did I see one sweat mark on anything that they wore. Did these men even sleep, or were they government issued robots? They were good at what they did. And, by god, they relished it.

"You've got five minutes to muster! Five minutes!"

Up and down the aisle they would strut, barking out insults indiscriminately, occasionally stopping to berate someone who had an obvious imperfection. It could be a big nose, buck teeth, or acne. You name it, they had ready-made insults for every defect a human could have.

"Private Stewart, get your fat ass out of bed and bring your chin with you!" No one was spared.

"You should all be on your feet! Pushups await those who hesitate! If one hesitates, then you all hesitate!"

At 0605 hours we were all standing at attention in formation. Heaven help the late arrivals, but there was always someone.

Sergeant Jones stood in front of the formation looking at his watch. He knew he was about to get his jollies, that somebody would be delayed. He never took his eyes off his watch, except to glance at the steps coming down from the front door of the barracks.

Talking out loud to himself, "Zero six zero four hours, and 45 seconds."

"Zero six zero four, and 50 seconds."

"Zero six zero four, and 55 seconds" He knew there was a straggler. "Five, four, three, two, one, 0605 hours."

Sergeant Jones put both his hands behind the small of his back, looked straight ahead, and rocked back and forth on his heels. Like a shark that could smell blood he knew he would soon have a victim, and we would not disappoint him. A satisfied smile came over his face as Private Walter King came running out of the barracks trying frantically to button up his shirt. In panic King ran to the formation, fell in, and stood at attention, his cap still in his right hand at his side.

Sergeant Jones let the tension build with a moment of dead silence. We all waited. He calmly walked over to King and stood in front of him. The other two sergeants slowly meandered towards where King and Sergeant Jones stood. The sharks were circling their bait.

"Good morning Private. Beautiful mornin', isn't it?"

"Good morning Sergeant Johnson. Yes, it is, Sergeant Johnson." Sergeant Jones winced, but he remained calm. After all, he had all day.

"You're late. Jerkin' off?"

"No, Sergeant Johnson!"

"I think you jerked off in your cap, or otherwise it would be on your head." Kings quickly realized his mistake and put on his cap.

"Feel better Private?"

"Yes, Sergeant Johnson!"

Sergeant Jones tilted his head left and right, pursing his lips together. His wince was becoming permanent.

"That hurts me every time you say that Private King." King had no idea what the sergeant was talking about.

"Private, were you the man who took my mother to the prom?"

"No Sergeant Johnson!"

"Did you ever have sex with my mother, Private King?"

"No, Sergeant Johnson!" King was sweating profusely from his brow.

"Then you aren't my daddy, are you?"

"No, Sergeant Johnson!"

You could feel King falling apart and the pressure building. Sergeant Jones, calm and collected for now, was an expert at what he did. He let Private King dig our grave, deeper and deeper. He put his nose an inch from King's ear.

"Then what the hell are you doing giving me a new goddamned last name if you ain't my daddy, you moron? All you suckers drop and give me twenty!" Without a word we all assumed the push up position.

"Now when you count 'em off I wanna hear, one pushup Sergeant JONES, two pushups, Sergeant JONES! You all got that?"

"Yes, Sergeant Jones!"

"Then ready, begin!"

And so, it went. King would learn the given surname of our Sergeant Jones the hard way, and we would all help him. But, that's how it always went. One screwed up, all paid. That's the way we would be trained. All for one, one for all. No man did his twenty pushups alone. We did them with him. Over, and over, and over again, until we got it right.

We wouldn't understand it, and hated it at first, but it this would mold us into one unit. We would learn to care of one another, think the same, overlook minor flaws that each man had, and we'd help one another. That was the bottom line.

Later in our training we would gladly drop for pushups alongside another recruit who was picked out for punishment for his indiscretion.

This was the way of the military. This was the way of soldier. In the meantime, it would be pushups. Lots and lots of pushups.

Chapter 9

A black guy named Ding Rhodes was made my squad leader. He was about 5'9" and thickly muscled with huge hands. Ding looked older than the rest of us. I guessed 22, or 23. This made him seem out of place as most of us were in our teens. He didn't look like anybody you'd want to mess with, but he did have an infectious smile. and whenever I saw him, he appeared to be laughing about something. Ding was from Harlem and his real name was Dingham Arville Rhodes, Junior. He didn't like either Dingham, or Arville, so gave himself the name Ding when he was in grade school. Nobody would ever argue with him that this wasn't a good choice of names.

I would have my first opportunity to really get to know this man during pugel stick training. We were marched to a field and took our seats in bleachers that bordered a circular sand pit. Sergeant Jones stood before us, immaculate as ever in his uniform, even after marching a few miles with us. He continued to stand ramrod straight in front of us.

"In combat there may come a time when you run out of ammo. I expect most of you will turn tail and run. However, for those of you who choose to stay and fight, and that will be all of you by the time I get done with you, you'll have to use your rifle to bludgeon your enemy to death. For those of you from Oklahoma, bludgeon means hit somebody over, and over again until they cease to be standing before you. Your rifle butt may be all you have between living and dying." This guy was funny.

We had previously practiced what were called vertical and horizontal butt strokes. The butt was the end of your rifle stock. A vertical butt stroke meant swinging the rifle in a vertical manner to strike the enemy. A horizontal butt stroke, of course, was swung horizontally toward the targeted bad guy. We were now going to use pugel sticks on one another to apply this training.

Pugel sticks were wooden poles about the length of a rifle with rounded padded cylindrical cones on both ends. This training would involve putting two soldiers inside the sand pit and having them throw butt strokes at one another. Close combat fighting that would measure our aggressiveness.

My first fight would be with Benny Tinkerman. "Tink" was a little guy from St. Louis. He was no taller than 5'8" and must have weighed about 135 pounds. He wore glasses and was really a shy, likeable guy. Tink took his glasses off and handed them to Sergeant Jones. Sergeant Jones then threw them on the ground.

"What am I, your mother?"

Tink looked down at his glasses, picked them up and stuck them in his fatigue pants pocket. We both put on our head gear and snapped the chin strap to one side. This head gear was simply a football helmet with wire mesh covering the face to protect your eyes, nose, mouth, and chin. When you had it on it was sort of like looking through a screen door up close.

"You privates ready?" Sergeant Jones stood with one arm extended between us.

We both answered Sergeant Jones with a hardy, "Yes, Sergeant Jones!"

Other privates could be heard hooting from the bleachers, egging us on.

Well, it was a mismatch. Tink was willing, but I was an athlete, despite my girth, and a lot bigger than him. It was over in a matter of seconds. A horizontal butt stroke sent Tink cascading clumsily to his knees. As he tried to get up, I nailed him with another on top of his helmet, and he went down face first. It was a shallow victory on my part, and I reached one hand down to help Tink up. Sergeant Jones grabbed me by one arm and spun me around.

"What the green-eyed hell do you think you're doing, dickhead? You givin' that little yellow VC bastard a chance to stab you through your heart."

Tink was on one knee, groggily trying to stand up.

"Now you hit that VC bastard again, Private Stewart!"

With that I gave Tink one final blow, and he fell back down to the ground. Sergeant Jones stepped in, grabbed me and raised my right hand.

"We have a star-spangled warrior here! A killer of VC! The winner, Private Stewart!" Cheers and hoots followed. I helped Tink up, and we smiled at each other.

"You okay, Tink?"

Tink, never much with words, took off his helmet, winked at me, and walked towards the bleachers.

"Who's next to challenge this gladiator, this killer of men? Who'll it be? Step up if you dare!" Sergeant Jones, obviously enjoying himself, looked around for volunteers. Dozens of hands went up.

I heard the earth tremble as Ding Rhodes stepped forward off the bottom row of the bleachers, his smile brandishing those big white teeth. Ding didn't stand up like most men. He uncurled, unwinding slowly, stretching and flexing his huge muscles through his skintight T-shirt. Sergeant Jones was visibly excited.

"Okay, okay, we got ourselves a giant killer! David has arrived and needs his sling shot!"

Sergeant Jones helped Rhodes on with his helmet and tightened the straps. I needed someone to keep my knees from knocking. I'm guessing Rhodes had 19" arms with a 19" neck. His hands wrapped around the pugel stick like he was grabbing a toothp i c k .

Ding was laughing and saying, "Gonna get some, gonna get some!" I couldn't see his face through the mesh, but knew he was smiling, and about to enjoy himself immensely. God, why me? I looked over at Tink, who was now sitting, pointing at me, and laughing. I'm sure everyone was laughing, but I got tunnel vision, fixated on the hulk in front of me.

Sergeant Jones checked to make sure the straps were tight on both helmets. There was no getting out of this. I was thinking to just not embarrass myself, just to stay on my feet for more than a few seconds. If I moved parallel maybe I could get in a few shots when he lunges. There was really no reason for Rhodes to kill me in front of all the troops.

I heard my bunk mate yell out, "Say your prayers, Stewart."

61

The laughing was starting. Not out of ridicule or dislike for me, but what was about to happen to me. To them, this was going to be a comedy show and I was the straight man. A lamb was being sacrificed to the god of war, Ding Rhodes. Ding may have looked like an Olympic body builder, but, hey, he **was** human just like me. He bled, too. At least I thought so. Sergeant Jones motioned us to the center of the ring.

"All right David, Goliath, you ready?"

Rhodes was chuckling. "Yes, Sergeant Jones!"

"Private Stewart?"

I was silent, planning my first strike. Would I hit him with the horizontal butt stroke, or wait for him to lunge and upper cut him with the vertical butt stroke?

"Private Stewart, goddamn it, are you deaf? Are you ready?"

"Yes, Sergeant Jones."

Sergeant Jones stepped between us with his right arm extended. He looked at me and did a quick look at Rhodes. I had already decided on a quick horizontal stroke followed by the vertical stroke.

"Ready?" Sergeant Jones looked at me again, as if he was saying his last goodbye.

"Fight!" His arm jerked back, and the duel was on.

I remembered opening my eyes and shaking my head to get rid of the rush of smelling salts. Things were blurry. I could see the brim of Sergeant Jones's hat as his eyebrows came into focus. His face was down very close to mine. I was on my back and could see the mesh from Rhodes's helmet over the back of Sergeant Jones's face. He continued to move the packet of smelling salts back and forth in front of my nose until he thought my eyes were adequately focused.

"You ain't dead Private Stewart, just almost." He helped me so that I was able to sit up with my elbows still on the ground. Rhodes had his helmet off now and was, well, smiling.

Looking up at Ding, "You ever kill any white men before?"

"Just two." He laughed and extended his huge right arm. I grabbed it and he pulled me to my feet.

"You okay, Stew?"

"Except for hating you, yeah."

Sergeant Jones knew he didn't have a cadaver on his hands, and quickly turned and asked for two more volunteers to fight. I picked up my protective helmet, as Rhodes and I walked to the bleachers to watch the next fight. Ding put his big hand under my left arm to make sure my wobbly legs didn't give out on the way out of the sand pit. He was a good man.

"Sorry." he said with a chuckle. "I guess I got a little carried away."

"That's okay Ding, I don't remember anything anyways. How many times did you hit me?"

"Oh, I don't know, three, maybe four. The first time I hit you, you stood there like the Statue of Liberty. Everybody was laughing. I think you were out on your feet, but you didn't fall, so I just got in a few more smacks, and over you went. I never saw anybody look so stiff when they fell." Ding couldn't control his laughter.

"Laughin', huh? I guess I'm a funny guy." I turned to Ding as we sat down, "Well, I want you as a friend now, because where I come from friends don't kill their friends. How 'bout it?" I stuck out my right hand and Ding grabbed it with his. My hand disappeared within his massive grip.

"Ding you weren't serious about the two white men you've killed, were you?"

Ding put his elbows on his knees, clasped his hands, and just looked straight ahead. After a few seconds he looked over at me, winked and gave a chuckle.

We all started to get used to the routine after the first few weeks of hell.

Most of us found our own little clique, but in general we all got along. My first paycheck was for $78.00, one month's army pay, after deductions. Considering we got free room and board there were no complaints. It gave us money to go to the base PX, and even get off base to hit some of the night spots, if we were lucky enough to get a pass. I never did go off base while at Fort Jackson. I was content to take what little free time I had and just hang out, play a little ball, and chat with the new friends. Of course, there were letters to write, and most importantly, letters to read.

If we weren't marching, we were running. Rain, snow, wind, or freezing cold, nothing stopped training. We had a hill just outside of the barracks area that led to the rifle range, and other training sites. It was affectionately known as "Drag Ass Hill." It was true to its name. Going down in the morning was the easy part, but after a long day of marching, shooting, or other training it was major heartburn on the way back. Good army planning.

At the end of week ten I got pneumonia. I had been coughing and wheezing my way through week nine, and it finally hit me good while in the mess hall eating breakfast. Ding was the first to notice.

"Hey Stew, you sweatin' golf balls, man. It's gotta be 50 degrees in here, and you look like you just ran in the rain."

I could see two of Ding. Each one of his heads was rotating around the other. "Yeah, maybe you're right. I oughta have this checked out."

I got up and proceeded to fall face first on the end of the table. Every plate of food that was being eaten looked like flap jacks being tossed in the air. Ding and a few others started cursing, but then realized that this was no joke, and came to my aid. I was carted off to the base hospital.

The sick bay that I was in was full of ill recruits. Upper respiratory disease was the biggest culprit. I had been diagnosed with pneumonia, had a high fever, and a terrible hacking cough.

Sergeant Willits came to see me on my second day in. "Morning Private Stewart."

I sat up as best I could. "Good morning, Sergeant Willits."

Sergeant Willits looked young. I would guess he was no older than 30, six foot tall, stout, though not an ounce of fat on the man. Although strict, he didn't have all the bluster that accompanied Sergeant Jones and was even giving out praise when we performed up to standards. Maybe that was his roll.

"How are you feeling, private?"

"Not too good, Sergeant Willits, but I'll be out of here as quick as I can."

I would have loved to have asked him where he was from, and how he got into being a drill sergeant, but it wasn't appropriate to fraternize with the NCOs.

He knew it, and I knew it. They asked the questions; we gave the answers. Never the other way around. There was a line that wasn't crossed. That's what discipline was all about.

"Private Stewart, there's a chance you don't get out of here quick enough we'll have to rephase you."

"Rephase me, Sergeant Willits?"

"Yep, you'll be falling behind in training. You'll be sent back a few weeks with another training company."

Oh, no. This was unthinkable to me. I had gotten this close to graduation. It would be maddening to have to go through an additional three, or four more weeks of training. All those friends I'd made would be lost.

"How long until I'm better, Sergeant Willits?"

"Well, that's up to you, and the doctors, I guess. I just wanted to come in and let you know. You take care of yourself, and hopefully we'll see you back at camp." He patted me on my arm, turned and left. I was desperate.

"Sergeant Willits, would you put in a word with the nurse for me? I don't want to be held back?" He looked over his shoulder, nodded, and walked out of sight.

Nurse Bennett walked down the aisle with a chart in her hands, stopping at the foot of my bed. She was very pretty and looked wonderful in her white nurse's uniform.

"Nurse Bennett, what do I have to do to get out of here?"

"Well, private, you have to get better first. You see that small pitcher of water on the stand? You need to drink one of every hour. You think you can do that?"

I reached for the pitcher and poured the water into my glass. I chugged it down, followed by another. I poured another glass.

"Private Stewart, you are in here for pneumonia. I don't want to have to include drowning too. Here take these pills. If you drink every ten minutes, or so, you should be okay. Do you have your bed pan handy?"

Embarrassed, I reached down and showed her my bed pan.

At lunch I passed out again while going through the chow line. I had insisted to the nurse that I would be fine walking to get my food. I had picked up my empty metal tray, placed a bowl of Jell-O onto it, and BANG! Ding himself couldn't have knocked me down any better. I was helped to my feet, insisting I was fine. Back in my bed I looked up at a concerned Nurse Bennett.

"I tripped." She gave me a sour look.

"Drink your water, Private Stewart, drink your water. You aren't leaving here until I say so, so drink, sleep, drink, sleep. Got it?"

I went into the hospital on a Friday night. The first three days were rotten. It felt like I would be sick for some time, however, by Wednesday I had made remarkable progress. It would still be touch and go for me as far as re-phasing. I continued to drink gallons of water and slept as much as I could. That was in between all the peeing I was doing.

The following Friday morning I saw Sergeant Willits coming toward me down the aisle.

"Hey, Private Stewart, you're looking better. How you feel?" He didn't let me answer, but continued, "We hit the rifle range on Monday morning. Now this is an important week and you can't miss it. Monday is the day. I'll check back with you Sunday, and we'll see how it goes." He didn't give me any time to respond but turned and walked away. I guess this was it.

Saturday and Sunday came and went, and I felt better. I had been showing off by walking to the latrine rather than using the bed pan. I had lost a few extra pounds from all the water and Jell-O, was light on my feet, and hadn't fallen into any other food. I'd just have to wait for Sergeant Willits, and Nurse Bennett.

Later in the day Nurse Bennett told me that I was good enough to be released on Monday. I was jubilant. This was great news. We would have to be at the rifle range at 1300 hours to join everyone else. Sergeant Willits would come and get me. I threw both my fists straight into the air.

"Yes!" I let out a loud laugh. "Nurse Bennett I feel like dancing', and I don't even dance."

She looked at me matter-of-factly, "If you try dancing with me, I'll have your ass thrown in the brig."

I caught myself, knowing I was way out of line. "Sorry, Nurse Bennett. It's just really good news."

"Well, except for falling into my food, you've been a good patient. You know Sergeant Willits has been sick, too. Just so happens he's getting released Monday morning also. You two try to take care of one another on the way down to the range."

I hadn't known he was sick. He hadn't told me that he had also gotten pneumonia and had been laid up all week. He hadn't shown it at all. These drill sergeants were all spit and shine. Men who didn't complain. Men who knew what it meant to be leaders. We needed them, and I guess he figured I needed him. So, he did what he was supposed to do. Lead by example and motivate his men.

Monday morning Nurse Bennett came to wake me at 0700 hours to give me the last of my medicine.

"Get up, Private Stewart. You've got a rifle range to run to today." My mouth was dry as the heat in sick bay seemed higher than usual.

Jokingly she said, "Don't be hard on Sergeant Willits. Remember he's been sick, too." I promised her I'd take it easy on him.

I had some eggs, toast, Jell-O, and a glass of orange juice for breakfast. Later, when I got dressed, I noticed my pants were a bit baggy from the weight loss, but I was happy, and ready to go. Sergeant Willits came in, stood in the doorway, and motioned me towards him.

"At least Drag Ass Hill is downhill on the way out. Shall we, private?"

We began the trek walking, and even walked down Drag Ass Hill, but once on flat ground we started jogging. It didn't take either of us long to start coughing. It was now late April, and not as cold as when I first arrived, but the air was cool enough to get an unenthusiastic reaction from our lungs. We hacked and wheezed as we ran side by side towards the rifle range. It would be a five-mile jog. I felt so much lighter from my stay in the hospital, but I could tell I wasn't fully recovered. I'm sure Sergeant Willits felt the same way.

"Let me know when you need to stop and puke, Private Stewart."

"Yes, Sergeant Willits." He had said nothing about being sick in the sick bay, and I didn't ask. At about the three-mile mark I began dry heaving.

"Okay, Private Stewart, stop, stop! Head off the roadway and chuck it up."

I walked off the road, bent over, hands on knees, dry heaving violently. I had tears in my eyes as I struggled with it. Standing upright I wiped the spittle off my chin.

Glassy-eyed I looked back at Sergeant Willits.

Standing, hands on hips, he hocked up a big ball of mucus, spitting the greenish/yellow wad over the roadway onto the dirt edge. True to form he maintained his drill sergeant prowess, not complaining, and appearing to take it with a grain of salt.

"Not much farther Private Stewart. Let's keep it up. Fall in, let's go." I put my steel pot back on my head, and off we went.

After about 20 more minutes I could see the range ahead and make out figures that appeared to be milling around. It must have been break time. We both arrived to cheers and applause. I wouldn't be rephrased, and I was a happy lad. I was greeted with pats on the back, and sarcastic remarks of 'slacker', and 'freeloader', but I loved it. I was back with the guys. I really didn't know how much I had missed them. I guess they missed me, too.

Sergeant Willits stopped his jog in front of Sergeant Jones to report in.

Sergeant Jones then turned to me.

"Welcome back, Private Stewart."

"Thank you, Sergeant Jones." I saw the faintest of a sincere smile on his face.

"Okay troops break over! Everybody in second squad now get online, and ready to shoot. Hustle up, hustle up!" I grabbed my rifle and got online.

I was ecstatic. Everyone looked so fine. This was the happiest I had been since the start of training. I was going to make it. I loved everybody, even loved Sergeant Jones. I got online and commenced firing at his command.

"Private Stewart, you are the worst fucking shot I've ever seen in all my years as an instructor! Every VC you see will surely escape to breed again!" Well, love was fleeting.

Exhausted from my run and still weak from the pneumonia, my unsteady hands barely qualified me as a marksman. My shooting was a far cry from my days of hunting groundhogs back home, but I chalked it up to being sick and still weak from the pneumonia. Most importantly, I had made it back. Completing the rifle shoot qualification was just the beginning of the end. The rest of the training we had to wrap up would all be gravy, and unlike Drag Ass Hill, it would all be downhill.

Everyone would be graduating. Not one recruit fell through the cracks. We'd all hold on the next seven days until graduation. We'd all proudly stand before our families with our new physiques, and confident statures. All of us would make it through the screaming of Sergeants Jones, Willits, and Edwards, and were the better for it. They would now look at us with pride and feel good about themselves knowing they had, once again, turned a bunch of selfish, undisciplined, boys into soldiers. Not an easy task. They had pulled it off, and we would be forever grateful. *We* had pulled it off. I was proud that Sergeant Jones was my lead drill instructor.

The graduation that followed was all pomp and circumstance. None of my family members were able to attend, but that was all right. It was a proud day for me, and I would be home soon enough to strut my stuff. The field was adorned with dozens of American, Battalion and Company flags. There was a slight wind blowing, and all the flags flapping in the breeze only added to the splendor of the moment.

Bleachers had been set up, and a podium was planted in front for the obligatory congratulatory speeches by Commanding Officers, who we had not even seen during our training. The stalwart drill instructors that got us here merely stood by our sides as praise was heaped on our parents about our accomplishments. Moms and dads, brothers, sisters, aunts, uncles, and girlfriends were dressed in their Sunday finest. Smiles were everywhere.

After the ceremony we all casually walked back to the barracks to pick up our personal belongings. I walked upstairs and saw some of the guys packing their duffel bags. Proud parents and siblings were by their sides, pulling on sleeves, touching the rifleman's badges adorned to their chests. Little brothers held onto their big brother's arms, so proud to be standing next to a real soldier. Fathers stood at a distance snapping pictures. Sergeant Jones approached me.

"Well, Private Stewart, you should be proud of yourself. Your folks couldn't make it down?"

"No, sergeant, too far. My dad died a couple years ago. My mom couldn't drive it herself."

I saw a sadness in his eyes. "Well, son, sorry to hear that. He'd be proud of you. I'm proud of you. You done good son, real good."

"Gee thanks Sergeant Jones." He had called me son. "You're not mad at me anymore Sergeant Jones?"

"Son, I was never mad at any of you. You go on and make the Army proud, you hear? Make me proud along the way. You were my kids." He shook my hand and walked up to another family and began to chat.

There was a lot of laughter and back slapping from the troops. This place had been our home. I looked over at Ding. There he stood, all smiles with a younger black kid at his side. It had to have been his brother. Ding was packing his duffel bag too and looked over at me and gave me a thumbs up, flashing that big white-toothed smile of his. I did my best John Wayne strut and walked over to him. He began to laugh.

"Well pilgrim, looks like we got ourselves a PFC Ding here." I extended my hand to him,

"How 'bout that. Not even gone, and you got a stripe already. Whoa! You deserved it Ding. It was really good being here with you." I looked down at the boy who appeared to be about 10 years old.

"Who's this good lookin' guy? Your brother?"

"No, Stew, that's my son Kenny."

His son? It then dawned on me. As much as I thought I knew Ding, I didn't even know he had a son.

"Son? Ding, how old are you?

"Twenty-eight, my man. Will be 29 next Tuesday." Twenty-eight years old? I'll be darned."

Ding had been an inspiration to us all. Now I know why. He wasn't a kid.

He had real responsibilities at home, and somehow, he ended up in the Army. I didn't even know if he was here by choice, or just necessity. His son was beaming. This was his dad with the stripe on his sleeve, looking so sharp in his uniform. I really felt proud to know this man. There were tons of questions I now wanted to ask him, but it was just too late.

"Geez, no kiddin'? Man, Ding you're old enough to be my father." Ding laughed that big laugh of his.

Kenny chimed in, "my dad's a soldier!"

"Kenny, your dad's a great soldier. He'll probably be a general one day." Kenny's eyes got wide. "A general? That right papa?"

Ding looked proud and embarrassed at the same time.

"Well, maybe a major, but we gotta check with your momma first." Ding stuck his big right hand out toward me.

This wasn't a time for a handshake. This was family. We had all made it, and had all become brothers forever. Although most of us would go our own ways, and never see one another again, these faces and names would be indelibly etched in our memories. We shook hands, exchanged addresses, and then gave each other a bear hug. His big hand slammed down on my back a few times.

"Stew, you take care of yourself, hear?"

I stepped back and looked Ding square in the eyes. "Yeah, you too, Ding. Make your son proud."

Ding picked up his duffel bag and took his small sons' hand in his. "Ding, where you headed after this?"

"Well, A.I.T. at Fort Knox. Gonna be a tank driver. How 'bout you?"

"Fort Gordon, Georgia. Military Police Academy."

"MP? Man, you really know how to hurt a brother."

Ding winked, gave me his big toothy smile, threw his duffel bag over his shoulder, and walked away hand in hand with his son. I watched as he got to the doorway and turned the corner out of sight. I expected him to be a career soldier. Ding would have been a great leader.

Three days after I last spoke to him, Dingham Arville Rhodes was killed in a car accident while at home on leave.

Chapter 10

After basic I got two weeks leave to go home and show my stuff. I had dropped 40 pounds of lard and must say I felt pretty good about the way I looked. I was in excellent shape and the uniform only added to the glory of it all. My mom and friends were all proud of me, of course. I even went to church, in uniform, and felt good about myself for the first time in a long time. I took the time to visit my dad's grave. Life wasn't hurting as much now. Maybe he was looking down at me with a smile on his face, proud of his son.

I had confidence about the upcoming MP Academy at Fort Gordon, Georgia.

I had confidence about a lot of things. I raved and joked about Sergeant Jones saying things about my double chin, no longer considering the things he did to me as evil, but as necessary. He made men of boys, did his job well. Perhaps we all need help shedding our teenage years. If I could make it through Sergeant Jones riding me hard, everything else should be easy.

The two weeks I spent at home were wonderful. Chip, Terry and I spent time together, but I never saw Dee. Dee was out on the road with some band and I missed not being able to see him. Chip had told me that Dee had gained an incredible amount of weight. He had to go for an induction physical and had gained so much weight that the scale would not accommodate him. REJECTED! Rejected for duty. He was terrified of going off to war, and I never blamed him, or looked down on him for it. He was a gentle soul, and would have been a danger to himself, and others. I stopped by hoping to see him, but his dad said he was on tour down south somewhere. I gave Mr. Clay my next duty station address and asked him to pass it along to Dee, but I never heard from him. I packed my bags and headed for the Military Police Academy at Fort Gordon, Georgia.

MP Academy was fairly uneventful, except for the first day. I had met up with another soldier on the way down to Georgia by the name of Mike Sherman. He and I chatted on the plane ride into Atlanta, and from there on the bus to Fort Gordon. When we got there, we basically just sat around waiting for the arrival of all the men who would be attending this academy. Young men were arriving every hour. Not much to do, and no one was yelling at us. So far, so good.

Once we had been mustered, and met our new drill sergeants, we were shown our barracks. Sherman and I decided to head up the second floor. The double bunks were first come, first served. I took the first bunk on the right, throwing my duffel bag on the bottom bed. Sherman threw his on the top. We'd be bunkmates. It was good to have a friend already.

It must have been around 1900 hours when a guy in disheveled khakis walked by us with this crazy, wide-eyed stare. He looked like he'd been sleeping in his uniform for days. Sherman nudged my arm to take notice.

Sherm whispered, "Whoa, the twilight zone."

This guy looked completely disconnected. He dropped his duffel bag in the middle of the floor halfway down the center of the room, and kept walking, never looking from side to side.

"What's his problem?"

The soldier then opened the back door and stepped out onto second story landing. Without skipping a beat, he vaulted over the railing.

THUD!

"Holy shit! Did I see what I thought I saw?" Sherman jumped down from the top bunk.

Everyone was running for the balcony, elbowing and nudging each other aside to get a look. The soldier was face down with his left leg grotesquely bent from the knee the wrong way.

Sherman and I glanced at each other in disbelief. "Geez, Stew, looks like he doesn't want to be an MP, huh?"

Sherman let out an uneasy laugh. Everyone was shocked and chattering about what they just saw. Some chuckled, some just shook their heads in disbelief and walked away from the balcony.

"Geez, I guess not. What a dumb fuck."

Two soldiers came running out the back door of the first floor and yelled up to us, wanting to know what had happened. Sherman and I just shrugged.

"Jumper!" Sherman yelled down. "I'd give him a nine, but the Russian judge is giving him a seven." I jabbed Sherman in the ribs.

"Sherm, you are cold, man." I turned and walked back inside. There wasn't any reason to watch anymore. The guy didn't want to be here, and he would get his wish. We never heard anything else about him after that.

We spent most of our time in classrooms learning about the Uniformed Code of Military Justice, or the UCMJ. Unlike high school I found myself enjoying this, but unlike high school I didn't have a guitar to divert my attention. The physical training rigors of basic training were also behind us. Previous fat bodies had already been finely tuned. Everyone came in fit and trim. We found ourselves exercising only three days a week for one hour at a time. Most of the guys, me included, would even exercise on our own to keep that edge. My choice was usually running, running for long distances A five-mile run was now easy for me, and I enjoyed the feeling it gave me.

The drill instructors were still very strict and insisted on self-discipline, neatness, and dedication. If you appeared to be a slacker they would come after you. I found out during a routine inspection. Our lockers had to be immaculate. The contents had to be laid out in specific order, to include the rolling of socks and underwear. However, one day I flunked inspection, and learned that there were dues to be paid for inattention to detail.

A drill sergeant, wearing a white glove, unscrewed the lid off my metal canteen, stuck his finger as far inside the small opening as he could, swirled it around, and pulled his finger out. There was the smallest amount of discoloration on the tip of his index finger. This set off the chain of events, but I wasn't the only one to pay. Several of us spent the day removing wax from the barracks floor with razor blades. The floor was then waxed again. Of course, this all took place on our day off. Bitching was not allowed.

This was part of life, part of learning. Could we take it? I had learned from Sergeant Jones and learned well. We all had. We whistled while we worked.

None of us knew what was in store for us after graduation. Some got orders for Germany, Korea, Japan, some stateside. About 25 of us got orders to report to Fort Benning, Georgia, for counter-guerilla warfare school. Warfare? Guerillas? Not the zoo kind, but the kind that hides and shoots at you. It was clear that we were going to be trained to get in the fight.

It was all made perfectly clear when we got off the bus at Fort Benning and were greeted by sergeants wearing olive drab t-shirts. Standard issue was white. Olive drab meant camouflage. Camouflage meant Vietnam.

We would be part of a group of men forming the 552nd MP Company and had a couple months to get ready for the war zone. That's all we knew, and we were to keep it "top secret." Our mothers were not even to know. It was not to be mentioned to anyone in letters, or over the telephone. We had no reason as to why, except orders were orders.

Training was nothing but flat out fun. We ran, did pushups, ran some more, doing it all with a sense of team spirit and camaraderie. We played war games, setting up ambushes at night, and generally scaring the hell out of any civilians who happened to drive by close enough to hear the rapid fire of M60 machine guns firing blanks. This was more like it. I could have spent my entire enlisted time right there at Fort Benning, but these were just games, more training. We had no idea while we played, laughed at the sound of blanks being fired at one another, there were men 9,000 miles away getting a dose of real life, real bullets. We still had a lot of growing up to do.

You would have thought we were the only unit in the country that was training for Vietnam. The MPs who pulled garrison duty at Fort Benning were in the 139th MP Detachment. They were all spit and polish in their class A uniforms. We felt we were better than them. After all, we were going off to war...they weren't. We showed our contempt for them in our morning jogs in front of their barracks. We sang in unison and as loud as we could.

"If I had a yellow spine, I could be in the 1-3-9! Sound off! Sound off! One, two, three, four, one, two, *three four*!"

It was here I met men like John Prahl, Jim Peterson, Jim Troupe, Mike Ramirez, Tom Likely and Doug Dragert. It was a company of about 100 men, and it was hard to get to know everyone, but we did bond as a unit. It was probably the beginning of August 1966 when we got our final orders to ship out. We'd be leaving for Vietnam on the largest troop carrier in the world, the USS Simon B. Buckner. Most of us got about a month's leave to go home and say goodbye before our one-year tour of duty. What was next?

Destination, Vietnam.

Chapter 11 Vietnam

Our journey had begun in Oakland, California, in September of 1966. We sailed parallel to the coast of California and made a brief stop in San Diego to pick up a large contingent of Marines. I was in awe of the beauty of San Diego as seen from the ship. I can remember the pastel colors of the houses on the hills that gently dropped down to the bay, and how picturesque it all was. I remember wanting to come back to this city one day. Never did I realize that I would one day live there. We would not see land again until we got to Okinawa. From Okinawa we'd head for Danang, a port city in northern South Vietnam. Here we'd drop off the Marines and then head south along the coastline for the port city of Vung Tau.

What do MPs do on a ship for 21 days? Well, for one, put up with a bunch of Marines. It was decided to show how *elite* we were, so we would be the first to start having PT (physical training) on the ship. Now, if you've never tried doing jumping jacks in a choppy ocean, I suggest you try it. One blustery day, with a rough sea, we began doing jumping jacks. We also did a little cadence in respect to the Marines we were sailing with.

"One, two, three, four, we don't like Marine Corps!"

Now that brought out every jarhead on the ship. We were hooted and harassed the entire time. These guys were the real meat and potatoes of combat, and they weren't about to put up with it. Off came their shirts, and they fell in right next to us with hoots and laughter.

They were especially delighted when they saw that every time our feet left the deck of the ship, the ship would move a bit, and we would land a foot from where we started the jumping jacks. We could have jumped ourselves right off the side of the ship had we kept it up. We learned about jumping up and down continuously when the sea was choppy. We chose more pushups and dumped the jumping jacks.

Our only respite from the cruise was a one-day stopover at Okinawa. The Marines were given liberty and the MPs were given their first duty assignment. We'd police the Marines. Big mistake. The beach was clearly marked **"contaminated, do not swim."** To a drunk Marine that meant **"diving contest here today."**

Never did I believe that alcohol and contaminated water mixed. It didn't. Well, the Marines thought it did. We pulled out dozens and dozens of "swimmers" from the ocean. Mix that in with all the vomiting and we were officially baptized. But nobody was killed, no animals were hurt in the filming of this movie.

It took us 21 long days to arrive at Vung Tau. Needless to say, we were anxious to permanently put our sea legs behind us. If we grunts wanted to sail the seven seas we would have joined the Navy. All of us were all anxious to get onto solid ground once and for all. We had been ordered to gather all our gear in our duffel bags, put on our steel pots and have our M-14 rifles ready to go. We were to carry no ammunition. This would be a friendly debarkation.

The Navy LCTs, troop landing crafts, came alongside in the calm sea, hugging the side of the ship. One by one we climbed over the side, and down the large rope nets that extended into the guts of the crafts below. We were packed in like traffic in Los Angeles at quittin' time. The sandy beach shoreline was about two hundred yards away. It looked like we could have just walked to shore on the water, it was so flat. Not a ripple, or a wave.

I don't remember a sound from anyone as we made our way slowly towards dry land. We were still uncertain about the order of no ammo in our rifles.

And then a faint sound of a brass band playing, and a lone drummer. I could see a large crowd on the beach but couldn't quite distinguish what was going on. The heavy doors of the LCT dropped into the shallow water. Now it was clear. I could see a military band lined up on the sand. Beautiful, slim girls with long straight hair, and beautiful long silk dresses, carried leis forward to us as we clumsily lugged our duffel bags out of the water onto the beach.

Each surprised soldier bent over to receive his welcome and was hastily ordered up onto a roadway to assemble. There was a contingent of high-ranking Army officers greeting our officers and NCOs. They were all saluting, shaking hands and seemed pleased at what they saw.

John Prahl walked up to me. "Man, it's fucking hot."

"I don't know, beats the snow. Wonder where we're going now?"

"To our base camp I suppose. Man, I don't know about you, but I'm damned glad to be off that stinkin' ship."

"Yeah, I know what you mean."

Sergeant Aguirre was now yelling for us to muster near the busses. We filed in until each bus was packed with men and gear. I sat down next to John and then saw my first MP.

There were two jeeps with three MPs in each jeep. Mounted on the back of each jeep were M-60 machine guns, each manned by an MP. They had serious looks on their faces and wore flak jackets. The sun reflected off the colored bands around the sides of their shiny black helmets. The number 560 was on one side of the helmet, and an indistinguishable multi-colored insignia on the other side. There was a big white **MP** embossed right in the middle of the helmet. I was impressed. I nudged John and pointed over to them. These guys looked bad. That would be us in due time.

As Sergeant Aguirre gave the thumbs up, one of the MP jeeps pulled in front of the lead bus, and off we went. The other MP jeep took up the rear. Sergeant Aguirre jumped in the lead bus, closed the door, and looked back at us.

"Welcome to Vietnam, boys." He had a big grin on his face.

We arrived at our new home, Long Binh, the last week of September 1966. It was obvious that much work needed to be done. Long Binh would one day become the largest military installation in the world, but we had arrived in the early days, and it was still growing. In fact, it looked like it needed a lot of work. Our compound, unfortunately, was not to grow unless we made it so. Much physical work and filling of sandbags needed to be done.

The mess hall was already built, so eating wasn't a problem. There was also a latrine. Now these "shitters", as we called them, were not state-of-the-art. Instead they took me back to my outhouse days at Iron Hill, Delaware. They were nothing more than holes cut into wooden benches. Positioned under each hole was half of a 50-gallon metal drum to catch the waste. There was no flushing. The only way to get rid of the waste was to drag the drums out from under the benches, douse the contents with gasoline, and burn it. There was no shower, but it was under construction, but not yet useable. There was no housing for us to sleep. Men worked busily to put up the large tents that we'd call home.

John and I were told by Sgt. Aguirre that we'd be pulling perimeter duty from 2200 hours until 0200 hours. In the meantime, we were to assist other men who were filling sandbags. The sandbags would eventually be piled one on top of the other to become the four walls around our tents that would protect us from mortar shrapnel, or rifle fire.

John and I had been hanging together since Fort Benning. He was a soft-spoken cowboy from Laramie, Wyoming, blond hair, blue eyes, a chubby cheeked kid who talked with a slight stutter. John and I both loved baseball and talked a lot about our favorite teams. He was a popular fellow with everyone.

Sergeant Aguirre had shown us where we would be pulling perimeter duty. It was nothing more than a half-dug foxhole with some sandbags piled around it. About all you could do was lie on your side and stare straight ahead.

There was a highway about a hundred yards in front of us that was well traveled. This highway led to Saigon, about 25 miles to the west of us. Just beyond the highway was the small village of Tam Hiep. In between us and the highway were rolls and rolls of barbed wire. Perimeter security was still being upgraded, and that was all that was between us and the local population. That night was our initiation, our welcome to Vietnam. John and I were concerned, to say the least. We were thinking it would be nice to have those Marines with us from the ship. Vomit and all.

The night was very calm, not a breeze in the air. It was intensely dark, except for the faint lights from houses across the highway. The area in front of us was sandy and pocked with low lying shrubs. As a breeze came by the branches of the shrubs would stir and we would give our full attention to this movement. Was it the breeze, or someone crawling? We spent our four hours of perimeter duty wide awake and attentive. It turned out to be quite uneventful. When we were relieved at 0200 hours, we both went back to our tent and crashed for the next several hours.

I woke to the shouts of, "Rain, rain!"

It was about 0900 hours. I pulled myself from my cot and peered through the tent flaps. It was pouring outside. Standing in front of me was John, stark naked, with a bar of soap in his hand. His hair was wet and foamy from the soap. He had a big grin on his face.

"Stew, hurry up! Shower time before it stops!"

I tore off my underwear and threw them on the cot. The coolness of the down pour was a welcome relief. I grabbed John's bar of soap and began to lather up. John's helmet had filled with water, and he bent over, picked it up, pouring the contents over his head. There must have been 30 butt naked MPs standing in the rain bathing. Everyone was laughing and singing.

"Yahoo! Man, this is great!"

I was busy lathering up, hoping the rain wouldn't stop before I rinsed off. It didn't. It rained hard for the next two hours. Our glee turned into gloom, as the rain turned our compound into an ankle-deep quagmire.

We were not allowed off base during the entire time that we were working to get our compound ready and livable. It was one day after another of filling sandbags, helping with construction of certain buildings, and so on. We were not pulling any MP duty, except for perimeter duty around our own compound.

As is Army protocol, our finished work on the compound had to be inspected by the base Inspector General. It was more or less for show, but nevertheless we had to make sure everything was spit and shine. The Inspector General would walk through, give his blessings, and complement our Commanding Officer, Captain Kennedy, and his subordinates for a job well done. Early on the morning of the inspection Lt. Morris approached Tom Likely and me.

"We've got a pile of crap jeep in the motor pool that I want you guys to get out of here. Don't want it around for the inspection. The inspection begins at 1000 hours and will probably last a couple hours.

You two take it off base around 0930, and I don't want to see either of you back here until about 1230 hours. The I.G. should be heading up to the officer's mess by that time. It should be clear by then. Got it?"

Tom and I looked at each other with mischievous smiles. We saluted Lt. Morris. "Yes, Sir, Lt. Morris."

Lt. Morris halfheartedly returned our salutes and said mockingly, "Don't screw it up you goofballs. You wreck even a piece of that crap jeep and it's gonna be your heads."

We were getting off base. We knew that there was a town called Bien Hoa about five miles north of Long Binh. All we needed to know is that it had bars and girls. We both checked out our handguns just to make sure we had some protection in case anything happened. We had no idea what to expect. The other guys were glad to hear that someone was getting off base after three hard weeks of toil and labor, but they weren't happy it was me and Tom.

"Brownnosers, kiss asses!"

That was the typical refrain we got when we spread the word about our good fortune. There wasn't one guy who didn't want to be in our place. A few hours of freedom after filling all those sandbags. Wow! Tom and I hurried to the motor pool.

Tom was from Brooklyn and brought along his heavy accent with him. Tall, lanky, and equipped with a quick wit, I'm sure he had to be his schools class clown.

Tom also liked to sing and had a good voice. One of the guys had an acoustic guitar and Tom and I enjoyed entertaining the troops with our renditions of The Beatles "We Can Work It Out", and "Ticket to Ride", among others.

"You got shotgun, Stew. I'm gonna show you how a real New Yorker navigates. You'll be safe with me behind the wheel. Plus, I can't shoot worth a shit. If something does happen, we'll need your exemplary expertise with a sidearm, coupled with my proficiency behind a hog such as the M151 Army issued jeep, to get us out of the kill zone."

"Tom, I feel so much better now. Do you even know how to start it?" Tom gave me a playful slap on the back of the head.

"You just follow along with Mr. Fireball Roberts here. Let's gas her up. We've got about 15 minutes to split this place, and the women are waitin'."

When we left out of the main gate, we realized we hadn't a clue where we were going. Everything did look like, well, home. Everything except the people on the roadway driving their cars, trucks and riding bikes, were Vietnamese. Surely this couldn't be that difficult. Tom stopped before pulling out onto the roadway.

"Where is Bien Hoa?" He asked while looking up and down the highway. "You asking me, Fireball? I wouldn't have been able to find my way out of the Alamo."

Tom gave me his famous raised eyebrow look and smirked.

"Well then, Mr.Wisenheimer, I guess I'll just have to turn on the ever-reliable radar that is imbedded in this superior brain of mine."

I took this to mean that he didn't have a clue either. Tom licked his right index finger with his tongue and stuck the finger into the air. I guess I'll just follow the stars.

"Uh, the stars were out.....last night!"

"It's this way." Tom turned left onto the roadway and gunned it. The jeep backfired, stalled, and coasted to a halt on the side of the road. He looked straight ahead, hands on the steering wheel.

"I did that on purpose, just testing this baby's strengths and weaknesses."

"Yeah, Fireball, this is real assuring."

Tom cranked her up again, and off we went. My life was in his hands. If we turned up missing-in-action it would be his fault.

A small clapboard sign on the side of the road read **Bien Hoa**. A faded arrow pointed north from the highway that we were on. Tom stuck his arm out and gave his best left turn signal but turned right. Tom **was** a character. He had been waving casually to everyone he saw, as if he was nobility visiting his serfs. Most of the people actually waved back, but most with looks of dismay on their faces.

The road we turned onto was considerably narrower, and traffic was much slower than on the main highway. Bicycles slowed things down considerably in Vietnam, and this roadway was no different. I was amazed to see a family of five on one 50cc motorcycle.

Miraculously one child could be fit between the open space between the driver and the handlebars. Mom sat side saddle behind dad with a baby in her lap, and another child sat behind her, holding on for dear life. Traffic was slowed to 10 miles per hour, at best.

I noticed that there were quite a few small shacks that had signs advertising that they were car washes. Some of the car washes had military jeeps sitting out front being washed by small boys. Strangely there were no soldiers around. The boys couldn't have been any more than nine or 10 years old. When they saw us, they quickly turned and flung their rags over their heads in a circular motion.

"Hey, G.I., car wash! Numba one car wash!"

One boy ran into the roadway after us, still shouting, "Two dolla! Two dolla! Come on!" He ran beside us for several yards. We continued down the road at a snail's pace.

"Shit, it's going to take us all day to get to Bien Hoa at this rate." Tom's eyes lit up. "No shit? Look at this."

The makeshift sign said, 'New York Car Wash, Cheep'. Tom had a big smile on his face, as he looked at me.

"Ah, a little piece of home. Let's check this place out. Maybe we can get a beer." Tom pulled off the road onto the yard and stopped.

There was a small shack with no door. The place looked like it had been barely spared by a ferocious hurricane that had passed through a hundred years ago. Half the shingles were missing off the roof, a leaky hose laid in the front yard next to a bucket, and some rags were strewn about. A kid of about 12 ran out of the front of the house where a door used to be. He was happy to see us.

"Hey, hey, numba one, numba one!" He picked up one of the rags and the end of the hose. Another boy, maybe ten or so, came out and joined him.

"You want car wash?"

Tom had gotten out of the jeep. "How much?"

"5 dolla. Everybody else ten dolla. You neva get better."

Tom raised that eyebrow of his and looked down at the kid. "Everybody else say two dolla small pint. I'm from New York."

The 12-year-old looked up at him quizzically. "What New York?"

85

Tom pointed to the sign. "Your sign says, 'New York Car Wash'. You know, New York City?

"Oh, yeah, New York numba one, numba one! All other car wash numba fuckin' 10 car wash. This one numba one car wash all Vietnam. Five dolla get you good wash."

Tom turned to me. "Obviously a New York discount is out of the question. I'm gonna have to work on this kid for a few minutes."

He was bartering with the kid when his small buddy came up to me. I was still seated in the jeep. The kid looked dead serious. He put both of his hands on my right knee.

In a hushed tone, "You want short time?"

This kid was really cute, "What is short time?" I had no idea.

"You know, boom-boom." The kid then balled up his right hand and pounded his opened left hand onto the top of it several times.

"You know, short time, boom-boom, fuckie fuckie." He continued to pound his opened palm onto his fist. It dawned on me that he was talking about getting laid.

Getting laid, oh, my. Back in the states my girlfriend's favorite words to me had been, 'Keep your stinking hands off me'. Even if I had a gun to my girlfriends head it wouldn't happen. But now it all seemed just too easy.

All I had to do was say 'yes' and he, a child, was going to make it happen. A child was going to introduce me to the greatest of all imagined pleasures. I had no idea Vietnam was so glorious. The Army had not told me this. My groin was alive with the thought of it. This couldn't be true. This was how easy it was going to be away from home? Heck, I'd have to think about moving here.

Why had I chosen to live in America when this was here? Shotgun weddings were a reality back home, and reputations were everything. Not a guy's reputation, but the girl's reputation. Boys were in constant heat, but the girls of that era were in constant retreat. There was no reputation here. This was good. I was trying to be cool. You know, experienced, nonchalant, the 'why would I want boom-boom' kind of cool? I could see Tom was still busy finagling over the cost of the car wash.

"How much?" I asked, trying to look disinterested. "5 dolla! Cheap! Best boom-boom Long Binh!"

I gave him my best annoyed look and for no other reason blurted out, "Two dolla!"

"Okay!" The kid took my hand and tugged at me to leave the jeep.

Okay? That was it? No bartering back and forth? What kind of salesman was this kid? I expected at least a small clash over this, but 'okay'? Just like that? Was this a great country, or what?

"Hey, Tom, I'm gonna get laid."

Tom turned his head quickly. "You're what?"

"Yeah, something to do here while you get the car washed." I tried to act blasé, maintaining my cool.

"Oh, sure, yeah, sure. You sure?" Tom stared for a second and then turned his attention back to the other boy.

I was fumbling through my pockets for cash. I had left my wallet in my locker and didn't have a dime on me.

"Tom, you got two bucks?"

"Two bucks? *Two bucks?* What are you going to screw, a dead buffalo? Even at that you'd think a dead buffalo would be worth at least three bucks. Jesus man, two bucks?" Tom was going through his pockets as he talked, pulling out a wad of cash.

I just stood there trying to look cool. The little kid was pulling on my right hand and was telling me to come with him. Tom handed the two dollars over to me. The boy snatched it from my hand and pushed it into his shirt pocket.

"Hey, payday, I want that back?" He stuffed the rest of the cash into his front pocket.

The kid was pulling hard on my hand now.

"Hey, soon as we get back to the hooch buddy, soon as we get back. I promise, I got money in my locker."

I wasn't surprised to find that the shack was one small bare room. A rickety looking wooden chair sat against one wall. Half of the back wall was missing. The windows were hollow frames, the floor nothing more than dirt. This place had seen better days.

A disheveled looking unshaven man of about 40, cigarette hanging from his mouth, approached me and the boy. Sweat was all over his

87

brow and beaded on his thin hairless arms. He looked annoyed at the little boy.

"You got money?"

The boy extended his hand with the two dollars in it. The man snatched it and motioned uncaringly with his head to follow him. He turned and walked through the hole that used to be part of the back wall.

Behind the shack was an even smaller one. The outer walls were made of soda cans that had been flattened and welded together. Coca Cola and Pepsi cans, how colorful. The roof was a sheet of tin nailed to the thin wooden frames that held up the prefabricated soda can walls. There was no front door, but a bamboo shade that extended to the dirt floor.

The man turned to me, and without emotion, "Boom-boom numba one. You go inside, you hurry." He walked away, followed by the little kid who was now looking over his shoulder glaring at me.

I just stood there unsure of what to do. Did I just go in? Did she come out? Was she going to call for me? I felt a little push from behind. It was the little kid again. Looking irritated, he lifted a corner of the bamboo shade and motioned with his head for me to go. I grabbed a corner of the shade and the kid retreated out of sight. Pulling the shade back I expected the room to be very dark. It wasn't. Half the roof of this shack was also gone.

There she was. A very pretty, petite young girl, lying on her back on a bamboo mat on top a very rustic looking wooden table. She was completely naked and pushed herself up onto her elbows as I walked up to her. I nervously looked around.

Without saying anything she motioned for me to come over to her.

As willing as I thought I was, I was now just as unwilling. I stood there frozen, admiring how pretty she was, and at the sight of seeing my first completely naked girl. She motioned to me again.

"Hurry."

I unfastened my belt and slid my pants down. During my few uncomfortable rushed moments with her she laid with her eyes open, her head turned to the side. She fanned me with a tattered looking fan held in her right hand. I don't know if it was to keep me from sweating, or to keep the sweat of this big American from dripping on her. It was over in moments. It was not romantic, and I had lost my virginity.

When it was over, she got up and quickly walked to a bucket of water in the corner of the room. She squatted next to the bucket, took a cup and washed herself, splashing the water between her legs. She never looked up at me. I hurriedly began putting on my clothes. I was waiting for her to say something. Instead, she kept her head down and just motioned me toward the door.

If I was supposed to feel invigorated, born into manhood, I didn't. How old was this girl? Was that her father who wanted to know where the money was when I entered the shack? Were these boys her little brothers? Was she much older than them? I felt guilty. I had always been an emotional kid, and never meant harm to anyone and this bothered me already. I knew I had to keep my cool when I saw Tom, but the pit of my stomach was burning from the regret I felt.

I walked out and through the front shack, a forced false smile on my face.

Tom was still haggling with the other kid over the price of the car wash. "Hey! I thought you were going to get laid?"

"Ah, let's get out of here." I hurriedly jumped in the passenger seat and just stared straight ahead.

Tom got in behind the wheel. "No, seriously, I thought you were gettin' laid, man."

"I did."

"Holy shit! Uh, you left me like about a minute ago."

Tom started laughing but stopped when he saw that I didn't think there was anything funny about it. He raised his eyebrow. He couldn't help but get in another barb.

"You pay two dolla, or one dolla?"

I broke a tiny smile, putting my hand on the grip of my gun as if to pull it out.

"Okay boss, okay. Hope you ain't in love is all. Hey, look at it this way, at least you didn't take up much of her day." Tom laughed at his own joke.

Tom began to back up the jeep. The kid he had been haggling with then conceded.

"Okay, okay, one dolla! Car wash one dolla!" Tom just waved at him and backed out into the road. The kid looked irritated now, having lost his sale.

"You numba fuckin' 10! You numba big fuckin' 10! You neva come back you fuckin' cheap Charlie son of bitch!" The kid gave Tom the finger.

With a smile, and a wave, Tom joined the slow-moving traffic headed toward the town of Bien Hoa. I looked back thinking of the young girl. Both the boys were now giving us the finger as we drove away. We had had our first bonding experience with the Vietnamese.

I looked over at Tom. "You been laid?"

"Well, it's the law in New York. You have to get certified. You get a certificate. The Mayor gives it to you."

I let out a half-hearted laugh, folding my arms in front of my chest. "Just get me out of here."

"Hey, I'm serious about the certificate. I'll show it to you when we get back. Got it framed and everything. Signed by John F. Wagner himself, my man. Remember it like it was yesterday. It was a beautiful, sun filled sky, family was there…

"Will you shut up and drive?"

"Okay, but don't say I didn't tell you."

For the next half hour, we just drove around the countryside making tourist stops as we went. It was our first real look at the landscape outside of the base camp. The terrain was beautiful, very flat, and very wet. Canals crisscrossed one another through far reaching rice fields. Palm trees dotted the land just off the roadway, and people could be seen in their conical shaped hats working in the knee-deep water of rice paddies.

Water buffalo lulled about nearby, chewing on reeds as they waded lazily through the water.

Little boys saw our jeep and ran to us waving. Girls in traditional Vietnamese dresses walked hand in hand along the roadway, turning shyly from us when we looked at them. It all seemed so relaxed. How could there be a war with all this scenic beauty and tranquility? But through all this I still couldn't get the girl off my mind. I was hoping she didn't hate me. More than that I felt sorry for the life she had been forced into by her father.

Later as we got near the base camp I began to worry about my little adventure and had to speak.

"Tom, pull off the side of the road for a minute."

"Tom, I know it's going to be extremely difficult for you, but I'd appreciate it if you don't mention this to any of the guys when we get in."

He looked up at the sky, looking right and left. "You think it's gonna rain?" I slapped him on the right shoulder. "Man, you do, and I'll kick your ass." Tom turned to me. "Who's your man? Hmm? Who's your pal of all pals, hmmmm? Me. Hand in hand we'll get through this, triumph over the Viet Cong, and hand in hand we'll march home together."

With his raised eyebrow, and his best Franklin Delano Roosevelt imitation, "You have nothing to fear, but fear itself."

When we arrived back at the compound it was obvious the inspection was over. Guys were milling about, but for the most part everyone was in their tents. There were letters to write and sleep to catch up on. The compound was finished, got its seal of approval from the Inspector General, and all looked quiet. Just what I wanted.

We dropped the jeep off at the motor pool and headed for our tent. After all there was the matter of 'two dolla' that I owed. I went in the tent followed by Tom.

"Stewart got laid! Stewart got laid!" Tom had his left arm extended with his finger pointed accusingly right at me.

"The buffalo was three dollars, the girl two dollars. He chose the girl!" I could hear the groans from some of the guys.

I had my hands on my hips and could only shake my head back and forth and smile. This was Tom, but I probably would have done the same to him. I looked at Tom, now with *my* eyebrow raised.

"Oops!" He put his extended fingers of both hands over his mouth. "I was only concerned for your welfare. The more people who know, the more we can help you through this."

I just looked and shook my head. "No shit, thanks."

91

Tom's announcement made the guys in the tent stop whatever it was they were doing and stand up. They started slowly toward me, some with mouths agape. Now I knew that most of these guys were probably cherries too, but I knew I was about to get blasted. They were going to have some laughs, at my expense.

Jim Peterson came over to me and put his right hand on my shoulder. "Did you use your dick, or Tom's?"

"Well, I used mine this time."

Jim laughed and bent over his footlocker, reached in and pulled out a bottle of Jim Beam whiskey from the bottom of the locker.

"Hey, Jim, no time for celebration for me. I don't drink whiskey anyways."

"Drink, Stew? Who's gonna drink it? You're gonna go in the shower, strip down, and wash your dick off with this stuff. The alcohol will kill the germs. Man, you would have had better odds with the dead buffalo. Don't you know you were probably about the one hundredth guy she did today? You get the black syphilis and there's no hope for you. They'll have to cut your dick off and quarantine you in the Philippines for the rest of your life. Try screwing your girlfriend back home without one. It ain't easy, just ask Tom."

Everyone laughed as Tom took a swat at Jim's head and missed. "The Philippines?" I put my hands in my pockets.

"Yep, scary place too. A bunch of little islands, an archipelago actually. Cannibalism, all sorts of weird shit goes on there. A perfect place to quarantine people with the black syph."

Jim was halfway through college back in Cincinnati when he joined and was probably the smartest guy in our company. I had barely made it through high school. I was not about to ask him what archipelago meant, but anything coming from him had to be true. It all sounded very threatening.

The black syphilis? This had been mentioned to us in movies we had watched about communicable diseases on the ship ride over. No one had ever really heard this term before, but the instructors assured us it existed. It was also incurable. And the Philippines, cannibals? Shit! I grabbed the bottle of whiskey, threw my hat on my bed, took off my fatigue shirt, grabbed my towel, along with a bar of soap, and scurried out of the tent.

Tom looked at Jim. "What the fuck is an archipelago?"

"A group of islands. I think Stew thought it meant prison. He sure tore out of here in a hurry, didn't he?"

I was hopping all the way while reaching down clumsily unlacing my boots. Maybe these germs were just milling around on my foreskin waiting for the appropriate time to invade. I was taking my clothes off as fast as I could and noticed I was alone in the shower. I stripped down and got under the spray of the cold water. Hot water, where's the hot water? Doesn't hot water kill germs? We didn't have hot water.

There I stood, alone in a panic. I lathered up and began to clean myself. After rinsing the soap off I took the bottle of whiskey and poured more over my penis. I put the bottle down and rubbed the whiskey around as much as I could, picked up the bottle, and poured on more whiskey. I'd probably have to buy Peterson a new bottle, but heck it was worth, it if it worked.

Looking up I saw PFC O'Hara, a company clerk, standing naked in front of me, as I continued to pour. He had his towel over his shoulder and a bar of soap in his hand. He was looking at my groin area with a puzzled look on his face.

"What are you doing Stewart?"

"Getting it drunk. What's it look like I'm doing?"

O'Hara turned, shaking his head, and walked out of the shower.

I would spend the next two days worrying about the Philippines. I had begged the guys who were present in the tent not to spread the word around about this, and they agreed. But there was always Likely, and he assured me he wouldn't blab.

On the third day the discharge started. A pus-like substance was coming out of the end of my private part. No, it couldn't be, but I knew I had the clap. I thought back to the grotesque educational movies about venereal diseases as part of our indoctrination. The videos were very revolting, and I was now hoping a little exaggerated. Some of the victims had huge pockmarked testicles. Some had tumors the size of oranges on the ends of their penises. It was enough to convince anyone to not take any chances. No chances whatsoever. Except me, of course.

I knew I had to get this taken care of. I went to see Sergeant Aguirre, telling him I was feeling sick, and needed to go to sick call. He wrote out a slip for me and off I went to the infirmary.

The medic took a cotton swap and stuck it up the opening of my penis. He placed the mess onto a glass plate and disappeared into another room. He returned in a few minutes to confirm what I already knew. I had gonorrhea. I was given a shot of penicillin and told to return for additional shots. It took two more trips, and two more shots of penicillin to clean me up. Each time I lied that I just wasn't feeling well and needed to go to sick call. It was embarrassing to say the least, and I was scared as I didn't want to go to an archipelago.

At the end of November, I was called into the Executive Officer's office.

"Good morning Private Stewart."

"Good morning, sir."

How you feeling?"

"Okay, sir?"

"You over the bout of whatever you had?"

"You mean a couple weeks ago, sir?"

"That's it."

He placed a folder in front of him on the desk and opened it. "Private Stewart, before me in this folder is the monthly infirmary report. It lists all the findings and treatment for each soldier who went to sick call. Care to make it a matter of record again exactly why you went to sick call?"

I was speechless. I had been caught lying. Caught lying to my sergeant, and now I was standing before the XO. I had nothing that I could say to him. I was busted.

"Private Stewart? You have something to say? You'd better say it now."

I had to talk. "Sir, I was scared. I didn't know what to do. I thought I'd be thrown out of the Army if anybody found out. I was really scared and thought I'd have the black syph and wind up in the Philippines the rest of my life. Sir, please, I can't be kicked out of the

Army. I wasn't thinking and will do anything to correct this, but don't kick me out."

I was almost in tears. I was young and naïve, and learning life's lesson about telling the truth. I could only throw myself on the mercy of this man. He cleared his throat and looked down at the report. Hopefully he would understand my youthful indiscretion.

"I ought to bust your one stripe away from you. You know that, don't you? I could throw an Article 15 at you for lying to your sergeant. You've got shit detail for the next month. Every day for the next month. You got that PFC Stewart?"

"Yes, sir, yes, sir. Thank you, sir." I wiped the sweat off my brow. I had gotten off lightly.

"You'll report to Sergeant Aguirre and explain to him why you lied. You understand that?" I nodded in the affirmative.

"You're a good man Stewart, but you fuck up again and I'll transfer you out and you'll wind up a door gunner on a chopper. You're dismissed." I saluted and left.

I found Sergeant Aguirre walking towards the mess hall.

Approaching him nervously, "Sergeant Aguirre I need to speak to you."

He stopped and turned towards me. We had a great group of NCOs. He was a career soldiers and set a good example for all of us. He was affable and easily approached with our problems. He was well respected amongst the men.

"Yes, Stewart."

"Sarge, I just came from seeing the XO. I'm on shit detail for a month. I'm on it because I lied to you about sick call. I want to apologize to you. I was just scared, didn't know what to do, and panicked. I'm really sorry and hope you won't trust me because of this."

Sergeant Aguirre gave an understanding smile. "Whiskey never works, never."

He patted me on the shoulder, winked, turned, and walked towards the mess hall. My story had obviously gotten around. Sergeant Aguirre paused and turned to me.

"Always tell the truth Stewart. No matter how hard it hurts, tell the truth, son."

"Yes, sergeant, thank you sergeant."

Sergeant Aguirre was about 40 years old, a career soldier who had also lied once. During World War II he had enlisted at 16 to go off and fight the Germans. He was found out, shipped back to the states, but joined again when he turned 18, serving in Korea and now Vietnam. He was a good man.

Chapter 12

It was Christmas eve 1966. My first Christmas away from home. That was probably true for most of us. I had just gotten off duty and was not scheduled to work on Christmas day. I'd catch up on some letter writing. Tom was not scheduled either, so we could sit around and practice a few tunes.

I had just gotten my gear off and put away when Tom stuck his head through the tent flap.

"Hey, Stew, tonight drinks are on you!"

"Bullshit, Likely! It's your turn to buy."

"Screw you! It's Christmas, a time for giving. It's better to give than receive. Come on, buy me a beer. The Playboy Club is open all night."

"Tom, you ever wonder why you only have one friend? That friend is me. Do you think this friendship is free? Hell man, I've been writing down every minute of our friendship in my little black book just savin' it up for Christmas. By my calculations I have let you hang with me since the USS Buckner, protecting your butt from all the guys who have commented on how fine an ass you have. I'd have to estimate the bill at about $600.00. You can start payin' the bill tonight Thomas."

He raised that eyebrow. "They really think I have a fine ass?"

I had to laugh. Tom had a comeback for everything. The guy was unflappable, and I always seemed to wind up being the straight man.

Tom now showed feigned interest. "Who said I have a fine ass? Johnson? I've seen the way he looks at me sometimes, man. I bet its Johnson." Tom gave me his best deep-thinking look.

"All right, all right, I'll buy. But, let me warn you, I don't drink much, so I expect you to keep the bar tab d-o-w-n."

"Who, me? Hey, I wanted to be a priest before an MP. It will be like communion, just a little bread, and a sip of wine."

"Yeah, right, that's why you have the tattoo 'fish' on your left shoulder?"

"Well, I have 'go' tattooed on the right one. I'll be good, I'll be a cheap Charlie, promise. I'm hittin' the shower, so I'll see you at the club in about half an hour."

"Ah, give me a minute and I'll take a shower too. I need to see you naked so I'll feel a lot better about the size of my pecker."

Tom laughed and ducked out of the tent. I had gotten him, and this was the first time he wasn't able to give me a good comeback. Something told me I'd pay for that.

We had a big club. Well, a big tent. It was one of many clubs in country designated as *The Playboy Club*. It could have said *Our Drinking Tent*, but everything was a tent, so that would have been redundant. So, *The Playboy Club* it was.

Tom and I found the place packed. Smoke filled the air, and I could hear the sound of The Beatles singing "I Want to Hold Your Hand" playing from the jukebox in the corner. We had a tent for a club, but we had a jukebox. Nobody knows where the jukebox came from, but we were certainly glad to have it. Everybody knew where the tent came from, government issued. Go figure.

Salutes went up from those already drinking. Raised cans of Black Label and shot glasses filled with spirits.

"Five-five-deuce! Five-five-deuce! Fuckin' best, man!" I don't know who yelled it out, but it got a hardy round of affirmation from all who were there.

"Fuckin' five-five-deuce! Hooh, hooh, hooh!" Men were drunk. Tom and I saw John wave us over to his table. Mike Ramirez and Jim Troupe were sitting there along with Doug Dragert and Jim Peterson. Tom and I grabbed a couple chairs and pulled them up to the table. He looked at me and snapped his fingers.

"Get me a Budweiser. You can have whatever."

"Uh, excuse me, but the maid service is closed for the evening, bozo. If I'm buyin', you're gettin'."

"I'll pay."

"Whoa! You'll pay? Tom Likely? Holy shit! Let me see the money."

He took a wad of bills, rolled and wrapped with a rubber band, out of his pocket.

Doug Dragert's eyes opened wide. "Who the hell did you kill?"

"Kill? Kill? My talent has always been in the cards, my friend. A sucker is born every day, even in the five-five-deuce. You will notice that some of our comrades will not be attending this Christmas eve as they are awaiting the arrival of their pay warrants coming at the end of the month. Their wallets are a little lighter because of me."

"You got them to gamble away their money? Just before Christmas?"

"Yep, and I only cheated a couple times." Tom slammed down a five on the table, throwing a panatela between his lips, and lit it.

"Drinks on me, men. Merry Christmas!" I scooped up the money and headed for the bar. John yelled out, "Make that two more beers, Stew!"

I had never been a drinker. Although I'd had a beer now and then since joining the Army, I had never really acquired a taste for it. I returned to the table with everyone's order.

"Four Black Labels, gentlemen."

"I wanted a Budweiser." Tom said.

"Well, they ain't got Budweiser. It's Black Label or Pabst Blue Ribbon."

I laid the change down in the middle of the table. "We'll keep the pot here. I'll keep getting', as long as you keep payin'."

"Stew, we all know you're a cherry boy when it comes to the brew, so let's start doing some serious Christmas celebrating."

Doug leaned over in his chair and picked up a bottle of whiskey, putting it on the table.

"Boilermakers all around, gentlemen!" He unscrewed the cap.

I put my elbows on the table and leaned in towards him, "What is a boilermaker?" I had never heard the term before. "Stew, observe and learn."

Doug took the whiskey bottle and poured it into a shot glass that had magically appeared on the table. He picked up the shot glass, put the shot glass to his lips, tilted his head back, and swallowed the whiskey in one motion. This was followed by several large gulps from his beer. Doug slammed the can down on the table. Everyone was silent. Doug's cheeks turned red as he pursed his lips together.

"Ahhhhhhhhhhhhhhhhhhh! And then belched.

"You want me to do that?" Doug slid the shot glass over in front of me. "Well, there's a different way." He poured another shot of whiskey. This time he poured beer into a cup, filling it halfway. Doug carefully dropped the shot glass into the cup, picked it up, and chugged it down.

Oh, my! This was new to me, but part of male bonding *is* giving up all sensibility and reasoning. You had to be willing to go that 'extra step'. Everyone was looking at Doug admiringly. He picked up the bottle and poured the whiskey into the shot glass, shoving it over to me.

"How many sips of beer I have to take to wash it down?" Everyone chuckled.

"Sips?" Mike Ramirez was laughing at me. "Sips?"

"Stew, chug about half the can, or the whiskey will rot the inside of your throat out." Doug let out another belch.

I'd never tasted hard liquor before, only sipped beer. When I was growing up neither of my parents were drinkers. My dad and mom would go out once a year, and dad would take that time to get plastered. He'd get out of the car, falling over himself, laughing as he stumbled toward the house. I'd help him up to his bed while he giggled, speaking unintelligibly all the way. Other than that, the only time there was beer in the house was if my dad was watching the Friday Night Fights on television, and only if he had enough money left over from paying the bills to buy a six pack. I would be offered a sip and would oblige. I remember the taste being pretty good, but thanks to the legacy of my Aunt Corrine I never I had an appetite for drinking. She gave me all the education about drinking that I needed.

Aunt Corrine was the wife of my dad's brother, Uncle Fred. She was a nice lady, but sadly my memories of her were of her visiting our house, arriving drunk, bringing her bottle inside with her, and leaving after she urinated all over herself. She would be sitting on the couch, or chair in the living room, and then it would happen.

Slowly a urine spot would appear in her pants, or dress, and spread all the way down her leg. Uncle Fred was always patient with her and would help her up and leave embarrassed, apologizing all the way to the car. You could not help but like Aunt Corrine, her drinking aside. She died an alcoholic, way before her time.

Jim Peterson had started a drum roll on the table with the tips of his fingers. "Okay Stew, the time is here."

I picked up the shot glass and threw the whiskey back deep into my throat.

I swallowed, choked and spewed a small spray of liquid through my nose. It was awful. My chin went to my chest and tears came to my eyes.

"The beer! The beer!" They shouted, as Jim continued the drum roll.

I reached down, grabbed the can and began chugging the beer. One gulp, two gulps, three gulps, four. That was it. The foreign taste of the whiskey was gone. I brought the can down hard on the table, beer spewing out of the top of the can like a small volcanic explosion.

"Holy shit!" I was grimacing, my eyes involuntarily shut, as I looked down at the table trying to overcome the burning in my throat.

The guys were all laughing and hooting. I put both hands squarely on the table in front of me, palms down, fingers spread. My eyes were closed, and my throat was on fire. My face must have looked like a dried-up prune.

Gasping for breath, "May I have another, please?"

More hooting, more cheers. What was I thinking? Well, it **was** Christmas eve. I'm not sure what that had to do with what I was doing, but I guess it was a good enough excuse. Plus, we were bonding, and it seemed everyone was pleased. I would try at least one more. One more for the guys.

I would remember nothing after the fifth one.

I felt a gentle nudge at my shoulder. I was certainly in R.E.M. (rapid eye movement) and dreaming. They say your dreams are more vivid during R.E.M. I'm not sure who said it, but it was certainly true in this instance. I was lying on a wooden bench and Aunt Corrine was straddling my stomach. There was a big urine spot in the middle of her dress. She raised a large boulder above her head with both hands and slammed it down on my skull.

"Wake up, little nephew, wake up!"

She raised the boulder over her head again and bounced it off my temple. The boulder would recoil, and with each hit she would say to me sweetly, "Wake up, Jimmy! Wake up!"

When would the pounding stop? Another gentle nudge on my shoulder, as Aunt Corrine slammed the boulder down on my forehead again.

"Wake up shithead, wake up…" She had a benevolent smile on her face and her breath reeked of stale whiskey. I looked up at her and pleaded.

"Please don't pee all over me!"

This time she dropped the boulder onto my head, and it bounced high into the air, and out of sight. She flew off of me and disappeared along with the boulder.

"Private Stewart!" I heard a male's voice as my shoulder was nudged again, harder this time.

"Private Stewart!" I was coming out of my dream, but the voice was still very, very far away. I was trying to force my eyes open, but they were stuck together like glue. As I struggled to open them, dim light seeped into the area of my brain where my dream of Aunt Corrine had just been.

"Private Stewart, wake your ass up!" The nudging was almost violent now. My right eye struggled open, half clogged with sleep. "Aunt Corrine?"

I focused enough to see a silhouette. Definitely not the emaciated outline of my dead, drunk Aunt. It was Lieutenant Morris. I was lying on my stomach and struggled to turn on my left side.

"Lieutenant Morris, good morning, sir. What time is it, sir?"

He had his hands on his hips and appeared to be fighting back laughter.

Things were coming into focus and it was very bright. I struggled to get onto one elbow. My head continued to throb. Lieutenant Morris's demeanor turned serious.

"What the hell are you doing out here Private Stewart? And, who the hell is Aunt Corrine?"

"Out here, Lieutenant?"

"What are you doing sleeping out here on the perimeter?"

My god, I wasn't in my tent. My footlocker was at the foot of the bed, my wall locker was at the head. My boots were neatly placed under my cot. I was also naked. I looked to my left and saw the perimeter fence about five feet away from me. Reaching down I picked up a boot and placed it over my private parts.

"Private Stewart, didn't you learn from your sick call episode?"

"Well, sir, I'm not totally sure I'm responsible for this. I don't feel too well, and don't remember much. Do you know how I got out here, sir?"

"Well, I was hoping you'd tell me."

"Well, sir, I don't know. I just don't know." I shook my head trying to shake off the effects of the night before.

"Don't you have a shitter to clean?" I staggered to my feet, the boot still covering my privates.

"Uh, yes, sir. Yes, sir, I do." I picked up my other boot and held it behind me, covering my buttocks.

"Sir, if you don't mind. I'll get dressed and get on that right now, sir."

"Jesus, Stewart, see that you do. Who is Aunt Corrine?"

"Sir, it's hard to explain."

"I bet it is."

Lieutenant Morris turned and walked back towards the tents. I could have sworn I heard him chuckle. I was still struggling with my focus and balance. How'd the hell did I get out here? How'd all my stuff get out here? I flopped back down on the cot and put my head in my hands. Then it was all clear. Tom Likely, John Prahl, Doug Dragert, Jim Peterson, Mike Ramirez, Jim Troupe and the rest of The Playboy Club had given me a Christmas present. A free night on the Long Binh perimeter, compliments of too many boilermakers, and the five-five-deuce.

I looked back toward the row of tents, squinting to try to get them to come into focus. Looking down at my watch it was 0900 hours.

Geez, it was Christmas day, 1966. Laughter was coming from the tents.

I heard Tom yell out, "Everybody get a picture?" It was only December for gosh sakes. This was going to be a long year.

Chapter 13

Christmas had come and gone. It had been an uneventful first three months, except for the adventures of PFC Stewart.

I could hear the sounds of footsteps and the thud of boots hitting the wooden floors of our tent. Slowly waking from my sleep, I rolled over in my cot and pulled the sheet up over my face not wanting to awaken fully. I wanted to sleep more, but could now hear faint chattering, then more voices. It couldn't be dawn already. I pulled the sheet back and fought to open my eyes. It was still pitch dark. What was happening here? I heard John Prahl's familiar voice.

"Holy shit!" I heard rapid footsteps approach my cot.

Almost whispering. "Hey, Jim, get up." I could hear John chuckle. "Jesus man, you didn't hear all the shit? You need to get up."

An unrecognizable voice spoke, "Jesus, guys look at Stewart."

I got up on one elbow and looked at what was a silhouette of his face against the light of the moon coming through the open tent flap. Doug walked over and looked down at me.

"You've got to be kidding!" John turned to Doug and put his index finger to his lips.

"Shhh! Jesus, they find out about this...."

"Find out about what, John" Sitting up, rubbing at my eyes with the knuckles of my hands.

"You just slept through a fucking mortar attack."

Now I was awake and alert. I got up and hurriedly began to put my pants on, hearing the chuckles of a few of the other guys who had also entered the tent. I began lacing up my boots as quick as I could as Doug was taking off his flak jacket.

"Hey, it doesn't seem to matter much now Stew, you're safe. We went out on the perimeter and protected you." Doug and John began to laugh. John took off his helmet and threw it on his cot.

My fingers were shaking trying to put the small round buttons into the vertical slits on my shirt. Where was my helmet? Under the bed, yes. My gonorrhea caper, my being carried outside unconscious to the perimeter after a night of too much booze, and now this? My ass was in a sling now if the brass found out. I didn't want a lieutenant or sergeant walking in and seeing me undressed. It wouldn't take much for them to figure out what happened. I didn't need this. Thank god there is no roll call when under attack.

Lights had been turned on in the tent now, and the rest of the guys could see me. "Hey, Stew you didn't want to get your uniform dirty laying in the mud out on the perimeter?" Jim Troupe was placing his flak jacket in his wall locker.

John turned and issued his, "shhhh" warning again. The other guys complied, sensing the seriousness.

"What the hell happened?" I was now putting my flak jacket on.

"Well, the VC decided to throw in several mortar rounds, so we decided that tents were probably a target, and it would not be a safe place to stay. So, *we* all decided, except for you, PFC Forever, to get out while the gettin' was good."

"PFC Forever, huh?" I chuckled at the thought but had to admit that there was a distinct possibility this could follow me, and I would never get promoted again.

"Jim, how in the name of the good Lord did you not hear the incoming?"

"For the same reason I got gonorrhea. For the same reason I woke up on the perimeter Christmas day?"

John and Doug began to laugh. Mike Ramirez threw his pillow at me and began laughing.

"Where were you raised again? Retard Hill, Maryland? Oh, wait, Fair Hill, that's it." I threw Mike's pillow back at him.

Everyone was out of their gear now, and I began to calm down a bit. Other guys were slipping into their cots, pulling their sheets up over their shoulders. I sat back down on my cot somewhat relieved, letting out a sigh.

John was in bed and pulled the sheet up over his head. "Good night, PFC Forever."

I threw my helmet onto his stomach and it ricocheted off onto the floor. "You're nothing but a dumb Wyoming cowboy."

"Yeah, but when I make sergeant, you'll still be a private." I laid back on my cot and pulled the sheet up to my chin.

John was still chuckling. "Wake me when the shooting starts. If you hear it, of course."

Dragert sat up in his cot. "Oh, I forgot. Goodnight dear. Sleep tight. You want a tuck in, pillow fluffed?"

I just chuckled. There was no reason to answer. These were a bunch of good guys.

It was nice to know that you could mess up and they would cover for you. We had all screwed up something at one time or another in this man's Army. Wouldn't be the first time, wouldn't be the last. However, it did seem I was trying to set some kind of record.

Maybe I could go to sick call and get my hearing checked. No, no more sick call for me. Plus, I already knew how hard of hearing I was. Mortar attack? How would I ever explain this one?

I let out a soft sigh and closed my eyes. How in the name of god *did* I sleep through a mortar attack? It wasn't important now.

Sitting up in my cot, "Hey Dragert honey! You mind not calling me dear?" All I could hear was gentle snoring. I laid back and drifted off to sleep.

Chapter 14

The perimeter of Long Binh had several towers that were manned 24 hours a day by two MPs. Our job was to keep watch. Simple as that. It was long and boring duty.

The tower on the northeast perimeter at Long Binh looked out over a gently rolling speck of land of mostly marsh and shrubs. An occasional tree could be seen sticking up on the horizon, but for the most part it was devoid of heavy foliage. The road to Xuan Loc could be seen far off in the distance.

The tower itself was a large concrete structure that looked as if it was left over from the French occupation of the '50's. It was in the shape of a hexagon and stood about 10 feet high. Sandbags, two or three deep, were piled on the top of the tower giving it a total height of about 15 feet, including the roof. The roof consisted of corrugated steel secured to wooden supports. More sandbags were piled upon the steel roof for extra protection against any incoming mortar rounds.

John and I had been assigned to tower duty together on this night. Our 10-hour shift would be from 2200 hours until 0800 hours. An MP patrol jeep dropped us off along with our ammo canisters and other gear. John and I both had our M14's, plus a 12-gauge shot gun for good measure. We also brought along binoculars, several flares, c-rations and canteens of water. There was a radio that was already in the tower in case we needed to contact anyone.

The two MPs that we relieved were happy to see us. The best thing about tower duty was getting off tower duty. As we got out of the MP jeep they jumped in, sarcastically wishing us a good late-night tour. We would at least be pulling duty at night, and not during the day when the heat would fry an egg on the hood of a jeep.

John threw his duffel bag full of equipment over his shoulder. "Well, Sir James, our castle awaits."

"No shit. Ladies first."

John lumbered through the rear of the tower and took the spiral stairs to the top.

The tower gave you a really good view of the surrounding countryside during the day, but at night it was limited by the light of the moon. Rolls of concertina wire, in large circular rolls, were secured to metal stakes hammered into the ground laid around the entire perimeter. Anything on the other side of this wire at night would be considered hostile.

"You know I hate this duty." John threw his duffel bag down on the wooden floor and began to take out the supplies he had brought along.

"Hey, John. Just think, we've only got about ten more months of this. Geez, could things be any more boring out here? Maybe one of these days we'll see some action. Who knows, maybe tonight's our night."

"Jim, dream on, and you know it. I'm hot to do some town patrol. I wonder if we'll ever get to patrol Bien Hoa?"

"Well, I heard through the grapevine that we're supposed to start some convoy escorts. I guess the 720th MPs are stretched thin and we'll be assisting them. Now, that's something that can get us into some shit, and it'll be better than sitting around in this stupid tower. That's for sure."

"Amen to that brother, amen."

John and I had become as close as brothers. It was impossible to get to know every man in the company, so men usually hooked onto two or three guys in their squad and stuck with them. John and I each grabbed one of the two wobbly wooden chairs and pulled ourselves up to the sandbags, and looked out into the night.

We never ran out of things to talk about, but we also knew we had to keep watchful. John took it upon himself to keep the binoculars in his hands and routinely gaze out into the terrain.

It was about 0400 hours when the wind began to pick up. It was these hours that the VC would be their most active. Between now and daybreak was the time your senses would be demanding that you shut down and fall asleep. It was a struggle to keep your eyes open, especially in the closed environment of the tower. Especially in all this boredom.

Every hour or so a duty sergeant would drive by and shine his spotlight at the tower. We would take a flashlight and flash it back at him a couple times to let him know we were okay, and awake. It had been pounded into us since MP Academy to never even think about sleeping on duty.

Everyone at the MP Academy was introduced to static post duty during academy training. We would be taken to locations away from the mainstream and told to guard a most insignificant building. We'd be alone and didn't have the luxury of a companion to prattle to, to keep us awake. This duty usually started at midnight and would last until 0800 hours. Again, during those hours between 0400 and daylight your body would struggle to stay awake. I'm not sure man was made to stay awake all night. More than a few MPs in training were caught napping, or standing with their eyes closed, only to be awakened by a drill instructor just inches from their face. So, no sleeping while on duty.

It was a good learning experience. The consequences were severe enough to discipline yourself to stay awake, and no one in their right mind wanted to deal with the consequences. You'd do anything you could to stay awake. Slap your face, pour water from your canteen over your head, sing sweet love songs, anything.

It was almost 0400 hours and our conversation had slowed to a minimum as both John and I felt the effects of our bodies wanting to sleep.

"Stew!" I looked over at John who was holding the binoculars to his eyes and motioning me to move the few feet that separated us. "Come here."

"What's up?"

"There's something moving. Take a look." John pointed to where he wanted me to look, as I brought the binoculars to my eyes. "About a hundred yards out. See those low shrubs all bunched together? Right in there."

The excitement had started the adrenalin flowing and I was now wide awake. "John, what am I looking for? I don't see anything."

"Look for movement in the high grass to the right of the shrubs. Just look."

I kept focused. "I'm not seeing it, John."

"Here, give 'em to me." I handed the binoculars back to John. He put them up to his eyes impatiently. "Damn it! Where? There! Damned, Jim look off to the right of that big growth of shrub, there's fucking movement."

I took the binoculars back and gazed out towards the night. Yes, there it was. Movement. It looked like a steady stream making its way through the high grass. Slowly, slowly the grass was parting. It was heading our way.

"Shit! Are they fucking crawling, or what? Fuck John, something's out there, for damned sure."

John was standing, half crouched and had grabbed a flare.

"Stew, keep looking!" John's voice was hushed, as if it was possible for whoever it was a hundred yards out into the night to hear us. "Keep looking!"

My heart was pounding knowing how big of a target this tower was. Flat terrain and a tower that stood fifteen feet up into the air was a perfect silhouette in this moonlit sky. If these guys had any RPGs (rocket propelled grenades) we might not see the light of day.

I heard a thump and then a whizzing sound. John had shot off a flare. Like a firework going off at a 4th of July celebration, it shot into the night sky toward the shrubbery. Then the faint sound of a pop. The flare went off and we could see the parachute open, as it gently began its decent, lighting up the night sky.

John was now pointing his M14 down field toward the shrubs. I hastily put down the binoculars and followed his lead. The flare was descending very slowly as the wind carried it across the lit-up field.

We had gone through dry runs with the flares but had never actually shot one off while on duty. It was an eerie sight. I expected machine guns and mortars to open up.

John had his M-14 raised, concentrating with one eye closed, as he aimed out toward the field.

"Fuck this." John protested in a hushed tone. "We're sitting ducks up here."

I heard the static from the radio first. "Tango bravo, tango bravo, what is going on out there? Tango bravo answer, over!"

John and I glanced quickly at one another; our attention drawn from the field in front of us.

"Tango bravo, tango bravo, answer your radio, over. I repeat, answer your radio!" The duty officer had obviously seen the northeast perimeter light up like New York City at night.

"I'll get it." I laid my rifle across the sandbags and slouched back to where the radio was sitting.

"This is tango bravo, over."

"Who is this!"

"Uh, this is Private Stewart, 552nd MPs, over."

"What is going on out there? I've got the 11th Armored Cav calling me here wanting to know if they're needed. They can see the flare too, over."

I looked back at John, who now seemed more concerned about the duty officer than what might possibly be going on outside of the perimeter. He urged me to say something.

"Uh, we thought we saw movement outside of the perimeter, over."

"Movement? Well, is there, or isn't there, over?"

I looked at John, who glanced back towards the field, and then back toward me. "Well, there was." he whispered.

I brought the radio back up to my mouth. "Wait a minute."

John looked at me in amazement. "Jim, you can't say fucking 'wait a minute'. Say 'stand by', Jesus!"

"John, what's going on? What do I tell this asshole?" I put the radio mic back to my lips. "Uh, correction, stand by one, stand by one."

The flare was flickering out as John strained his eyes looking back out toward the shrubs.

"Tango bravo, tango bravo, what are you doing? Give me your status, over?" John looked at me and shrugged his shoulders. "Tell him everything's okay."

"Uh, this is tango bravo, everything seems to be okay. All clear here, over."

"Tango bravo, you stand by there, the duty sergeant is on his way."

Stand by? Where were we going? I was now sitting on my butt, radio in one hand, helmet tilted back, looking at John disgustedly. He had dropped from his firing position, and laid his rifle on the wooden floor, as he squatted next to it.

For all we knew, half a battalion could have been crossing over the wire now and it just didn't seem important. We were doing our job and now it seemed all hell was going to break loose. Not with the enemy, but the duty sergeant.

I saw the beam of light peek over the sandbags just above John's head. A silhouette of a jeep stood out on the horizon.

"Where's the fucking flashlight." I looked around on the floor and saw John give me a nod. He flipped it over to me. Standing up I flashed the light back in the direction of the patrol jeep. I could hear feet already rapidly stumbling down the incline toward the tower.

Out of the darkness came Sergeant Michaels and his driver. "Hey! Hey, get your asses down here!"

John and I got up, picked up our rifles, and slowly walked down the staircase and out the back. Sergeant Michaels had his hands on his hips.

"What the fuck is going on out here?"

"Well, sarge, we thought we saw movement, so we shot off a flare."

"Shot off a flare? You ever think of calling it in before you shot of the fucking flare?"

"Call it in, sergeant?" I looked over at John, who looked none too happy. "Yes, what's your name?" He leaned forward to check my name tag.

"Private Stewart? Call it in? Get on the radio and call it in so that the whole goddamned base doesn't go on alert and start shooting every goddamned thing that moves. You know how many people you woke up? The fuckin' Cav was getting saddled up to head out here."

"We woke up the Cav?"

"Don't be a fucking smart ass. I'm going to have to answer for this, not you." John chimed in.

"Sarge, we thought we really had VC coming at our perimeter. To tell you the truth, we still aren't so sure that we didn't. What were we supposed to do?"

"Call it in private, call it in!" Sergeant Michaels took a half-smoked cigarette out of his pocket and lit it up.

John and I just stood there speechless.

"You guys get yourselves back up in that tower and put a clamp on those fucking flares. You shoot those off again without calling it in and I'll have both of your asses in the morning."

It was no use arguing. The rules of engagement, previously unknown to us, were now clear. No flares would be set off without permission. If we were shot at, we'd have to get permission before we shot a flare off. No matter if we were under attack, we'd have to get on the phone and let them know and ask permission. Would we win the war this way? If there were VC out there in the bush, they must be laughing their asses off.

I could envision them huddled low around the shrubbery now with one class clown cradling his AK-47 sarcastically chattering in Vietnamese, "call it in, call it in!"

The sergeant and his driver got in their jeep and spun out, heading back toward camp. I looked over at John and raised both my eyebrows and puffed my cheeks out.

"We gotta get out of Long Binh."

John and I made our way back up into the tower, both depressed. We had done our job. We had hurt no one. We had only used one Army issued flare; parachute included. What sense was there for both of us to struggle to keep awake and ever alert? Both of us had aged a bit thinking we might see our first fire fight. With the adrenalin rush now gone, we were both exhausted. John took one last look past the perimeter with the binoculars.

"The VC must have fallen asleep from laughing so hard."

"I say we do the same. You want to sleep in one-hour shifts?"

"Sounds good to me. You go first."

All that MP academy training we went through now seemed like a distant memory, ancient history. John sat back in his chair, pulled up to the sandbags and stared quietly out at the perimeter. I took my helmet off and folded my empty duffel bag like a pillow, curled up on my side on the hard-wooden floor. I would get some sleep for an hour and then John would sleep. We'd do this until relieved at 0800 hours by the morning shift. No sense in losing sleep over this. It was just a war.

Chapter 15

Right after New Year's Sergeant Aguirre came to us during guard mount and said that the 1st Infantry Division, and the 9th Infantry Division, were looking for volunteers to escort convoys, and generally assist them for an upcoming operation against a VC stronghold.

John was standing next to me and I nudged my shoulder. We had both been talking about how boring our work was on base and were looking for something more exciting. We both quickly raised our hands. Dragert and PFC Baxter quickly did the same.

"Okay, Stewart, Prahl, Baxter you were the first three, so I'll see you go to the 1st Infantry Division at Dian. Dragert and Gary Hurley, you'll be going to the 9th Infantry Division at Lai Khe. Start gathering your gear. You'll leave tomorrow. Stewart, Prahl, Baxter, there's a chopper heading out of here for Dian at 0900 hours. You guys will be on it. Dragert and Hurley, you'll be catching a convoy at 0800 hours. Keep your heads down and don't embarrass The Deuce." He winked and smiled at us. I knew he was proud of his men.

We would be taking part in Operation Cedar Falls. Elements of the 1st Infantry, 25th Infantry, 9th Infantry Divisions, 173rd Airborne, 196th Infantry Brigade, and the 11th Armored Calvary would eventually surround an area known as the Iron Triangle, heavily inhabited by the Viet Cong. A huge contingent of Vietnamese army forces, ARVN, would also be involved in the fight. The idea was to push in on the VC from all sides and destroy them and their base camps.

Dian (Zeon) was the main base camp for the 1st Infantry Division and was south of the area of operation. The 1st Infantry Division would have to be re-supplied by running convoys from Dian to Xuan Loc and Ben Cat. That's what John and I were excited about. A chance to see some action.

"Hot damned!" John did a little jig.

Dragert, Baxter, Hurley and I gathered around John, and were as happy as school children at recess. What an adventure we all would soon be going on. This was the Vietnam we wanted to see. We had no idea about death and the suffering of the troops in combat. We were naïve, and like little boys playing army, we wanted to be a part of it.

But we also were excited because of a sense of duty. We were, after all, soldiers.

That morning John, Earl and I waited at the helipad for our flight. I had never been in a Huey before and this was especially trying for me because I was afraid of heights. We sat on our duffel bags waiting with our shiny MP helmets adorning our heads. A soldier wearing the patch of the Big Red One, 1st Infantry Division, ran up to us and instructed us to follow him.

I was the last in the chopper and had the honor of occupying the seat next to the door. The machine gunner was to my left and just a bit behind me. His M60 machine gun sat on its tripod, barrel facing down. He tapped me on my shoulder.

"Belt up!" pointing down toward the seat belt that was secured around his own waist.

I reached down and strapped mine on. John and the other guys did the same. We were all a little nervous not knowing what to expect. The engine of the chopper began to rev, and the rotation of the blades started slowly. Thud, thud, thud, thud, quicker and quicker until the sound became one steady whir. Dust was swirling madly off the tarmac. Suddenly the chopper shot upward about 20 feet off the ground. The rotor blades churned loudly. I turned to the machine gunner and screamed over the roar of the blades.

"When are they going to shut this door?"

"They aren't!"

Holy shit! Less than one foot to my left was nothing but wide-open spaces. As far out and as far down as the eye could see. I didn't join the Air Force. The doors would remain open during the flight. I was so glad that my stomach was empty but wouldn't know what to tell the guys if I fainted during the flight. I had to muster some strength. I would do this by staring straight at a spot on the back of the pilot's helmet during the entire flight. I grabbed the bottom of the metal seat with both hands at my side, digging my fingers into the metal. The chopper lifted, tilted left, and sped off north to Dian.

John was sitting to my right. I could hear him yelling in my ear.

"Stew, ain't this great?" John then gave me a nudge.

I nodded my head up and down a few times, but kept my eyes glued to the back of the pilot's head.

"Yeeeeeehaaaaaa! So long, Long Binh!" John was having the time of his life.

The chopper ride aside, I felt like a kid fulfilling a childhood fantasy. How many times had we reenacted famous battles as kids? Custer's last stand, the battle of the Alamo, Pork Chop Hill. To every kid play fighting was a reality. Now, removed from all those childish things here we were going out into the field. Headed for the Big Red One, the First Infantry Division.

The First Infantry Division had a glorious history and we were to become part of it. From General John "Blackjack" Pershing arriving in France during WWI, the D-Day landings on June 6, 1944 during WWII, and in the summer of 1965, the Big Red One being the first division called to fight in Vietnam. We were to be a part of their history.

As I was in thought, I could still hear John whooping it up. I managed to look over at him. He gave me a wink and flashed a big white smile.

"Isn't this fucking great?" John couldn't stop his enthusiasm.

Back to the reality of the flight I had forgotten how to speak. I struggled, keeping my eyes straight ahead. Finally, I got the words out. "I'll let you know as soon as we touch ground."

When we arrived, we were housed next to the First Infantry Division MPs but did not share a tent with them. We were "FNGs" to them (fucking new guys). They didn't have much to say and weren't eager to meet us. After all, they were infantry, we were rear-echelon, and hadn't seen or done a thing to earn their respect. Just the way it was.

Our first duty assignment was gate guards. John and I were disappointed. We had done this at Long Binh. It was nothing more than monitoring the traffic in and out of the base. At Long Binh there was a very small wooden kiosk at each gate entrance. Just enough shelter to keep you out of the midday's sun. At Dian, there were large heavily reinforced sandbagged bunkers. John and I pulled our first shift from 2200-0800.

Sounded just like tower duty to us. But first, in the morning, we would go into town as security for a deuce and a half truck picking up laborers who worked on base.

Every morning before 0800 hours military trucks would go to a designated spot in town and pick up laborers and bring them onto the base. An MP gun jeep would tag along for protection. It was a busy time of the morning with people going to work, kids going to school. Most all the girls wore the beautiful long traditional áo dài dresses. Boys all seemed to be dressed in short sleeved white shirts. Kids were pedaling bicycles, some had two or three piled on for the trip. Our jeep had pulled behind the last truck as it pulled from the curb and headed back to base.

The dirty bursts of diesel fuel clouds from these trucks was stifling. It's a smell that has never left me. Till this day I still have flash backs whenever I get a whiff of diesel fuel. That, and the whirring of helicopter blades.

Some of the kids held onto the sides of the trucks to help them navigate their bikes through the traffic. The convoy of trucks couldn't have been going any more than five mph, the traffic was so thick. We came to a turn in the roadway, and the loaded truck in front of me made a sharp turn at the corner.

A lithe girl on a bike, perhaps 10 years old, and wearing a conical hat, was pedaling by the huge right rear wheel of the truck. She continued straight as the truck made its turn and I watched in horror as she flipped off the bike and fell under the monstrous wheel. The wheel knocked off her conical hat and pinched her head, spitting her fallen body sideways, and up on the sidewalk. I couldn't believe what I saw. People in the rear of the truck screamed out in horror. I didn't even wait for my jeep to stop but jumped out of the shotgun side and ran towards the girl.

She was on her back with her head tilted to the left. The back of her skull was missing. A trail of blood and scalp had splattered the roadway from where her twisted bike lay. There wasn't a drop of blood on her anywhere, just the exposed portion of her brain.

Her school pack laid open in the roadway. Homework papers from the previous night clung to a three-ring spiral notebook thrown from her backpack by the impact. A lipstick case slowly rolled towards the curb, stopping in a small puddle of water.

People were screaming, but I could do nothing but look. She was obviously dead.

There was no sign of trauma on her face. Her mouth was slightly open, eyelids half closed.

How could this have happened? This was just a little girl on her way to school.

Was she looking forward to reciting her essay today? Was there a boy she would nervously flirt with? I just stared at her face. She had become another statistic of the war that no one would ever know about, except for her family and friends.

I helped place her in a body bag, and she was whisked away by an ambulance.

That was it. That's the way it always was with war. Innocents got killed. Accidents happened. Accidents claimed so many lives in Vietnam, not just the innocents, but for the soldiers, too. I got back in the gun jeep and we continued with our work. No time to really dwell. That would all come later in my life. The driver said nothing to me, nor I to him. We drove on in silence.

At night the roads into the base were closed. Unlike Long Binh, nobody left, and nobody came in. We were, after all, out in the boondocks compared to Long Binh.

Concertina was strung across the roadways and claymore mines were laid out in the road beyond the wire. The detonators for these mines were in the bunkers under our control. If we were attacked, and VC came up the road, we could detonate the claymores from the safety of the bunker. I don't think there was any "calling it in" that needed to be done here.

Next to our bunker was a tent and a mortar pit. There was a three-man mortar crew that stayed on the perimeter at night. During the night, and at random hours, they would awaken, drop a few rounds into their mortar, and fire out into the night. Then they'd go back to sleep. They were firing at nothing in particular. This was harassment fire that let the VC, who might be meandering about in the dark, know that someone was on duty and watching.

On our first night John and I took the chairs from the bunker and placed them in the center of the dirt roadway. We sat and began to chat. There wasn't a cloud in the sky. Every star that God had laid out was staring down at us. It couldn't have been any more beautiful and serene. It must have been 0200 hours, as John was leaning back in his chair, that he noticed green lines in the sky making their way toward us. They were coming up the roadway and about 10-15 feet off the ground.

"What are those?" The lines would then fade into the night. Distant crackling, very faint, could be heard.

"Hey! Hey!" A voice from off to our right and behind us. "Hey, MPs!"

John turned in his chair. "Yeah, what's up?" It was the mortar crew.

I could see three silhouettes in the dark against the clear night sky. One of the silhouettes was in front of the other two.

"Hey! You might want to get up and move!" John leaned towards them, "What?"

"You might want to move!"

"Why?"

"They're shooting at you. Those are tracer rounds!"

Holy shit! Were we raw, or what? John and I got up hurriedly, grabbed our chairs, and headed back into the bunker. We could hear the laughing coming from the mortar crew. We deserved it.

The rest of the night was spent *in* the bunker. We agreed right then and there that we needed to get our heads out of our butts. Claymores had been put out, for a reason.

The mortar crew fired off rounds into the night, for a reason. We'd stay close to the bunker, for a reason.

The next night I found myself on POW (prisoner-of-war) guard duty. VC that were captured in combat were transported back to Dian by MPs and placed in a small secured compound. It was there that they were interrogated. Our job was to maintain perimeter security. The VC were all clad in black, most barefoot. The men were small, wiry, and hardened looking. The girls were completely the opposite, petite, feminine with long straight black hair. The girls didn't look any older than 15 or 16 years old. Girls their age back home were learning to dance, become cheerleaders for the school football team, worrying about pimples, and their first kiss. These girls belonged in school. Instead they were out killing American soldiers.

One girl looked at me and gave a reserved smile. I couldn't understand the complexity of it then. John was approaching me in the distance. He had hurried quick steps, and a big grin on his face.

"Ha, ha, it's time. Convoys tomorrow my friend. Can you believe it? Just what we came here for. What time you off?"

"2200."

"Well, get some sleep, we'll be up at around 0630." With that John happily turned and headed back to our tent.

Now I was excited. Everything John and I had been talking about was coming with the break of day. I just hoped I could sleep when I got off duty. Why had we trained in Georgia? For this, that's what.

Chapter 16

The day had come. We were chattering like children as we donned our flak jackets and steel pots. Our brightly colored MP helmets wouldn't be worn, for obvious reasons, although we'd still have our MP brassards fastened to our left shoulders. Three MPs would be in each jeep. A driver, shotgun, and machine gunner. The M-60 machine gun was mounted on a steel tripod in the middle of the back of the jeep, where the back seat used to be. The MP manning this would have to stand for the entire trip.

Beating John to it, "I got first dibs on the 60 guys."

The First Infantry MP, who would do the driving, yelled out, "Just like a fucking new guy!" He gave me a quick smile.

The driver usually had his M-14 rifle, plus a .45 caliber automatic pistol strapped to his side. The shotgun carried the same equipment, but also carried a 12-gauge Remington pump shotgun. Several cans of ammo were placed on the back floor of the jeep. John and I made sure we hooked extra grenades, and smoke grenades, to the loops on our flak jackets.

"Look out VC, here we come." I said wryly. The driver turned to me with an annoyed look on his face.

"Listen, we take fire, you better just be bustin' caps with that hog you're on. I'll point and you just start firin' that thing. You got it? Keep it level and don't shoot anybody who's in front of you, unless they're VC. That includes me. Don't be blowin' off the back of my skull, okay? This isn't a game guys. We'll get along fine. Got it?"

I was a bit embarrassed at what I had said. "Yes, yes, sorry. You can count on us." Play time was over. The driver turned and laughed.

"Ah, don't worry, I was the same way on my first convoy. Just make sure you're on the team. Stay alert. You're gonna get leg heavy standing up back there. You need a break just sit back on the spare tire for a sec."

I pulled myself over the spare tire into the back of the jeep and stood behind the 60. I saw a metal bar that was welded to the front of the jeep. It was about two inches thick and went straight up about six feet, and then angled out at 45 degrees.

Tapping the driver on the shoulder. "Hey, what's the metal bar for?"

"Well, the VC like to knock the machine gunners out of the back of the jeeps. They string wire across the roads. That bar will snap any wire before it hits you. At least it's supposed to." He winked at me and chuckled.

"If you do get knocked out of the jeep, and aren't unconscious, start rolling towards the edge of the road so that the rest of the convoy doesn't run over you. The big trucks don't stop so fast." He looked at me and winked again.

"You're shittin' me, right?"

"Nah, man. Want to test it out? Once we get goin', jump out of the back of the jeep, and see how long it takes a flatbed loaded with ammo to stop. Just let me know when you're gonna jump, so I can turn around and watch." He winked at me yet again. This guy liked to wink.

I looked down at John. "Hey, wanna trade places?" John gave me the finger.

The driver let out a satisfied laugh and looked back again. "You'll do fine. I'm just messin' with you, man. But, do roll if you get knocked out though."

The driver continued with his humor. "Don't worry, legend has it they only go after the handsome gunners!"

John tapped the MP on the shoulder and pointed at me. "So, he's safe then? Stew, you're safe, buddy." Now John was winking at me. Was this winking contagious?

I kicked John in the back of his steel pot with my boot.

"You know John, I'm a terrible shot with this 60. Seems I always jack my first rounds down, and to the right." John smiled a big grin and gave me the finger again.

We were to be the lead vehicle this day on a large convoy of munitions and supplies headed for Lai Khe.

Convoys usually traveled at a speed of about 20 miles per hour, if we were lucky.

Usually an MP gun jeep would be in the middle of the convoy, and another gun jeep would bring up the rear. Constant radio communication was kept with the lead vehicle to make sure the convoy didn't split up due to a mechanical failure, or some type of obstacle in the roadway.

Our lead vehicle had just made it through the main gate at Dian. There were quite a few deuce-and-a-half and flatbed trucks falling in behind us. I was impressed and ready to go. Jokes were over, time to get serious. We were probably a couple hundred yards outside of the gate. One of the ammo cans was sliding around next to my foot, so I leaned over to secure it. As I did, one of the hand grenades fell off my flak jacket. It hit the floor of the jeep and began to jump around like a hot potato.

It would have been easy to just tap the driver and have him pull off the side of the road, but I had to save face here. I was still performing like the city slicker that I was. I reached down, while holding onto the M-60, and tried to retrieve it. The grenade would *not* cooperate. It did not want to be picked up. I could actually hear the grenade laughing at me like a child trying to flee in a game of tag. Another grenade fell from my flak jacket. Now there were two hot potatoes that were fleeing my grasp. I couldn't believe this. Why me? One of the grenades then managed to escape. Yes, escape. It jumped out of the rear of the jeep, landed in the middle of the road, continuing to bounce around, as if happy to be free. Nobody would pull his pin and cause him to explode. No, siree. I frantically put my boot on the other one, hoping no one was watching. Looking over my shoulder I saw the entire convoy begin to run over the grenade. Shit!

I waited for the explosion while the other grenade remained trapped under my boot. I waited, tried not to look back. The 1st Infantry Division MP glanced back at me and smiled, not knowing what had just happened. I returned an uncomfortable smile still, anticipating an explosion. I could hear him talking to his MP buddies later.

"Those dumb fucks from the 552nd. You wouldn't believe what this one dumb fuck did."

I looked over my shoulder again and it appeared that the convoy had cleared the road where the grenade was last seen dancing about. I hoped the grenade, danced its way into the woods, escaping from this place, saving me from major embarrassment, and the terrible reality of casualties from friendly fire.

It was a windy day and the convoy was trudging along at a snail's pace. We were doing ten miles an hour, at best. The dust kicked up from the roadway and coated our clothing like a cold December snowstorm. I was still standing in the rear of the jeep, manning the 60-caliber machine gun. We all wore large goggles, as we wouldn't have been able to see without them, the road dust was so bad. My eyes would have been blistered by the dust and dirt being kicked up in my face.

We drove slowly on a long stretch of dirt roadway. On both sides of the road were rows and rows of rubber trees. Workers could be seen at the trees cutting at the bark to drain the expensive liquid that dripped down the side of the trunks into waiting buckets. The convoy was slowing dramatically. Something was obviously happening behind us that was slowing us up. I looked ahead and could see a break in the roadway. It appeared to be a small roadside village on both sides of the road. The convoy behind us appeared stopped. A call came over the radio to pull off the side of the road.

Twenty or 30 feet off to our side were small neat houses. One stood out above the rest. It was a large two-story French style building. There was a large balcony jutting out from the second floor, and I could see huge pottery overflowing with an assortment of beautiful flowers. There were two large circular pillars at each side of a very large opened front door. The windows on either side of the door were shuttered and protected by steel bars on the outside. A few people were milling around. I didn't pay much attention to what they were doing. Several children ran out to our gun jeep shouting curiously in Vietnamese. John had already taken a chocolate candy bar from his jacket and the children ran to him with their hands out shouting gleefully. Candy bars, soldiers and kids. Timeless.

"Hey, maybe this is a store. I'll go see if I can get us a couple sodas." I jumped down from the back of the jeep, brushed the dirt from the sleeves of my shirt as best I could, took off my helmet, and pulled off my goggles. I threw the goggles down in the back of the jeep, put my helmet back on and walked to the front door of the large house. This house looked oddly out of place. It was stucco and nicely painted a pale-yellow color. The pillars on each side of the door were painted a light green with ferocious, but faded dragons climbing upward toward the overhang. The place looked like a palace compared to the other surrounding dwellings.

As I reached the frame of the door I stopped and peeked inside, not knowing what to expect. My eyes had not adjusted from the harsh light of the convoy, and I squinted as I looked in. I took one slow step inside of the house.

"Hello." I said quietly. There was no answer.

I took another step, as my eyes began to slowly adjust to the subdued lighting. The place was beautiful. This was definitely not a store. The floor was solid dark green tile that stretched as far as I could see. The ceiling was quite high. There were several large ornate oriental paintings on the walls. One that stuck out was of a fierce warrior on horseback brandishing a sword, as he lunged forward toward horrified soldiers carrying large lances at their sides. Several large fans hummed, as they twirled quietly overhead. I could see several pieces of furniture, as I continued to squint, trying to focus.

"May I help you?" A soft voice spoke.

It startled me, as I had not seen anyone in the house. A feminine figure was sitting on a large high-backed sofa near a large window off center of the room. I could see that her legs were tucked up under her.

"Oh, I'm sorry, I thought this might be a store. I was going to buy sodas. Sorry to disturb you."

"No, please come in for a moment."

"Ma'am, I'm really dirty." I must have been a sight to her. 6' 2", with a flak jacket adorned with hand and smoke grenades. My face was dark with dust, except for the area around my eyes, which were protected from the dirt by the goggles. I must have looked like a Martian to this lady. Not a fashion statement, for sure.

"No, please, do not worry."

I walked over to her and saw that her hair was pulled back straight into a bun.

She was fair skinned, beautiful, had on a red silk blouse with a high mandarin collar, and black silk pants. She didn't move as I approached her. There was a book sitting open on her lap.

"You speak English very well."

"I speak four languages actually." She leaned forward in the chair.

I was very nervous, as I was really outclassed by this lovely woman. She seemed to be about 40 years old, not a wrinkle on her face. Her face looked almost porcelain.

"Oh, what are those? I just speak English." Man, what a dumb thing to say. She laughed and said, "English, French, Chinese, and of course, Vietnamese."

"Oh, wow!" Another dumb country boy statement, but I was quite in awe. "Is this your house?"

"Yes, it is. My husband owned it when we were married. This was his rubber plantation. He died ten years ago from malaria, and now I run the plantation. Would you like a cold drink? Please, sit down." The lady stood up, closed the book and sat it on a small rattan table in front of her. I looked down at the title of the book.

She saw that I was looking at the book. "Lady Chatterley's Lover, by D.H. Lawrence. Have you read it?"

I couldn't believe it. I could remember seeing this book in my brother's *collection*, including his Tab, Sunshine and Health, and Playboy magazines. Bob hid them in his gun cases and warned me that this particular book had been 'banned', and we had to be careful not to be caught with it. I remembered opening it and peeking at some of the passages. It was quite sexually graphic. I would furtively glance over my shoulder as I read, hoping my mother wouldn't somehow walk in the room and surprise me.

"Well, yes. Read it all." I lied. The last thing I had read all the way through was a Superman comic book.

The lady was standing in front of me now. She was absolutely beautiful. This woman belonged with some aristocrat, not standing in front of a dirty MP.

"Did you like what you read?"

"Well, yes. Well written, I thought." I wondered if she could hear me sweating. I was reacting to the site of her just like I had reacted to the dirty parts in the book.

She turned slowly and walked through an open door to the rear of the living room and into another room. As I watched her walk away, I thought of the young girl in Tam Hiep. There is no way I belonged in the same room with *this* lady. I was way over my head here and feeling very inadequate. I looked down at the book, and then leaned over, leafing through a few pages. If for nothing else but to get my mind off how nervous I was.

"Can you come here?" I looked up and she was standing in the doorway of the other room. She was completely naked, and her hair was down over her shoulders.

I must have let out a loud gasp at the site of her. The only thing I could think to say was, "I'm awfully dirty."

She held out one hand to me and said, "I have a bath." From a distance, "Stew! Stew! Come on! Hustle it up!"

I could hear John yelling at me from the jeep. My mouth was agape, as all I could do was stare at the vision in front of me. It seems Lady Chatterley's Lover worked for her as it had for me when I snuck a look in my brother's bedroom.

"Stew! Goddammit, get the fuck out here! We'll leave without you!" She put her hand out and motioned for me. I turned and walked out of the house as fast as I could, not looking back.

"Hurry the fuck up, man!"

"Yeah, yeah, yeah, I'm comin'!" I hopped into the back of the gun jeep and righted myself behind the M-60.

"What the fuck were you doin' in there man? The convoy is rollin'. I thought you were going to get us some sodas?"

My eyes were fixed on the front door.

"Yo! Stew, you look like you've lost your best friend."

"Worse than that."

"What?" John frowned.

The gun jeep lurched forward, and I lost my balance, quickly tightening my grip on the 60 to steady myself. I couldn't take my eyes off the front door.

I turned towards John "You ever read Lady Chatterley's Lover?"

"You gotta be kiddin' me? What kind of book is that for a Wyoming cowboy to read? Who is Lady Chatterley? I read cowboy stuff, for cryin'out loud, but mostly comic books."

We were now back in formation and moving slowly north towards Lai Khe. I leaned over to John, who was now looking straight ahead. "John, I just saw a goddess."

"Where?" He looked over his shoulder. "In there?"

"Yeah. You think we can stop on the way back?"

"Uh, sure. Let me just jot that down in our schedule book here." John mimicked, taking a notebook from his flak jacket and writing down my request.

"Let's see now, that'll be Jim, two story house, visit, on way back. Hell, stay the night. Done, Stew. You're all set. What has gotten into you?"

John acted like he put the notebook in his flak jacket, and with a laugh turned his head back to the front. I let out a big sigh. Life was not fair at this moment. All I wanted to do was go back to this house, live on the plantation, and lay naked with this woman for the rest of my life. Instead, I was headed north again. North towards the Iron Triangle, and at best, a night in a tent with two other smelly MPs. Vietnam was just not fair. I let out another sigh, looking down at the sandbags laying on the floor of the jeep.

"Shit! Shit, shit, shit."

I could have made a mournful love song just using the word 'shit'. Maybe we would stop here on the way back to Dian. Maybe she'd still be there. Ah, geez, what was I thinking? I'm just a young, naive kid strapped to an M-60 machine gun, trying to act like a man. It was a moment that will not repeat itself. But I could hope. Would I dream of this woman later? I really, really hoped so.

The convoy went smoothly the rest of the way to Lai Khe. It was late afternoon when we arrived. The base camp itself was set in a heavily wooded area. I could see the tips of rows of tents off the sides of the dirt road. I could also see the long barrels of what must have been huge gun placements. There were three particularly huge powerful looking guns that I could see, with their blue steel barrels pointed outward at 45-degree angles. I had never seen guns as big as these. They were silent right now.

There wasn't much for us to do after the convoy was safely there. Trucks with equipment and munitions headed off to predetermined areas to be offloaded. Our three MP gun jeeps mustered together, as we took time to curiously look over the area. I could see an occasional one or two heads walking by off in the distance, but all in all the place looked like it was abandoned. I knew it wasn't. There were thousands of soldiers here ready to bring some hurtin' on the VC who were hidden within the jungles surrounding us.

An MP sergeant with a Big Red One patch walked up to us and pointed out the local chow hall. Chow sounded good. He also pointed to an area where our "living quarters", were located.

"If you guys want to shower, there are some showers located just east of the chow hall. Chow is served at 1630, so you've got a bit of time to relax and clean up."

We drove the short distance to where are living quarters were and parked our jeeps. I could see several tee pees looking tents sitting in a straight line. The tent material did not reach all the way to the ground, but was mounted on a center pole, the ends tied to ropes, and secured by stakes in the ground. I could see that each tent had two cots inside. The cots were sitting on the ground, unlike the wooden platforms at our base at Long Binh. Not all the amenities of home, but no complaints here. This is the kind of work we wanted.

Mosquito nets were folded and placed on top of the cots. They weren't hanging, so I guess we just pulled them over us at night to keep the mosquitoes from eating our bodies alive. No one complained. We all volunteered to help the First Infantry Division guys and weren't expecting red carpets, or valet parking.

John said he was bushed and threw his helmet down on the ground in front of one of the small tents.

"I'm going to sack out for a few, you guys. Anybody else? I claim this tent in the name of the great state of Wyoming." John plopped himself down.

"Well, cowboy, guess I'll take this one here." I bent over and entered the tent throwing my helmet next to his. "I've got a goddess to dream about."

John looked over at me as he loosened his boot laces. "What the heck happened back there, Stew?"

"Man, you wouldn't believe it. A beautiful naked woman wanted me. Not sure I saw what I saw, but I'm going to doze off, and maybe it will be so fresh in my mind that it will come back to me in my sleep."

One thing that we could do was sleep. Sleep took away the reality of being awake in a land so far from home. We pulled long work shifts, and anytime we could lay our heads down on a pillow and catch a few winks we would. Standing up in the back of the jeep the entire ride trying to balance yourself was tough. The road was rough, and it was physically tiring trying to keep your balance. We'd get an hour's sleep, go eat, and probably come back and sleep some more. We had nothing else to do. Sleep, precious sleep. It didn't matter how hot it was. John and I fell asleep almost instantly.

I was the first to awaken. My mouth was dry, and I was sweating. I looked over at John who was on his side, still sleeping. Doug Dragert walked by and peeked in.

"You guys going to chow?"

"Hey, Doug. How you likin' it up here at Lai Khe? Yeah, let me wake John and you can fill us in."

"Hey, John, John, chow time." John stirred, rolling over on his back.

"You ready for some chow, cowboy?" John opened his eyes and pushed himself up on his elbows. Then I saw it.

John turned his head my way. I recoiled and let out a gasp, "Holy shit!"

"What?"

"Man, a mosquito must have got you, and got you good, too." John had a ping pong ball sized lump in the middle of his forehead. He reached up and rubbed his palm over the bump.

"Holy, shit!" John sat up still feeling the bump. "Holy, shit! Did somebody hit me with a shovel? Does it look bad?"

"Well, it sort of gives you a unicorn look, but other than that it looks, well, huge. You know those Hindus with the spots in the middle of their heads? Sort of like them, but on a much grander scale. Maybe times a hundred. Plus, theirs have color. Yours is that washed out Wyoming, live in the snow, never see the sun look. Good thing you don't have a date tonight."

"No, shit. Holy shit now I guess we know why they laid out this mosquito netting."

"Geez, I hope the one that bit you died. I don't want him showin' up tonight. This guy that bit you could probably carry us out into a field. Maybe we can catch it and make it a pet." John chuckled and rubbed his bump.

"They should have given Purple Hearts for this kind of bite. I don't even know if my helmet will fit anymore. If the mosquito was a VC, I get a Purple Heart, for sure." John was chuckling and rubbing his bump as we walked off for chow.

I knew one soldier who told me about being bitten by a snake. He was with the 82nd Airborne. He and a platoon of men had gone on patrol into the jungle when a huge cobra struck out at him. The snake bit him through the mesh in his jungle boot, got his fangs caught up in the mesh, and couldn't let go. It unloaded all the venom it could into his ankle. A machine gunner came up and unloaded on the snake, killing it. He wound up in the hospital for a couple months, and later got a Purple Heart.

Our next convoy run near Tay Ninh proved to be an adventure, and one of pure luck for John and me. We had gotten within a couple miles of the Michelin Rubber Plantation when we heard a scraping noise coming from under our jeep. Something was dragging on the roadway. I leaned out from the passenger side to look but couldn't see anything. John was driving and pulled to the side of the road, leaning out to take a look for himself.

"Jesus Christ, run!" At the same time, he started yelling, "Mine, mine, get the fuck back!"

We ran off the side of the road and jumped into a canal. We both hugged the soil and looked back towards the jeep. I could see the antenna of a contact mine dangling from under the floorboard. A round metal canister was attached to the end of the antenna. We waited for an explosion, but it didn't come. The rest of the convoy behind us was stopped and began backing up a safe distance.

A grizzled looking sergeant came up behind the jeep puffing on a cigar. He had his flak jacket on and was shirtless, his hairy muscular arms dripping with sweat. He took off his helmet and scratched his bald head. He looked under the jeep, surveyed it for a minute, and then took the butt of his M-16 rifle and knocked the canister out from under the jeep.

"It's shit! It's a piece of shit, all come apart! No explosives, nada!" He looked over at us, waved for us to come back and turned and walked back to his truck.

I looked at John and let out a chuckle. "Now THAT takes some balls."

Breathing a sigh of relief, we got back in our jeep, but not before taking one last peek under the hood.

We continued to run convoys back and forth from Dian. It was a duty we relished. I never saw the naked lady again, although we passed her house several times. Her door was always open, but I just didn't have the nerve to step back inside.

After about five weeks our temporary duty during Operation Cedar Falls came to an end. Just over 700 VC were killed, but it had appeared that many had disappeared across the border into Cambodia. That said, thousands of tons of rice, hundreds of small arms, and various other types of weapons had been seized and were destroyed.

Our days with the 1st Infantry Division were over, and our temporary duty came to an end. We packed our duffel bags and caught a convoy from Dian to Long Binh. It had seemed like we had been gone for months. That short period of time for us had opened our eyes and let us gain the rightful respect for those who were doing the daily fighting in this hot, hostile country. We had grown up a bit and lost our "FNG" tag. The MPs of the Big Red One had even embraced us after we had learned the ropes. We worked hard and felt good about ourselves.

We were greeted as returning heroes once back at Long Binh, and wasted no time telling tales of our adventures, even though a tad bit embellished. Of course, I told the tale of the beautiful naked lady who tried to entice me to her bath. I was also readily reminded that catching gonorrhea once was probably enough.

Upon arriving back at Long Binh I had also gotten word that I was being assigned to the Cong Ly detail in Bien Hoa. Cong Ly was a converted hotel that housed officers and visiting dignitaries to the large Bien Hoa Air Base. I was glad for this. I would be right in the middle of the city of Bien Hoa, and not restricted to a base. The living quarters inside of the hotel were going to be nice. Goodbye tents. On my last day at Long Binh I saw John walking towards the mess hall.

"Say, Jim, how about some chow?"

"Sure. Man, I'm not working today and can use a sandwich. Let's see what they've got."

"My butt's draggin' a bit, how about yours?" John did look a little tired.

"Yeah, know what you mean. We never had to work like this before we joined the Army, that's for sure. I could sleep through the rest of my year here, honestly."

There always seemed to be someone in the mess hall for us. John and I walked in and saw a few other guys sitting at a table chowing down on sandwiches. We gave them a wave.

"Hey, guys! What's on the menu?"

One of the MPs looked up. "Shit on a shingle. Top notch stuff today. Just kiddin'. Bologna sandwiches. Yummy for your tummy. Just like ma used to make."

John and I grabbed some white bread and piled on a few pieces of bologna. Jars of mayonnaise, mustard, and ketchup were sitting on the counter along with salt and pepper shakers, and napkins.

"Man, I love ketchup on bologna." John swabbed it on with a little bit of mustard to boot.

"John, I don't know of any human being who puts ketchup on bologna sandwiches."

"Well, it's a cowboy thing."

"Cowboy? I think it's a poverty thing. There's something about your past that you haven't told me. How in the hell did you cowboys ever manage to tame the west?"

John gave me a serious look and held up his sandwich. "Ketchup."

John began to laugh, as we headed over to a table near the front door of the mess hall.

"Let's get the window view. Nothing like scenic Long Binh, and looking out on a luxurious shower and latrine facility while we eat. Ah, now that's my idea of paradise." John was standing at the door next to our table and raised his sandwich to his mouth.

BOOM!

The explosion was deafening. Standing just behind John I saw the shock wave moving across the perimeter and onto our compound. Tent flaps flew in the air, debris kicked up as if a twister was rolling in. Within a second it hit the front door of the mess hall. John was fell backward and tripped over a chair. I was able to maintain my balance but dropped, cowered behind the large mess hall table. Dust filled the air and I could hear people shouting as I tried to get my senses.

Jim Peterson ran through the door and yelled, "The ammo dumps been hit, everybody to the perimeter!"

Jim looked down at John who was still on his back. "Holy shit! Prahl's been hit, Prahl's been hit!" Peterson looked at me in panic. "Stew, take care of him, I'll get a medic!" Peterson disappeared out the door.

John propped himself up onto his elbows and looked at me groggily. "I've been hit?"

John's sandwich was now all over his face. Pieces of bologna and white bread were smattered on his jaw and nose. Ketchup was all over his lips, chin and nose. I started to laugh.

"What's so fuckin' funny man, I've been hit."

I got down on one knee and pointed at his face, "Ketchup."

John wiped the lower part of his jaw and looked at the ketchup on his fingers.

"You sure it's ketchup?"

"Taste it."

John was still unconvinced. "What are these little brown chunks? Skin?"

"Bologna."

John was beginning to recover from the shock of the blast, and rolled over on one elbow, righting himself.

"Holy shit, that was one strong blast." John's face looked awful, but I couldn't stop chuckling. He began brushing dirt off his shirt. "What's so funny?"

"Purple Heart."

"Purple Heart?" John looked at me quizzically. "Yep, you think you can get a Purple Heart for that?"

"For ketchup?" Most of the cobwebs were now out of John's head. KA-BOOM!

A second blast, this one louder and nearer our perimeter. The ammo dump was going up and it was shooting off explosives in every direction. John's eyes were as big as tires.

"Let's get the fuck out of here!"

We ran out the door and stopped to get our bearings. Sgt. Aguirre ran by and froze when he saw John.

"Jesus H. Christ, you been hit! I'll go get help. Stewart you see to him." I looked at John with tears in my eyes. "Purple Heart."

John turned his head slightly and squinted. "What? I can't hear?" I yelled back, "Purple Heart!"

John started laughing and gave me his cowboy yell, "Yeehah!" as we headed off towards the perimeter.

I would soon pack my bags and head off to Cong Ly. John never got his Purple Heart, and I'm not sure he switched to just mustard on his bologna sandwich. In late February of 1967 I would be transferred out to the 300th MP Company in Saigon. I don't know why I was one of the ones chosen. It could have been my embarrassing the company by being the first to catch VD, or perhaps someone ratted me off to the brass when I slept through the first attack on our perimeter. Maybe just the luck of the draw. It really wasn't important to me. I was happy to be going to someplace new.

I knew how a child of a divorce felt, however. The family was being broken up. It didn't seem fair, but I can't say I was totally unhappy about it. I was looking forward to Saigon. John and I didn't like the duty on base and wanted more involvement. We got that with the First Infantry Division. Maybe Saigon would hold some great adventure for me. I was ready to move on but leaving **would** be difficult. These were men I shared a bunk with at Fort Benning, sloshed through the Georgia swamps playing war games, huddled closely with on a troop laden Navy ship, and filled sandbags with. Thousands of words of encouragement, and all the good-natured hassling would be missed, but never forgotten.

I didn't realize that this was just the tip of the iceberg for me. It would never dawn on me that I had three and a half years left in Vietnam. Three and a half more years. I never would have guessed it. No one would have thought that Jim Stewart would stay in Vietnam for four years. Looking back, it was time I could have spent getting a college education. But the education I got from life from these four years would stay with me, and be far more important to me than college, in the long run.

I also had no idea at the time that I would hold these guys from **The Deuce** in my heart for years and years after the Vietnam War. Fifty years later still recalling and remembering the bond we had. I'd always remember **The Deuce**. Five-five-two, ho, ho, ho!

Chapter 17 Saigon

I wished I could have handpicked the guys who were going to Saigon with me, because John would have been dragged along with me. But I wouldn't be going to Saigon alone. My buddies Doug Dragert, who would be promoted to sergeant, Jim Troupe and Mike Ramirez, both from New York City, had also been transferred to the 300th MP Company. These buddies would lessen the feeling that all new friends had to be made. It was good. We were tight.

We caught a convoy headed for the large air base on the northern outskirts of the city, Tan Son Nhut. We would, more specifically, be billeted at Pershing Field. Tan Son Nhut was also the civilian airport, but it had mostly been taken over by the American military. American warplanes flew hundreds of daily sorties from here on bombing runs, and in support of the ground troops.

What can I say about Saigon? I had never seen so many people crammed into one area. Saigon was probably built for a population of 500,000 people. About 3,000,000 lived there or were huddled into the outskirts of the city. Many had fled the war in the countryside, and as a result, shanty towns had appeared everywhere. The convoy traveled at a snail's pace, fighting for the right-of-way against hundreds of taxi cabs, bicycles, and motorcycles. A thinking man would have thought that every citizen in Saigon was going to the same place, at the same time.

It was obvious that the rules of the road were that there were *no* rules of the road. Every pedestrian, bike, taxi, two-and-a-half-ton truck was fighting for space themselves, jockeying to move a few precious feet ahead of the person or vehicle in front of them. As we drove through intersections it occurred to me that the Vietnamese had to be color blind. I could see the light change from green, to yellow, to red. However, the Vietnamese obviously could not. City Police, dressed all in white, stood atop concrete podiums and frantically blew their whistles, waving their arms in desperation to try to persuade some semblance of order out of the traffic. No one listened, no one saw. To say this was folly was a huge understatement. It was certainly great theatre.

This was one city where rush hour was every hour. It was a terrific site, far removed from the relative peace and easy pace that was the countryside around Long Binh. If we didn't make it to Tan Son Nhut I would have enjoyed just being driven around taking in all the sights, sounds, and smells. We were acting like kids on their first visit to Disneyland.

"Hey, Troupe, can you believe this, man?"

"Just like New York City, brother. I think we're going to have a blast."

Mike had both arms draped over the side railing and was just smiling and waving to the people.

"Troupe, brother, we're home. New York City, part two. This is great." I could tell we were going to do well in our new home.

The 300th MP Company was mainly responsible for security at the Saigon Harbor. Foreign freighters and many American ships offloaded their munitions and supplies here. Our housing, however, was a step down, as Long Binh had quickly gotten away from housing us in tents and had put up prefab metal buildings. Here they were still in tents. It was great though that Jim, Mike and I would be living in the same tent. Doug would be moving in with other sergeants, but he was still Doug to us. The tents were large and spacious, with wooden floors, but they were still tents. That was okay though. This was Saigon, the Pearl of the Orient, not Long Binh. There was a big city out there for us, and we had the rest of our tours to take it all in.

I got my first duty assignment within two days. The main gate at the port. I had to screen all vehicles and personnel entering and exiting the facilities. Easy enough.

In the late afternoon, almost at the end of my shift, I was approached by a soldier who had a grenade in his hand.

"MP, can you help me out here?" He looked nervous, and a little unsteady from one too many local beers.

"Where in the hell did you get that?"

"A guy had it in the bar." He extended his quivering arm.

"Careful, keep your hand tight on the lever. Just let me take it from your hand. You know where the pin for this thing is?"

"Yeah." He held up his other hand and showed me the pin. "The pin won't fit back in."

"Okay, just wait till I get in into my hand."

I took the grenade from him, and then the pin. My partner radioed in what was happening to the duty sergeant. The sight of a grenade had attracted a crowd of onlookers. I told the soldier and others that they needed to back away. No one really listened. With that I walked over to the dock and had a seat on a bench, leaving my partner to man the gate. Within a couple minutes Sergeant Dragert and his driver sped up to the gate. Doug just happened to be duty sergeant.

"I got it sarge!" I extended my arm up in the air to show him the grenade.

"No way this stinking pin is going back in. It's not bent, but it's just not going back in the spoon. Doug, you'd better call EOD." (Explosives Ordnance Disposal).

He yelled back. "Already did! They're on their way. You want me to go across the street and get you a bottle of whiskey?"

"Ha, ha, very funny. You wanna come over here and hold this thing?" Doug just smiled back.

So, there I sat. I couldn't very well throw it in the Saigon River. I knew that frogmen could be in the water. So, I just sat and waited.

It took about 15 minutes for EOD to fight through the Saigon traffic. Once there they taped the lever tightly to the grenade, and I handed it over to them. It was all fairly simple, but, unknown to me I had just become one of the 'heroes' of the war.

I was put in for the Soldier's Medal, the highest non-combat medal for valor in the Army and decorated by a General whose name I've forgotten. I was also promoted to Specialist 4th Class. Not making light of it, but I never felt what I did was heroic. Just doing my job, but I'm sure even the most heroic grunt out in the field during combat would probably say the same thing.

I was proud of it, but the most exciting part of it all…a pay raise. The promotion also got me off harbor duty. I was assigned to a team of four other MPs, including Jim Troupe, to guard the MACV compound just outside of the main gate to the airbase.

It was easy duty. There was only one way into the compound and one way out.

We could make our own schedule as long as there was always an MP on duty. This was way too easy. This was also where I met Mai.

I was working the 1200-2400-hour (noon until midnight) shift. When curfew came, I usually stood just outside the gate on the roadway edge. Curfew was at 2200. No one was allowed on the streets between 2200 hours, and 0500, hours except the American MPs, Vietnamese MP's, and Vietnamese civilian police. All others had to be tucked away in their homes, or in the case of servicemen, on base. As a matter of fact, we seldom saw a civilian police officer on duty after 2400 hours. It always seemed to be just the American MPs and Vietnamese MPs.

It was an odd site to see Saigon during curfew hours. It looked like everyone had packed up their things and just abandoned the city. Saigon was a huge city. Thousands of citizens from the countryside had migrated to Saigon to escape the war in the hamlets, and rice paddies. This turned the outer regions of the city into areas where refugees set up shanty town after shanty town, but you wouldn't think anyone lived here after curfew.

You could hear a pin drop after 2200 hours. All that noise, movement, and confusion that was pre-curfew was now gone. Stand at the end of one long straight avenue and look down its length, and width, and you'd see nothing but shadows, streetlights and an occasional dog wagging his tail looking for food remnants. It was an eerie sight.

The speed of the cars and motor bikes increased dangerously 15 minutes prior to curfew, as people hurried to get home. Watching this from my position on the street was pure fun, as I was amazed at how adept they were at maneuvering their vehicles in, and around, but curiously, never over one another. This was people watching at its best.

One night a cyclo came galloping down the street at breakneck speed, spewing puffs of gray exhaust into the night air.

A cyclo was a wonderful invention by some imaginative motorcyclist who didn't' have the money to buy a car to make into a taxi. So, he turned his motorcycle into a taxi by welding a cart to the front. Two big Americans, or possible five to seven Vietnamese, could sit abreast of one another. They were highly maneuverable and could zip in and out of the heaviest of traffic. If you needed to get somewhere quick, the cyclo was your answer. Taxis, for the most part, had to wait in line. A cyclo went around everything.

This cyclo had a most beautiful girl sitting by herself. She was in a pure white áo dài dress. The dress was about as feminine an outfit that you would ever see. Tight fitting, flowing three quarters to the ground, with slits on both sides to the waist. Worn underneath were black silk pants. She was sitting up ramrod straight, her hands clutching the purse in her lap. She had long straight black hair and beautiful almond colored skin. I was quite fascinated by the sight of her.

I could see that she was looking at me and as she passed, she raised her right hand, gently waving. The cyclo zipped by so fast that I didn't wave back. It was too late. I watched it drive out of sight hoping she would turn around and look at me so I could return her wave. She didn't. An opportunity missed. I had not been with a woman, since I had lost my virginity back at Tam Kiep. Well, that's the *only* woman I had been with, and that experience had cured me, so to speak.

This woman had definitely caught my attention, but that didn't seem to matter much now. As was the beautiful woman on the road to Lai Khe, she was gone. I let out a sigh and just watched the traffic dwindle until there was no one on the street except me. Up and down the roadway I looked. Nothing. I was alone again.

The next night I worked the same hours. I had thought about the woman I had seen, so I would stand out in the roadway again, or the next night, and I would see eventually her. So, with curfew approaching I walked back to the roadway edge and stood, my hands clasped behind my back. This time my attention was steadfastly aimed toward the direction the cyclo had come from last night.

Sure enough, like a vision out of the sky I saw a cyclo darting in and out of traffic, coming towards me. This time her áo dài was red, and this time I acted. I had no real cause to do so, but I motioned the cyclo off the road. The driver must have been going about 20 mph when he saw me, pointing his finger uncertainly at his chest. I nodded and he hit the brakes, turned the handle, stopping on a dime right in front of me. The beautiful passenger grabbed the rail of the cart seat so that she wouldn't be thrown out of the cart onto the pavement. Now what?

The girl looked startled at the abrupt stop, and I could see that it scared her. I was searching for something reasonable to say but all I could come up with was, "Hello."

She looked up at me. "Hello."

The driver of the cyclo looked at me, "What you want? Curfew almost here."

"Oh!", clearing my throat. "My name is Jim. What's yours?" The driver put his hands on his hips, rolled his eyes, looking just a bit annoyed. "This no short time girl."

"Mai. I have to go home quickly before curfew."

"Yes, right." I wrote down my name quickly on a piece of paper and handed it to her. She took it and put it in her purse.

The driver pleaded, "MP, I go home now, okay?"

I looked at him apologetically. "Oh, yes, sure, sorry, sorry." I looked down at the girl, "What's your name again?"

"Mai."

"Yes, Mai, well goodnight." The cyclo pulled back onto the roadway and sped away.

Mai looked over her shoulder now and gave me a timid smile and wave.

I was in love. That's all it took. How simple was that? I felt so good that I waved to all the passing taxis and cyclos that went by me, waving casually until there was no one left. I was finally standing alone on the side of the roadway with a stupid grin on my face. My watch said 2201 hours. Up and down I gazed. Nobody but me, but that was fine, just fine. Saigon was now, well, just fine.

The next night I assumed my same anticipatory position from the last two nights.

I didn't know what to expect. I must have looked like a nervous groom waiting for his bride to walk down the runway of a church, looking about nervously, worrying that maybe the wedding wouldn't take place after all.

2155 hours came and I had not seen the cyclo, or, more importantly, her. Love was fleeting. Suddenly a taxi stopped in front of me and Mai put her hand out the back window, handing me a folded piece of paper.

"It's late, I must go." Off the taxi sped, the exhaust hurling more gray clouds into the warm night air.

I opened the note. It read, Nguyen Thi Ngoc Mai, 195 Troung Minh Ky Street. I tried pronouncing the name to myself;

"Nag-gu-en, Nig-u-yen? Geez! Nag-u-yen, Thi, Nah-gock? Man, this is tough. Let's see now, uh, N-go-see, Mai."

Who invented these names? This was difficult. Whatever happened to Nancy, or Mary, but that really didn't matter. I had a name and an address. All I needed to really know was Mai. Now what?

Well, for starters, I did not have to work for the next three days. Two, I had an address. Three, all I had to do was have the nerve to act on it. I had forgotten about the love I had left in the plantation on the convoy to Lai Khe. Tomorrow was my day off. I'd just have to see what would happen with this. I slept well after I got off my shift.

"Taxi, taxi! Hey, taxi!"

The driver pulled off to the side of the street just down from the main gate of the base. I smelled my armpits to make sure that I hadn't overdone it with the cologne.

"Where you go?"

I pulled the piece of folded paper from my pocket and showed it to him. "Ah, yes. Troung Minh Ky, very close here. You wanna ride? $300 piaster, I wasn't going to barter today. You could usually cut the rate in half without a whimper of complaint. I didn't want haggling to break the good mood I was in.

"Okay. $300 piaster is number one."

The driver gave me a grin full of gold teeth, and reached in the back opening the door.

"Let's go, G.I."

The ride was all of about three blocks. The taxi driver's easiest money of the day. "Okay, G.I. Right here. One-nine-five. You see number there?"

I looked up above a small alley that separated two three story apartments. The alley was very narrow, probably no more than five feet wide. In front of the apartment building was a small shop. A middle-aged woman sat behind a counter and must have sensed my unfamiliarity when I got out of the taxi.

"Can I help you?"

"Well, yes. This paper says 195 Troung Minh Ky, but no apartment number."

"You have name?" I passed the paper to the lady.

"Ah, yes, Mai. Very beautiful this Mai, very beautiful. You girl friend?"

"Uh, no, just friend, I guess."

The woman smiled. "You make Mai you girlfriend, you very lucky. She nice girl, very pretty." She got up from the counter, looked down the alley and pointed, "You go there, you go this way (pointed to her right) and upstair. You see two door. You go on this one." The lady pointed to the right.

"Thank you, thank you." I bowed slightly and walked into the alley. The woman spoke out. "She no there, she have sister name Hue, okay?"

I turned and waved thanks. At the end of the alley I turned right and walked up a flight of stairs that had no railing. There were two doors. One on the right, and one on the left. The door on the right was open. I slowed to a stop and took a deep breath, tentatively walked up and looked in the open door. Mai was sitting on the floor with her legs crossed. A younger girl with similar long hair sat across from her. There was a book between them. They both looked involved and didn't sense my presence.

"Ahem." I leaned in a bit.

Mai saw me and smiled, got up quickly, said something to the other girl in Vietnamese, and came towards the door and asked quizzically,

"You, Jim?"

146

I guess I looked a bit different out of my MP uniform and had my cap off and in my hands. I smiled and nodded.

"Oh, so glad to see you. Please come in. This my sister, Hue (Way)." At this time another girl, looking about Mai's age, walked out of the kitchen.

"This is my cousin, Dao (Dow)." Mai then said something to Dao in Vietnamese and Dao laughed.

"Oh, Mai said you were beau coupe handsome, and she is right." Dao looked satisfied and tweaked Mai's cheek. "How long have you been in Vietnam?"

"Well, about six months, is all."

"We were getting ready to eat. Please, you eat too."

So, I sat and ate a scrumptious meal of white rice, shrimp, and vegetables. My first Vietnamese food, and I must say, it was delicious. Hue did not speak English and was very quiet as we ate, occasionally peeking at me out of the corner of her eye. Mai and Dao both spoke good English, struggled with some structure, but I was able to understand everything they said.

Mai was from Phan Rang, about 120 miles north of Saigon, a small town on the coast. She was 18 and had been in Saigon about a year. Dao was a year older. They had come down from Phan Rang together to make money to send to their large families.

Many young girls had left the more rural settings to find work, and the safety that the huge city of Saigon gave them.

Dao worked as a secretary for a special forces' detachment headquartered in Saigon. Mai worked in a bar pushing drinks known as Saigon Tea. Saigon Tea was nothing more than Kool-Aid in a shot glass. For every $2.00 Saigon Tea that she got a G.I. to buy her, she received a portion of that money. She didn't like the work and hated the drunkenness and cigarette smoke. Mai did not drink or smoke. She said that the drunker she got the G.I.s, the more willing they were to buy her tea, and to buy more beer for themselves. So, the owner of the bar profited, as well as the girls.

She was strikingly beautiful, cocoa complexioned with high cheek bones, and beautiful sad almost black eyes. Her black shiny satin-like hair stretched down her back and touched her waist, full breasted with a small waste. I couldn't help but stare at her.

Mai said that she had had a boyfriend before, but he had returned to the states. "Do you have a girlfriend?" She asked looking shyly down at her food.

"No, no. I haven't thought of it, really. Not much time. I'd like to have a girlfriend though."

Mai took a mouth full of food, looked at me and raised both of her eyebrows and smiled.

"You never had a Vietnamese girlfriend?"

"No."

"You too good looking not to have girlfriend."

"Well, I don't."

It was as if it had already been decided. I would sit there and eat and talk with her and Dao until it got dark. As Hue did the dishes we went into Dao's apartment across the hall and out onto the balcony and sat. It was sprinkling and the air had cooled. Looking down on Troung Minh Ky Street there was still a lot of traffic on the road. There was a small shop immediately across the street where people were walking in and out. I couldn't tell what they were selling or buying.

Mai was sipping an iced coffee through a straw. "Do you like coffee?"

"Well, I've never had it with ice before." Iced coffee was a treat that the Vietnamese loved. I didn't try it, as I had never liked the taste of cold coffee in my cup.

We talked until late. Dao excused herself as she had to work in the morning. "Well, I guess I had better get going." I started to get up.

"Jim, its curfew." I looked down on the street and it was deserted now. Up and down the street, nothing was moving. I was in a bind. I guess I would have to wait on the balcony and shout out at a passing MP patrol, if one came by. They'd be able to give me a ride back to the base.

"Are you in trouble?"

"Well, no, but I don't see any taxis or cyclos now. I'm going to have to wait here for the MPs to come by."

"Jim, if you want, you stay here tonight. Do you work tomorrow?"

"Well, no, I can do that. What about Hue?"

"It's okay."

That night I stayed with Mai. It was official, I had a girlfriend. The next day I went to Pershing Field and to my tent and got as much stuff as I could and moved it into Mai's apartment. Housing directives strictly prohibited living in other-than-government facilities. However, it was quite slack for the G.I.s in Saigon.

Actually, it was nonexistent.

To drive through the areas north of downtown it looked like laundry day, every day. G.I.s green fatigue shirts, pants, underwear, and socks adorned clothes lines hung from one apartment window to the next. It had even been broadcast over the Armed Forces Radio Network that the mayor of Saigon was requesting that clothes not been hung out the windows as they were an eyesore. Seems everyone was living off base and no one, not even the brass, seemed to care. They couldn't care much when they were doing it themselves.

My time with the 300th MP Company was, except for the grenade incident, quite uneventful. This is the type of duty that so angered the combat troops in the field. I worked my shift, went "home" to my apartment, a good meal, and a beautiful girl. I was lucky and gave it no thought. To me it was just the luck of the draw. The combat soldier would have changed places with me in an instant, and not complained one bit about it. It wasn't fair, but that's just the way it was. I didn't ask for this duty, nor did some of them, but if the role could have been reversed, they surely would have reversed it.

There were far more soldiers like me, those who were in the rear and in support of those who did the real fighting. The ratio of support troops to combat was 10 to 1. For everyone who fought, there were ten in the background. To think that the all the soldiers in Vietnam were in constant danger was just not true.

The apartment itself was just one medium sized room where we had two beds. One was for Mai, and me, and the other for sister Hue to sleep in. There was a large ceiling fan above us, and the beds were draped with mosquito mesh and curtains for privacy. We had a television against one wall, and a couple of nondescript chairs. The kitchen was small with a cooking area and a small table and chairs. Our one window to the outside world was in the kitchen and looked upon the sprawl that was Saigon. While looking from this window you could see blocks upon blocks of apartments and other dwellings crammed as tightly together as space would allow.

The toilet was also located in the kitchen behind a closed door. I always had problems with this as it was *not* the standard G.I. issued outhouse, nor the more modern toilets that we were used to back home. The toilet area consisted of a hole about six inches in circumference, and two grooved imprints of feet in the cement on either side of the hole. The idea was to squat with your feet on the imprints, aim, and hope for the best. This was one aspect of apartment living that I didn't appreciate.

You see, the small framed, lithe Vietnamese were able to squat all day long with their arms draped over their knees. Conversations could be carried on leisurely in this position for hours. Lunch could be eaten at a curb side food stand in this position. For them it was a position of comfort. For the big, inflexible, thick Americans it was aposition of pure agony.

I never squatted fully when I went to the bathroom. Why? I physically couldn't. Instead I would place my feet in the proper placements and extend both arms so that the palms of my hands were pushing on the side walls. This would give me support. I would then squat as much as my body would possibly let me without cramping up, and, well...go. It was not pleasant. I dreaded it, but what was I supposed to do? While in Rome...

Mai had a table in the corner of our small apartment where she maintained a small shrine. There were a few pictures of family members, and some other ornaments. I never really took the time to pay attention to it. There were always several sticks of incense sticking out of a small ceramic pot.

Mai would occasionally light incense at the altar and get down on her knees, place the palms of her hands together in front of her face, and close her eyes. I was not yet a Christian and had only dabbled with Protestant churches back home, but never gave much thought to the worship of anything.

"Mai, what are you praying?"

She pulled her hands apart, and without opening her eyes tilted her head slightly in my direction, raising her right index finger to her pursed lips.

"Shhhhh."

Mai turned back and knelt in front of the altar for a few more minutes, quietly, peacefully. I had to respect her for this, even though I didn't know what she was doing. All I knew was that she was removing herself from everything that was happening right now. The war was not in her thoughts, or the hardships that she may have seen. She sat there kneeling, looking beautiful and serene.

When she finished, she put her hands on her knees and leaned forward slightly, turning to face me.

"The incense is so that I can remember the people that are gone. The people who are no longer on this earth, but are still here in, how you say? I don't know the word, but like a ghost."

"Spirit?"

Mai tried saying the word. "What does that word mean?"

"Well, it's like a sort of like a ghost, I guess. Somebody dies, but you know they are still here. Maybe you know they are standing next to you. Things like that. Maybe more an angel than a ghost though. I think most ghosts are bad."

"Oh, yes, spirit. What is the other word? "Angel."

"Angel," she repeated.

"Do you believe in angel."

"Angels? I don't know. I think so."

"You believe in ghosts?"

"Ghosts, yes."

"Ghosts, but no angel?"

"I'm just not sure."

"Are they same?"

"Well, ghosts can be scary. Angels are not scary."

"What is scary?" I made a devilish face at her and growled. "So, you scared of ghosts, but no angel to make you happy?"

I sort of felt inadequate and uneducated about this. She was right. I believed in ghosts, yet I wasn't sure of angels. Was there a difference?

One perhaps bad, one perhaps good. Believed in the bad, but not the good?

"What do your spirits do?"

"They come and go. They will look out after my family in Phan Rang. It is very important to remember your relatives who have gone because they are not really gone. They come back to help us, protect us, give us help."

"Do they say anything about me?"

"You? They say that many of you have come before, and many of you have left."

They say I should be careful with my heart."

"Did they say anything bad about me?"

"No. They care about protecting me."

"Do you think they'd like me?"

"You? No, you too hairy." With that Mai laughed, got up and ran to the bed and jumped on top of me. Mai began to pummel me with the pillow while she gleefully laughed.

"You are a number 10 American dog! Mai continued to hit me as Hue walked into the room through the front door.

Mai turned to Hue as she straddled my purposely defenseless body. "Cầu cứu!"

Hue grabbed another pillow off her bed and began to hit me while Mai continued to laugh and thump me with hers. Both were now chattering playfully in Vietnamese as I laid there at their mercy. They continued their attack until Hue's pillow burst apart, feathers going everywhere. Mai was laughing so hard there were tears in her eyes and laughed harder when Hue fell off the edge of the bed. Feathers were all over me, the bed, and in Mai's hair.

Hue pointed at Mai's hair and laughed uncontrollably. Mai threw the pillow at her, as Hue got up and ran out the door, Mai in hot pursuit. I was no longer the target. I could hear the scuffling and giggling on the stairway.

How could I not enjoy this? I sat there propped up on both elbows. Was there really a war going on here? Was I in it? It seemed I was living in another time, far removed from the hurt and pain suffered by so many in the rice paddies and jungles. I was very lucky. I had not asked for this, had not gotten special dispensation to be here. I was just here. Luck of the draw, I guess. I could have wound up humping for days on end in the heat and wetness that was the delta, but I was here instead. Safe in Saigon. Maybe I would stay here forever. Maybe I would prove Mai's ancestors were wrong. This would be one American that would not come and go.

One thing that really touched me about Mai and her friends was the inherent sense of family that they all seemed to share. I could have sworn they were all related. Their own family seemed to extend to everyone who was within arm's reach. I never saw a baby that wasn't picked up and coddled or played with. It was hard to really know who the mothers were, as the children always seemed to be in someone's arms.

I guessed that these women that I saw all around me had gotten used to their men going off to war. They all seemed like sisters, cousins, and nieces to one another. Mai would often have all her extended family of girl friends in our house at night to watch the televised Vietnamese soap operas. They all sat on the floor, drinking tea or iced coffee, kids on their arms. I never understood the excitement of watching the puppets shows on the TV, as they played out their ancient stories. The girls would all laugh and make fun of one another, and of what they saw. As I lay on the bed facing the television and watching them, Mai would occasionally look my way and say something in Vietnamese to me. As if I could understand her. She was happy having her friends here, and happy that I didn't seem to mind.

She would always talk to me in Vietnamese when she got mad at me. Sort of like Ricky Ricardo going on his Spanish tirade at Lucy when she messed up or made him mad. I found it quite amusing and would mock her until she started laughing, but she'd always get in a good shot to my arm. I tried my hardest to learn the language, but it must be one of the most difficult languages to master. So many of the words seemed to be identified by the particular pitch, length, and tone used. I was able to learn to count to one hundred and say such thing as "thank you", "you're welcome", "how much", but that was about it.

I never knew Mai's family. I knew her father was dead. She would occasionally go off for visits to Phan Rang for a couple days at a time. One day I came home from work and saw an older woman sitting on a chair in the kitchen. She had a cloth wrapped around her head. I would have guessed she was quite elderly and had black stained teeth from constant chewing of betel nut. Betel nut came from the betel palm, and many older women placed this between their cheek and gums. It was mildly narcotic and could relieve the pain of diseased gums. She spoke no English, and my Vietnamese wasn't even rudimentary. Mai respectfully introduced us, and we both shyly acknowledged one another. I guess I was being introduced for a purpose. Meet the family, meet my boyfriend, meet my mother.

The time in Saigon went by very fast. October of 1967 was upon me quickly. My DEROS (date of expected return from overseas) was less than 30 days away. I was officially a real short timer. One night sitting on the balcony Mai asked me when I was returning to America.

"Well, I have about 30 days left."

Mai took a sip of her iced coffee and looked straight ahead. "Are you fini with the Army?"

"No, I will have one more year, at least, and then I'm finished."

"You go back to girlfriend in America?"

"Well, I already have a girlfriend."

Mai, looked at me, not understanding what I had said. "What's her name?"

"Mai."

"No, you American girlfriend. What's her name?"

"I don't have another girlfriend. My girlfriends name **is** Mai."

Mai thought for a moment and took another sip of coffee. She pursed her lips and a tear came to her eye. I knew she hadn't understood my little play on words.

I leaned forward. "Mai, I'm talking about you. I don't have a girlfriend in America. I just want you. I'm not going to America. I'm staying here."

"What? Sạo quá. You lie, no?"

"No, I don't sao. I don't lie. I'm going home for two weeks next month, and then when I come back, I'll be going to Vung Tau."

"Vung Tau? Why not Saigon? You live here." I could see the disappointment on her face.

I had chosen to extend for six more months. Vung Tau was the R@R Center, Rest and Recreation, for those soldiers who wanted a three day in-country retreat. It was where the 552nd MP Company had originally landed, and it was quite a beautiful area.

I hadn't checked out other MP companies in and around Saigon. Another MP with the 300th had told me about it, so I signed the papers. I had not thought about Mai at the time. I didn't really know how deeply I cared about her until I was sitting on the balcony and saw her cry. No one had cried over me before.

"Well, you can come live with me."

"You crazy, I can't go to Vung Tau. What about Hue? What about Dao? What about my mother. She know I live here. Not Vung Tau. That's very far away. How long in Vung Tau?"

"It will be for six months."

Mai turned to me. "Jim, I cannot leave Saigon." Mai got up and walked back inside, turned to me, and said, "You don't understand. I cannot leave Saigon."

On the day before my flight back to the states for my leave Mai was very depressed.

"I think you never come back."

"Mai, I will be gone for two weeks. I will visit my family, and I will be back here in two weeks. All I can do is promise you that."

"You find American girl friend and then you won't come back."

"Well, if I don't come back the Army will come and get me, and they'll make sure I come back. I have signed papers to come back. You have to trust what I say." I fumbled through my wallet and found my expired Maryland driver's license.

"Here. You keep this and give it to me when I come back."

"What's this?"

"It's a very important ID. Don't lose it. I need it when I come back."

"No *sao*?"

"No sao. No lie"

I knew I was looking at a girl who loved me. I had been just a fun-loving kid up until now, but I was feeling different about my life, and different about her. I was even thinking about marrying her, though she didn't know it. Now, how would I convince my family, and would they understand?

Chapter 18

It was a two week leave that I could have done without. My mom didn't stop crying, and my brother John didn't stop persecuting me about my decision to return to Vietnam. John added uneasiness and intimidation to every aspect of life, and those around him. His way of solving a problem was through fright. If you cowardly shrank away in fear of him, he had just solved the problem. He could have been a knight among men. Instead he pounded your senses with rejection, intimidation, and inferiority.

"Jesus, you want to get killed? Don't you see what this is doing to your mother? You won't even be here for your birthday. Another missed Christmas! Grow up!"

It didn't stop. I counted the few days until I could get on the plane and return to Saigon. I wanted to be anyplace but "home."

That's all I remember about those two weeks. It was October of 1967.

It was when I went back to Vietnam, after extending my tour after my first year, that I grew to love Dao like a real sister. When I arrived at my apartment Mai was not there, and Hue was unable to tell me where Mai had gone. Dao took me into her apartment and sat me down.

"Jim, Mai went to Vung Tau."

"Vung Tau? She went down there?"

"Yes, she went down to wait for you."

"You're kidding? She did that?" She did that for me?"

"Jim, she loves you very much."

"I guess she does." I couldn't believe what she had done for me. She had so much love for me that she would leave the security of Saigon. Leave behind Dao, Hue?

Unbelievable.

"Wow, Dao, I can't believe it. I was so anxious to see her again, but she's not here. I must get to Vung Tau as soon as I can. How long has she been gone?"

"Well, you were to be gone for two weeks, so she left two days ago. She went by bus."

"Geez, I can't believe she left Saigon. Is there a way to get in touch with her?"

"Well, no phones that I know. The best way is to just go as quick as you can. When do you go?"

"Well, I have to go to Tan Son Nhut tomorrow at eight and take a helicopter."

"Do you want to eat? I have shrimp and rice?"

"Yes, that would be good. Mai always made me shrimp and rice."

"I know, I know. She gave me orders to feed you shrimp and rice, shrimp and rice." Dao had a good laugh.

"What else do you eat? I know, I know, just shrimp and rice?"

"Well, I did have *rice* and shrimp one time." Dao laughed out loud again. "You are too crazy."

"Yeah, I know." I paused for a moment. "Mai went to Vung Tau? Vung Tau. Just amazing."

The next morning, I was on a chopper headed towards the coastal town of Vung Tau.

Vung Tau means 'puddle ships. It was a long strip of land surrounded by ocean. Ships used to receive safe harbor here during the days of piracy. It was now an area where ships might stop before traveling up the Saigon River to the city of Saigon. Picturesque would have been an understatement. If there was any place where it looked like war could never occur, this was the place.

I had never been there, but I chose to extend my tour there hoping I could do some traditional town patrol functions. I was sure the town must have bustled with energy, and challenge that the 'vacationing' soldiers could bring. It was going to be six months that I looked forward to, and hopefully the experience would help me if I became a cop after Vietnam. I was having some reservations though. I knew it was a big sacrifice for Mai to pack up and move away from Saigon and her family. I just hoped I wouldn't let her down.

I arrived around 0900 hours but was not scheduled to check in until noon. That gave me three hours to find Mai. I asked a passing Air Force sergeant which way the main gate was, and he pointed behind me.

"Straight ahead, straight ahead. Going to town?"

"Yes, I have three hours to kill. Where's the 560th MP compound?"

"Right over there. You can see the sign from here."

"Oh, yeah, okay, thanks."

This should be easy. Once at the gate I waved to the MP and walked out on the roadway. Well, this wasn't Saigon. No taxis, nothing. I turned to the MP at the gate.

"How do I get to town?"

"Just stand here and thumb a ride." No sooner did he say this than an MP jeep pulled up to the gate. I could see him talking to the driver, and then point over to me. Another MP sat shotgun. The MP in the passenger seat motioned for me to join them, so Ijogged over to the jeep. He must have noticed my 18th MP Brigade shoulder patch. "Hey, you an MP?"

"Yeah, I'll be joining you guys come 1200 hours."

"All right, my names Webster, and the ugly guy next to me is Sams. Jump on board. You going to town to have some fun before you report? We'll give you a lift."

"No, gotta hook up with my girlfriend. She came down from Saigon. I just want to see her before I report in. How do you guys like town patrol? I'm sort of anxious to get started."

"Town patrol? Well, you won't be starting with town patrol. You gotta earn your way. You'll probably get thrown onto river security escorts for a while."

"River security escorts? What's that?"

Webster turned around to face me. "Well, you could wind up riding tugs down into the Mekong Delta, or supply ships up the Saigon River to Saigon. It can be dangerous, and it will take you away for days, maybe even weeks at a time." Webster laughed. "Saigon, right back where you came from."

Geez, right back up to Saigon? Trips down the delta? This had never crossed my mind. It looked like town patrol was out, unless for some reason I got lucky.

"Come on, let's get you into town to find your girl."

This news devastated Mai when I met up with her. She had gone to work in a local bar waiting for my arrival so we could get an apartment, and she could quit work. She had even talked about bringing Hue down later to be with her. Now it seemed that plan was in jeopardy.

When I checked in back at the base it was confirmed…ship security duty. My first trip would be back up the river to Saigon. I was crushed.

Mai stayed in a room at the bar. Several of the girls slept in the same room with her, so she wasn't without companionship. She wasn't happy with the situation but was going to be patient. It was thought that I'd be back in a couple days, and we would talk over what we were going to do. Little did I know that I would be on the ship and gone from Vung Tau for 10 days.

Two-man teams stayed with the ships during the trip until it dropped us off back in the port of Vung Tau. However long it took to offload their goods, we'd be there with them providing security. Twenty-four hours a day, seven days a week. Our shifts were usually ten hours on, ten hours off. It was sleep, eat, work, sleep, eat, and work. That was it. It was mind numbingly monotonous.

Although the ships usually provided excellent food, there was nothing whatsoever to do when you weren't pulling your work shift. Nothing, other than sleep. While I was in Saigon, I did manage to get off the ship and go to the apartment to see Dao and Hue. All I could think of was what Mai was doing. I was able to get word back to Vung Tau to have one of the MPs from the 560th go find her. He let her know I was stuck in Saigon and would return soon. I could tell this wasn't going to work out.

When I got back to Vung Tau after my first trip I was given three days off. This gave me time to be with Mai. The mamasan owner of the bar knew I was an MP and didn't say much, but she made sure that Mai worked the tables pushing Saigon Tea. I was able to buy Mai out of the bar so that we could spend time alone. I tried to convince her to give this a chance to see if I would wind up on town patrol sooner than I thought.

My second assignment was a trip down the Mekong Delta on a tug pulling barges.

I'm not quite sure why two MPs went along as these barge crews, all civilian contract workers, many Filipinos, were more heavily armed than we were.

Our job was to shoot anything in the water that could contain explosives that got too close to the barges and repel any attacks on us from the shorelines. The problem with tug escorts was that tugs moved very, very slowly. When I told Mai, she was mad and impatient. I couldn't blame her.

The shoreline up the Saigon River had been heavily defoliated with Agent Orange, however many of the small tributaries in the delta had not. I remember sleeping under the stars on the deck of a tugboat. The town of My Tho could be seen lit up on the shoreline. Every star in the sky was out and looking down on me. It should have been a lonely feeling, but it wasn't. We were a hundred yards offshore, the water was calm, and just a slight breeze in the air. I couldn't believe a war was going on in this country. It was a weird feeling to not be thinking of my family back home. I wasn't. I don't know why that was. Perhaps I was falling in love with this place. Could that really be? My thoughts turned to Mai back in Vung Tau, all alone. This trip lasted three days and two nights.

When I returned from this trip Mai was depressed. She wanted to know when I would be pulling town patrol duty, so that we could get an apartment, and she could bring Hue to stay with her to have company when I was working. I told her I didn't know, but to wait just a little while longer. It shouldn't be too long.

Then it was off to Saigon again and the battle that would be called The Tet Offensive.

The NVA (North Vietnamese Army) and VC (Viet Cong) had planned an attack on dozens of major cities and military facilities throughout all of Vietnam. From the DMZ (Demilitarized Zone) in the north, to the Delta region in the south.

I was in Saigon when the Tet Offensive started but stuck on a cargo ship. I had a ring side seat to the carnage, as I was able to listen to the action through the 716th MPs dispatch, WACO. It was unnerving. I could also hear the sporadic exchanges of gunfire and explosions, followed by exchanges between MPs in distress. The MPs were outmanned, but not out fought.

My partner and I were not allowed off the ship. Our orders were to protect the ship. The first twenty-four hours brought intense fighting with the MPs taking the brunt of it. Five MPs had been killed in the battle for the American Embassy. Twenty-two others would lose their lives before the offensive came to its close. We wanted so badly to get off the ship, but it would have been courts martial time for us if we had left the ship undefended. It was very frustrating.

The 716th MP Battalion had about a thousand men in its command.

Approximately 300 MPs were on duty that night. Five enemy battalions of between 2000 and 2500 had infiltrated into the Saigon area. Attacks were spearheaded by the C-10 Sapper Battalion. The plan called for 35 battalions of 4000 locals to attack the following six major targets

1. The Vietnamese Joint General Staff Headquarters
2. The Independence Palace (President Thieu's office)
3. The American Embassy
4. Tan Son Nhut Airport
5. The Vietnamese Navy Headquarters
6. The National Broadcasting Station

The following partial chronological account is taken from the Staff Duty Log of the 716th MP Battalion:

•**1:30 a.m.** Three vehicles, including one truck loaded with explosives, drive up to the National Palace staff entrance on Tu Do Street. They commence their attack with 34 sappers.

A B-40 rocket is fired against the staff entrance gate. An MP patrol responds to the palace, and the two MP's are killed. Their M-60 machinegun is stolen by the VC. The VC are forced across the street to a half-completed hotel complex. The VC hold out for 15 hours, and 32 are killed. Two are finally captured.

•**2:00 a.m.** Sappers begin an attack against Gate Number Five, at the Vietnamese General Staff Headquarters, just east of Tan Son Nhut Airport. They attack from the Long Hoa Pagoda across the street from Gate #5.

An American MP jeep appears on the scene and the MP's engage the enemy. The security force now has time to close the gate. Additional MP's respond and defend the compound.

The assault collapses and the enemy retreats back to the Long Hoa Pagoda.

•**2:40 a.m.** Nguyen Van Muoi drives a black Citroen sedan past the six story American Embassy on Thong Nhut Blvd. He carries a samurai sword in the back seat for luck.

•**2:45 a.m.** Mortar fire drops into city. Muoi drives by again. This time he shouts, "Tien" (forward)! A Peugeot truck and a taxicab drive west on Thong Nhut Boulevard along the south wall of the four-acre compound and stop. The sappers begin unloading weapons and equipment as others step out from the shadows.

Two military police, SP4 Charles L. Daniel, 23, of Durham, NC., and PFC William E. Sebast, 20, of Albany, NY., both from Company C, 716th MP Battalion, are at the east side entrance on Mac Dinh Chi.

•**2:46 a.m.** At the Embassy rear fence Commandos appear in civilian clothing and black pajamas, with red armbands. Carrying new AK-47s, three B-40 rockets and explosives, they climb into the compound.

•**2:47 a.m.** Part of the commando team attacks the side gate. SP4 Daniel and PFC Sebast close and secure the gate and radio "Signal 300" (enemy attack). The VC then blast a hole in the ten-foot wall, at the front of the Embassy, using a 3.5-inch rocket (B-40).

Daniel radios, "They're coming in! They're coming in! Help me! Help me!" They manage to kill two Viet Cong leaders before they are gunned down on the Embassy grounds.

MP SGT Jonnie B. Thomas, 24, of Detroit, MI., and SP4 Owen E. Mebust, 20, of Lynwood, CA., of the 716th MP Battalion respond to Daniel's call for assistance and drive east on Thong Nhut Boulevard. As they reach the main entrance they are ambushed and killed, by automatic rifle fire. Other military police and US Marines are now also responding.

On the Embassy roof, Marine SGT Rudy A. Soto Jr., 25, of Selma, CA, fires six .38 rounds at the commandos. Once he is out of ammo and with his shotgun jammed, he watches and radios situation reports.

Marine SGT Ronald W. Harper, 20, of Cambridge, MN and CPL George B. Zahuranic, 20, of Uniontown, PA., secure the main doors. A B-40 round hits the door and window wounding Zahuranic. A second B-40 round soon follows.

•**2:55 a.m.** The National Broadcasting Station is attacked. A jeep and two Toyotas stop in front of the station and a group dressed as Vietnam Riot Police attack. At the front gate they kill a police guard. A machinegun on the roof across the street kills a platoon of ARVN paratroopers sleeping on the roof of the station. The attackers hold the station for six hours.

At the Vietnamese Naval Headquarters, at Bach Dang Quay, 12 sappers attack by blowing a hole in wall. Within five minutes 10 are killed, and the other two are captured.

•**3:00 a.m.** BOQ #3, near Tan Son Nhut Airport, reports enemy action. The MPs are engaged with the enemy force which is retreating to the Long Hoa Pagoda after being driven from the Vietnamese General Staff Headquarters.

Rockets and mortars begin falling on the Long Binh complex, fifteen miles north of Saigon. A local VC battalion launches a diversionary attack against the eastern bunker line, while the 275th VC Regiment attacks the northern perimeter.

Sappers begin infiltrating into the ammunition depot just north of Long Binh. The VC 274th Regiment also attacks the Bien Hoa Airbase just north of Long Binh.

•**3:15 a.m.** The American Embassy is under attack.

•**3:16 a.m.** Explosion at the Phoenix City BOQ (Officer's billet).

•**3:17 a.m.** Explosion at the Townhouse BOQ.

•**3:18 a.m.** BOQ #1 under attack.

•**3:19 a.m.** MacArthur BOQ under attack.

•**3:20 a.m.** Marine CPT Robert J. O'Brien, 36, of Marshfield, MA, arrives with a six Marine "reaction force," at the east side Embassy wall. They get pinned down by fire and retreat across the street from the side gate.

•**3:21 a.m.** Rex BOQ under attack.

Three battalions of VC attack the western side of Tan San Nhut Airport, which houses MACV and Seventh Air Force headquarters. They attack from positions they have occupied since midnight at the Vinatexco mill, just across Highway #1 from Gate #51.

A consolidated VC attack takes place by the 269th VC Battalion attacking from the northwest, the 267th VC Battalion attacking from the southwest and one battalion attacking from the east. They manage to overwhelm the ARVN defensive force and enter the airfield.

MACV headquarters guards and members of the US Air Force 377th Security Police Squadron stall their advance until reinforcements arrive from the 25th Infantry Division in Cu Chi, at 6:00 a.m. The final enemy soldiers are not driven out until approximately noon.

•**3:25 a.m.** Explosion at BOQ #2.

•**3:40 a.m.** Automatic weapons fire and attack at BOQ #3.

•**3:41 a.m.** MPs at the Embassy want an urgent resupply of ammunition.

•**3:42 a.m.** Sniper fire at Metropole BEQ.

•**3:50 a.m.** Incoming mortar rounds into the Montana BOQ.

•**3:58 a.m.** The Saigon port area reports automatic weapons fire.

•**3:59 a.m.** Mortars and rockets are fired at the Embassy, and reinforcements requested.

•**4:00 a.m.** US Marines and MP's are dispatched to the Vietnamese National Police station to escort them to the US Embassy to assist. They refuse to leave their station.

•**4:07 a.m.** MP Unit C9A reports that a 716th MP Battalion alert force in two escort jeeps and a 2 1/2-ton truck loaded with 25 military police, have been ambushed by a B-40 rocket and machinegun fire in a narrow alley. They were responding to the reported attack at BOQ #3. Heavy casualties are reported.

•**4:08 a.m.** Unit C9A is hit. Both MP's are killed.

For the next sixteen hours the VC will battle these MP's and the two additional MP rescue teams sent to assist the initial alert force. In this one battle alone **16 MP's die in the alley and 21 are wounded.**

•**4:19 a.m.** BOQ #3 requests more ammo.

•**4:20 a.m.** At MACV Headquarters General William Westmoreland orders the 716th MP BN to clear the Embassy compound as the "first priority."

•**4:30 a.m.** Request for armored vehicles and helicopters for an Embassy assault. A reaction team is appointed.

•**4:45 a.m.** At the Phu Tho Racetrack an MP unit radios, "The driver caught a slug in the gut, and I'm under heavy automatic weapons fire. Can you give me some help?" Before help arrives, both MP's are killed by the attacking force, the 6th Binh Tan VC Battalion.

•**4:49 a.m.** Cleveland and Columbia BOQ's request ammo and assistance.

•**5:00 a.m.** At the Saigon Motor Pool, three claymore mines are detonated. Booby traps are discovered.

•**5:16 a.m.** Explosions and small arms fire at the Royal Oaks BOQ.

•**5:30 a.m.** Two platoons of 101st Airborne Division infantry, led by MAJ Hillel Schwartz, 33, of Tacoma, WA, attempt twice to land on the Embassy roof from helicopters. Each time they are driven off by VC fire.

•**5:35 a.m.** Automatic weapons fire at the Butte BEQ.

•**5:42 a.m.** MP shot in an attack at the Denbigh BOQ.

•**5:46 a.m.** Claymore detonated at the Flint BOQ.

•**6:00 a.m.** Camp Red Ball under attack.

•**6:02 a.m.** MP machinegun jeep captured by VC.

•**6:13 a.m.** Claymore mines detonated at several BOQ's.

•**6:15 a.m.** The area near Ambassador Bunker's home is hit by mortars and automatic weapons fires.

At the US Embassy a Medivac helicopter lands and deposits three cases of .223 ammo, none of which is usable by the Marines. It departs with Zahuranic, Soto and Army PFC Charles M. Fisher.

•**6:18 a.m.** Tent City B at Tan Son Nhut under attack.

•**6:45 a.m.** Mission Coordinator George Jacobson, on the second floor of his villa, at the northeast corner of the US Embassy compound, spots blood on his first floor. He calls for assistance.

•**7:00 a.m.** Marine LT Case shoots the lock off the front gate at the Embassy. It takes six rounds. MP's crash through the gate with a jeep.

At the Joint General Staff Headquarters, a second unit, the 2nd Go Mon Battalion, attacks Gate Number Four. They enter the compound, attack and seize one building before they are routed.

•**7:05 a.m.** At the Embassy front gate, 1LT Frank Ribich leads the MPs in a battle to regain control of the Embassy grounds. For approximately one hour they clear the compound grounds of the remaining enemy.

•**8:00 a.m.** Troops of the 199th Light Infantry Brigade attempt to take the Phu Tho Racetrack. They will fight all day until they finally capture it at 4:30 p.m.

•**8:35 a.m.** MAJ Schwartz, in seven helicopters with his platoon of paratroops from C CO, 502nd Infantry, lands on the Embassy roof.

•**9:00 a.m.** The lone remaining VC is wounded and trapped in the villa by MP. PFC Healy crosses the lawn and throws up a gas mask and .45 caliber pistol to Jacobson. MP's fire at the lower windows and toss tear gas. The tear gas drives the VC upstairs. He shoots three times at Jacobson and misses. Jacobson shoots the VC with the .45 caliber pistol that had been thrown up to him.

•**9:15 a.m.** The US Embassy is declared secure. From this one action four Vietnamese and **five American MP's are killed.** Seventeen VC are killed, and two VC, Nguyen Van Sau and Ngo Van Giang are captured.

Throughout the rest of the day the Viet Cong attack several targets in the Saigon area. Eventually military police of the 716th MP Battalion, including their attached units; the 527th MP Company; Company C, 52nd Infantry; and the 90th MP Detachment respond to many more of these attacks, along with back up forces from the 92nd MP Battalion.

*On this first day, after an estimated nine separate attacks are over, **20 military police have been killed and 21 are wounded** from the 716th Military Police Battalion.

I took no active part in this offensive. Would I have wanted to? I felt bad not being able to help. I knew the danger, I heard the gunfire, and explosions. I heard the hysterical radio chatter.

I would have preferred being in the fight with them. I had trained for it in Georgia. I had done my days with the Big Red One, but I know it would have been horrible seeing comrades down, bleeding and dying. Still, I should have been there. Every MP would have wanted that. For me, it just wasn't go be. I would be involved in the second Tet Offensive, as it was called, a few months later.

Chapter 19

Several days after the offensive started, I fell ill. I was on duty about 0100 hours and my partner was sleeping. I had become dizzy and was sweating profusely. I hadn't been feeling well for days. I didn't think of going in and waking him to relieve me. I decided I just had to fight my way through it and get through my shift. At about 0300 hours I got really sick. I was hanging onto the railing, starboard side.

I held on and walked port side and had to place both my hands on the railing to stay upright. I staggered to my room and sat down on the side of my bed, sweat pouring from my body, leaned back, reclined, and shut my eyes.

The next thing I know the door to my room opens, and an MP lieutenant and sergeant walk through the door. I had been caught sleeping on duty by the duty officer from the 300th MP Company, who also had the responsibility to check on the 560th MPs who were working the ship details. I sat up quickly and reached for my helmet but knocked it off the bed sending it spinning like a top on the deck.

The lieutenant looked upset. "What's going on here specialist?"

"Well, sir, not feeling too good, and I just meant to come here and sit for a minute."

"Relax? Looked like you were sleeping to me."

"Well, yes sir. I'm sorry it wasn't intentional."

"And what seems to be your problem?"

"Well, I'm not sure. I'm a little sick and have a fever and was pouring sweat a few ago."

The lieutenant walked over to me. I must have looked sick to him. He placed the back of his palm against my drenched forehead.

"Hmmm, you've got a fever. You look like crap. That aside, you're not supposed to be in here sleeping. Do you want me to get you a relief?"

"Uh, no sir, really, not that. I'll be okay, just let me get back to my post. I'll make it through the end of my shift."

The lieutenant had a pensive look on his face. "Hmmm, all right Stewart, get back out there. You look familiar. We're you with the 300th just a while back?"

"Yes, sir, yes sir." I clumsily picked up my helmet and rifle and walked past him to the door.

"Wait, you sure you're okay? You're not walking too steady."

"No, sir, I'll be fine. There's too much going on and I should be outside." The lieutenant didn't say anything but watched me as he walked off the ship.

Two hours later I was found unconscious by my partner on the aft deck. I was picked up by an ambulance, transported to Tan Son Nhut, placed on a chopper, and flown back to Vung Tau. I had mononucleosis.

I was going to have to spend the next two weeks in a hospital ward. I had one of the MPs pay a visit to Mai to tell her what had happened.

I was half asleep the next day when I saw Mai step through the front door of the ward. She looked beautiful in her white áo dài. Her hair was combed straight and hung down to her waist. Other soldiers who were awake took notice, and sat up in their beds as if a dignitary had just walked in. One solider hurriedly ran a comb through his mussed-up hair.

Someone uttered, "Whoa", and looked over at me with a smile.

Mai stood in the doorway petrified. All the soldier's eyes were on her, and I knew that being as shy as she was, she was overwhelmed by it. I held my hand out and motioned to her. She walked with small steps, her eyes diverted downward, seemingly afraid to react to the stares of those she passed.

She came to my bedside and put her hands on my left arm. One soldier said loudly, "Well, ain't you gonna kiss him? Dang!"

Mais eyes stayed fixed on me. I could tell she was embarrassed. "You don't have to kiss me here." Her fingernails dug into my arm. "You sick?"

"Yes, I got sick on the ship. Mononucleosis, but I don't know how to explain that in Vietnamese."

"When you get better?"

"Maybe about 12 more days, not really sure."

"Jim, you never here for me. I get very lonely by myself, and I miss Dao and my sister. I miss you too."

I couldn't expect Mai to stay here in Vung Tau, so I said it. "Mai, why don't you go back to Saigon."

"You want me to go back?"

"Mai, it's not good for you. Go back and stay with Dao and wait for me. I might even get another trip up to Saigon so I can see you then."

"But what happens when six months are finished? You go home?"

"No, no. Mai I'm going to go back to Saigon and work as an MP for another six months. I never should have left Saigon, and never should have let you come down here. It's been very difficult for you."

"So, you come back to Saigon, for sure?"

"Yes, I promise." Mai had a soft smile on her face. "I love you. You know that, right."

"Yes, and I love you too. Don't worry about me, I'll be okay. You have to go back to Saigon and just wait. It won't be long."

"You won't find another girlfriend?"

"I have a girlfriend, remember? Did you see the way all the soldiers looked at you when you walked in here? They would all like to be as lucky as I am."

Mai blushed, "Okay, I will leave tomorrow on the bus."

I sat up resting on both elbows. "But you have to give me a kiss before you leave."

Mai smiled, put her arms around me and kissed me. The hooting started. "Whoa! All right!" from down the aisle.

"Hey, me too!" from the bed next to me.

"Jim, I trust you. I will wait for you in Saigon."

With that she turned and hurried out of the ward to whistles and admiration. "Hey man! "Where did you land her? She's the prettiest Vietnamese I ever saw."

"Well, I'm wondering that myself. I wonder that myself."

I lay back in my bed, closed my eyes and fell asleep. It was better this way. I was no use to Mai like this.

I had written a letter to my mom letting her know that I was staying in Vietnam for six more months. I couldn't imagine the trouble that letter had to cause around the house but had come to realize that Vietnam was now more my home than home was. I was not in the least bit thinking of home. I was thinking of Saigon and Mai.

I was able to get up to Saigon a couple times during the remaining time left on my tour. Mai seemed very happy and content to be back with Dao, Hue, and the rest of her friends.

Mai didn't know the exact date that I would be back in Saigon, but I couldn't get there fast enough after my six-month tour with the 560th. I was heading for the 527th MP Company by way of a convoy that I caught early in the morning. When we hit the outskirts of town I needed only to hop in a taxi for a short ride to my apartment. My apartment, huh. I was now calling it 'my apartment'. The front door was wide open, as it usually was. She had no idea when I would be back, or if I would ever actually come back. Mai was sitting quietly on the floor, her legs folded in front of her, looking down and reading a magazine. I tapped lightly on the door frame.

"Jim!" Mai got up quickly, throwing the book onto the bed and ran over to me.

I was home. I was treated with a rice and shrimp dinner, and all the latest gossip from her and Dao. I was asked how many girlfriends I had after Mai had left Vung Tau, and jokingly fibbed that there had been hundreds. I had never cheated on Mai. Things were back to normal, the way things were supposed to be. Normal in Saigon.

I was supposed to live in the International Hotel, several blocks west of central downtown, but, as usual, nobody seemed to do much checking to see where we slept. The International was several stories high and had bars located on the first floor that catered to the MPs who were billeted there. I never set foot into these bars, as I was always off to my apartment when I got off work.

We used to get our jeeps out of the motor pool around the corner of the hotel and drive them to the front where we'd load up our gear for the shift. After Tet we mounted M-60 machine guns on the backs like the infantry MPs had done with the Big Red One.

One night an MP secured his machine gun onto the turret, slammed the cover down on the ammo feed tray, and the gun accidentally discharged several rounds into one of the bars. One soldier was killed, and a couple bar girls were wounded, as the bullets penetrated the concrete block structure. This was one of many accidental deaths that had occurred during the war. Unknown to people back in the states there were deaths such as these quite often. Drownings during R@R, traffic collision fatalities, heart attacks, and even murders at the hands of other soldiers. If it happened in the states, it happened in Vietnam.

I don't think I slept in my room more than a dozen nights out of my six months tour with the 527th. I occasionally made a token appearance just to keep on the safe side, slept in my bunk, and ate Army chow at the mess hall. I'm not sure anyone noticed.

The main duty of the 527th MP Company was town patrol. I had landed in MP heaven. We patrolled the streets and bars looking for any signs of trouble. Saigon was a huge city with alleys that crisscrossed one another, and it was easy to get lost in the maze of apartment buildings. I had also latched onto a lifetime friend, Per A.W. Christiansen, from Vancouver, Canada. He was a burly, blond, good natured fellow, and we became inseparable. If there was anyone whose Viking heritage showed, it was Per. We pulled many a town patrol duty together. One night I found luck was on my side again.

While on patrol Per and I got a call of a man with a gun at the Sunshine Bar at the end of Tu Do Street. Tu Do street was a couple blocks long and was full of bars on both sides of the street. This was the hot spot for night life in Saigon. The bars opened around ten in the morning and stayed open until curfew. This kept the MPs very busy. This street catered specifically to American servicemen and civilian workers.

When we arrived, we parked the jeep at the end of the block and walked up to the front door of the bar. I took off my helmet and peeked around the corner of the opened front door. I could see a Vietnamese soldier standing at the bar. He looked a bit upset. Two other soldiers stood behind him. They both looked scared. There was no one else in the bar.

I turned to Per who was standing to my side out of the sight of the soldier. "Well, don't see much. I'm going to go in."

"You sure? He have a gun?"

"I don't see one."

For some reason I didn't draw my own gun. I put my helmet back on and stepped in the doorway. I took about two or three steps toward the group and then saw that the angry looking soldier had a .38 special revolver in his right hand, holding it down to his side.

For whatever reason, I didn't stop, didn't panic. I gave him a sheepish smile.

That's all that came to mind. No backing out now. I walked slowly toward him as he kept an eye on me. One of the other soldiers seemed to plead with him in Vietnamese. He looked back at his companion, and then back toward me.

I got passed him and walked into the back of the bar into a hallway where the restrooms were. I saw a line of bar girls and soldiers huddled down against the wall. There must have been about 10 of them. They all looked scared out of their wits.

Very calmly, "Okay, everyone stand up and follow me outside."

They must have thought I was crazy, but they complied, all looking at each other questioningly.

"Everyone, calm, in one line and just walk out without looking, or saying a word."

They followed me around the corner. The soldier was still standing there with his gun in his hand. I could see half of Per's body in the doorway. I'm sure that he had his gun out at his side.

We all walked out the front door and the bar girls and soldiers scattered in the wind, running down the street. Vietnamese MPs (QCs) had just pulled up in their jeep. Two of them jumped out with their M-16 rifles at the ready. They ran into the bar and I heard them screaming at the three soldiers who were inside.

Per looked at me and said, "What the fuck was that?"

"What?"

"That?" He pointed his still drawn gun toward the front door. "You wanna get killed?"

"Well, I sorta got stuck. By the time I saw his gun, well, it was too late. I just kept walking and smiled at the bastard."

"I guess he liked you, geez." Per let out a laugh of relief.

"Well, shit, what'd you want me to do. He had the drop on me. I was in no man's land."

"I guess so. Now this one you need a medal for, not that dang grenade thing you did down at the docks. I don't know if you heroes got guts or are just plain stupid. You didn't piss your pants?"

"Lemme check. Nope, can't say that I did."

The QCs brought all three men out in handcuffs. It was highly unusual for a Vietnamese soldier to come to one of these bars, very unusual. I guess the beer and jealousy got the best of the one guy. What I did was tactically dumb, but I did get myself in the middle with nowhere to go, but forward. I was lucky.

A few weeks later two MPs from "A" Company of the 716th MP Battalion would respond to a similar radio call for a bar in the Cholon district of town (Chinatown). They were both gunned down and killed when they walked in the front door by a drunk Vietnamese officer. Nothing would happen to this officer; however, he did meet his fate during the fall of Saigon and was killed in action.

Saigon was also full of AWOLS, soldiers who were absent-without-leave. You were AWOL if you failed to report for duty within a short time limit. You were classified a deserter if you were gone without authorization *over* 30 days. In 1968 it was believed that as many as 5,000 AWOLS were in Saigon. That's a lot of potential trouble.

Many had gotten involved with ration card fraud. Ration cards were issued to soldiers, and they contained a list of items that could be purchased from the PX (Post Exchange) on a monthly/yearly basis. The following was allotted to each soldier/civilian for one year:

four cases of beer a month six bottles of wine or liquor
six cartons of cigarettes a month three cameras a year
one slide projector one movie projector three tape recorders two watches
typewriter
electric fan tv

one tuner one amp

one record player two radios

Now you might ask yourself what a soldier needed with three cameras in a year, three tape recorders, in a year? It became the standard to buy one, then purchase two more and sell them on the black market and make a healthy profit. The authorities had to know that all these goodies flamed the black market. They had to know. Or, perhaps it was by design.

Each time you made a purchase the clerk (all who were local nationals, i.e., Vietnamese) would punch out a hole in the card where one case of beer was noted. In some cases, they would mark an "X" over the item instead, if they didn't have a hole puncher. An AWOL soldier, working in cahoots with the clerk, could go into the PX, and have the same item purchased, and the same card hole punched over, and over, and over again.

These items would then wind up on the black market to be sold at three or four times the normal price. Martel cognac was a big item with the Vietnamese. You would know the day a shipment of Martel cognac arrived at the PX, as soldiers would be lined up around the store waiting to make the purchase. The cognac, sold for about $3.00 a bottle, would then be sold to the Vietnamese for about $12.00.

Quite a profit in those days. Martel cognac was sold out the day it was put on the shelves. Six bottles of liquor, times $3.00 a bottle, was purchased for a total of $18.00. That was a lot of money out of a soldier's pocket back then. But, when you sold those six bottles, times $12.00, for $72.00, it was very enticing. And don't think that it was just the privates lined up to make the purchases. Sergeants and officers also got involved. It was tacitly okay to do. It wasn't right, but it was widely accepted.

Otherwise there wouldn't have been so much cognac for sale.

Don't think that the liquor was sold in some dark alley. A Vietnamese friend might by it. A girlfriend would sell it at the market, etc. There was nothing clandestine about it.

It was on patrol of the alleys in one of the most congested areas of Saigon that Per and I ran into another problem with the AWOLS. Per had just turned into an alley off Troung Minh Giang Street. The alleys were quite narrow, and children were everywhere. We had driven very slowly for a few minutes, making a right turn into another alley that crossed the one we were on.

"Freeze, you motherfuckers, freeze! Put your fuckin' hands in the sky!"

We were staring down the barrel of an M-16 rifle. Neither Per, nor I had the time to respond. This was an AWOL, or a deserter. He had on his fatigue pants and a white tee shirt. A bandana covered his nose and mouth. His companion, .45 caliber pistol in hand, came around to the driver's side and stuck his pistol in Per's face.

"Get the fuck out of the jeep! Now, motherfucker!"

Per and I, hands in the air, got out of the jeep. We were made to strip down to our underwear. Everything we had on was thrown into the back of the jeep. Any Vietnamese who had been sitting out enjoying the day had quickly retreated into their homes.

"Okay, motherfuckers, down on the ground! On your faces, goddammit!" Per and I complied and spread ourselves out on the hot dirt in the alley. I heard the jeep speed off down the alley, got up on one elbow and looked over at Per.

"Shit!"

Per and I weren't the first and wouldn't be the last. We had been robbed of everything. AWOLS were getting so brazen that they would rob MPs, take all they had, and sell the spoils. Everything, jeep, guns, web belts, fatigues. Most of the goods turned up on the city streets downtown in the black market.

Neither the Vietnamese city cops, or the Vietnamese MPs, or the American MPs could confiscate items sold openly on the black market. The black market was not a clandestine operation. Stalls lined the streets in the morning, or a *merchant* simply displayed the items on a tarp spread out on a sidewalk. U.S. military canteens, mess kits, ammo pouches, helmets, fatigue shirts, and pants were sold openly. They were hard items to come by in the supply rooms of military bases, but easily purchased on the streets of downtown Saigon. And when I say downtown Saigon, I don't mean a side street, but right on the sidewalk in front of a legitimate shop.

The black market fell under the control of the Vietnamese customs police.

Occasionally they would raid the stalls, and street corners, and confiscate the contraband. We would always know when a raid was coming, because the black marketers would only put out a small *offering* the day of the raid. They would sacrifice some goods for one day for the privilege of keeping in business. The customs police would make their raids, pick up the token offerings, and be gone. The American press would cover the event, take photos, and report it in the papers. The next day the black market would be in full operation with their full stock of stolen goods displayed. It was a high stakes game with corruption all the way to the top. The papers would first page highlight the raids, show photos of smiling officials who had done their jobs, and everyone would be happy.

Cultural differences existed and it did cause dissension, at times, between the Vietnamese and Americans.

Young Americans did not understand the conservative and religious strictness of the Vietnamese. Many of the Vietnamese men frowned upon seeing their women walking with or living with American soldiers. You had to be very discreet. When I was a soldier Mai and I never went out together. Instead we were content to stay at home and meet with friends around the apartment complex.

One day we decided to venture out to the Saigon Zoo. We went in separate taxis. Taxis were subject to being stopped and searched by joint city and Vietnamese military police (QCs) checkpoints. We enjoyed our day at the zoo, but foolishly decided that we would take the same taxi back to our apartment. At a traffic light I saw several QCs and city cops standing just off the sidewalk in the street. One of the city police looked over at our taxi, saw me, and must have seen Mai sitting next to me. He flagged the taxi over to where he and the others were standing. He did not look pleased.

He stuck his head in the back window on Mai's side and asked her for her identification. Vietnamese were to always carry their ID cards with them. She said she had left hers at home. This was all he needed. He opened the back door to the taxi and ordered her out. Irritated, he pointed at me, and put his palm up motioning for me to stay in the taxi. The other men gathered around Mai. I could hear them chattering excitedly back and forth. A QC leaned over and looked in at me.

"She you girlfriend?"

"Yes, has she done something wrong?"

"She have no ID. Maybe she VC."

I decided to take a chance. "I'm an MP with the 527."

"You, MP?

"Yes, yes, can you talk to that policeman? "No, he very mad. He take girl to jail."

"Jail, for what?"

"She have no ID. Maybe VC for sure."

I started to scoot over to the open door to get out of the taxi. I looked out and Mai was gone. Panic came over me.

"She's no VC!" I shouted.

"Hey, you be nice. You better get out of here, or they take you to jail too."

I could see two other city cops looking at me with anger on their faces. The other QCs seemed unconcerned.

"What jail?"

"I don't know how to say, but over there." The QC pointed northeast.

I took my anger out of the QC. "This is bullshit! She's not a VC." It must have upset him.

"No, no booshit, man.! You better get the fuck out of here, or we take you too."

I got in the taxi and told the driver to hurry to my apartment. When I arrived, I ran upstairs to find Dao, told her what had happened, and that the white mice (a derogatory term for city cops) had taken Mai. Dao said that she would go to the police station to try to get her out.

"Try?"

"Jim, they don't like seeing Vietnam girls with Americans. Mai is very beautiful, and they are very jealous to see this. I may have to give them money. Do you have money?"

Mai had kept an envelope full of money in a small dresser next to the bed. I leafed through it. There was about $60 worth of Vietnamese

179

money, and about $20 worth of Military Payment Certificates (military money used to pay soldiers instead of regular U.S. currency).

"Dao, this is it. You think this will be okay?"

"I don't know, but I go now. You have to stay here."

Dao was gone for about three hours, returning without Mai.

"Jim, they won't let her go. They say she has no ID, and she might be VC."

"Dao, what happened to her ID? Is it here? You know she's no VC."

"She lose it long time ago. She never get new one. They told me not to come back for three days."

"Three days! That's bullshit, Dao. What will they do to her?"

"I don't know. You can get more money? I will go back tomorrow, if you get more money."

I had some money back at the International Hotel, locked up in my locker. I had to work the next morning, so would get it before guard mount.

"Jim, come to my house. Don't worry. Come to my house and just talk."

I didn't sleep much that night. It was a strange feeling not having Mai in the apartment. I tossed and turned and fretted over what I might do to the "white mice" if anything was done to her.

The next day I dropped off twenty more dollars to Dao. I worried about Mai during my entire shift. I checked back in with Dao later in the day and was told that they still would not release Mai, and she was to come back tomorrow. Tomorrow, what were those bastards up too?

I spent this night at the hotel when I got off duty and borrowed some more money off some of my MP friends, just in case. The next day I stopped by the apartment and gave Dao $20.00 more. Then I went back out on patrol, not in the mood to play army at all. I scowled at every white mouse that I saw.

When I got off shift, I went back to my apartment. It was empty. Hue was not there, and Dao was not in her apartment. I took some rice out of the refrigerator and ate it cold. Just then I heard footsteps coming up the stairwell. As I got up, Mai walked into the room.

Her face was expressionless, and she didn't make eye contact with me. "Are you all right?"

"Yes, fine. I need to wash and then sleep. I don't sleep for three days."

Dao was standing in the doorway with Hue at her side. Dao put her index finger to her lips as if to say, 'shhhh'.

"Jim, come to my house, let Mai wash."

Mai walked past me and around the corner. She ignored me and began to disrobe. I continued to watch her.

"Jim! Come, have some iced coffee. Mai will come later."

I looked at Dao, as she motioned for me to come instantly. I walked into her apartment and sat down. Hue stayed with Mai.

"Dao, what happened?"

"Jim, I pay all the money and they let her go."

"But why is she acting that way."

"Jim, she doesn't talk. You don't ask her, okay? You must promise you don't ask."

"Those bastards hurt her, didn't they?"

"Jim, you don't ask. Nothing else to say. Don't make Mai sad. Don't talk about this anymore. You must promise. You hear me?"

"Dao, I need to go back to Mai."

"No, no, you sit here. Let her alone for a while. Let her wash, go to bed, and sleep. You stay in my bed tonight, and I go sleep with Mai and Hue."

I laid awake most of the night, my mind running wild with horrible thoughts about Mai and the white mice. If I could have gone to the police station, I would have killed them all. I had promised Dao I wouldn't say anything. It must have been around four in the morning when the door opened, and I could see Mai's silhouette enter the room.

She got under the sheet with me and snuggled up to me with her back to me. I put my hand on her waist.

"Mai, you OK?"

Softly, "um hmm." My nerves frayed, and all my adrenalin spent I fell asleep.

When I awoke at 0730 Mai was gone. Dao was cooking in the kitchen. I sat up on both elbows.

"Dao, where is Mai?"

"She went to Phan Rang to visit her mother."

"Phan Rang? She never said anything."

"Jim, you never mention this again. She goes with Hue, and they come back in four days. You want to stay here with me?"

"No, no. I guess I'll stay at the hotel. Four days? Did she say why?" Dao put her index finger to her lips, "shhhh."

I never knew what happened to her. It was never discussed. Mai returned from Phan Rang, as if everything was normal. She didn't seem phased by it. I kept my promise to Dao and never talked of it. I had a hatred of the white mice from that point on and would have loved to have taken revenge. I would have loved to have been in the position to have had to help one of them, and then just walk away, leaving them to whatever their fate was. I knew that wasn't right, and I probably wouldn't do it, but that's how I felt.

Chapter 20

Mai was pulling at my shoulder. "Jim, wake up, wake up, something is happening." I rolled over and looked up at Mai.

"What, what's wrong?"

"The VC are in Saigon again. You need to get up. I can hear bombs."

Bombs? I wasn't sure that the VC had bombs and didn't know if Mai knew the correct word to say, but she had gotten my attention. I righted myself and sat on the edge of the bed, still not completely awake.

"Where are my clothes?" Mai handed me my shirt, as I walked into the kitchen. I was supposed to work today. What time was it? How was I going to get all the way back to the International Hotel for muster if the city was under attack? How close were they? Was this the same magnitude as the first Tet attack? Mai hurried back in with my freshly ironed pants.

"Mai, what time is it?" Mai handed me my watch and my wallet. "It's 6:30."

0630? I didn't need to be to work until 1200 hours, noon. We had no telephone, so calling in was out of the question. I pulled my pants on and reached under the bed for my boots and socks.

"I'm going to have to try to get to the hotel."

"How are you going to do that? You don't have a gun, and you don't know where the VC are. I don't want you to go."

"Well, the lieutenant will be expecting me, that's for sure. I'm sure all the MPs are getting ready to fight right now. They'll be waking up everybody. I'll be in real trouble if I'm not there when they call my name. I need to get there. Do you know if there are any taxis on the street?"

"I don't know, I don't go outside."

I finished lacing up my boots and grabbed my hat.

183

"Mai, I don't know when I'll be back. I'll try to stop by and see you, but I don't know where they'll send me in the city. Don't worry about me, okay? I'll be back, just don't worry. I've got to get down to the street to try to get a ride to the hotel."

Mai reached up and put her arms around my neck and kissed me on my cheek. I could see the worry in her eyes. She had the most expressive eyes. Dozens of MPs had been killed or wounded in fighting in and around Saigon during the first offensive, and I'm sure this weighed heavily on her mind.

"Do you have any piaster? I might just have to take a cab to the hotel. If there are any out there working."

Mai went to the dresser and opened the top drawer. She pulled out an envelope and took out a handful of piasters.

"Here, because you might need more."

"I don't need all that. "

"Maybe you get hungry."

I put the money in my pocket and walked out the front door. Mai walked with me. As we walked down the stairway, I tried to envision what might be happening out on the street. As we got to the alleyway, I could hear exploding mortar rounds.

They weren't close, but I feared that I would be out of luck finding transportation to the hotel. I walked to the end of the narrow alley and could see that the streets were pretty much empty. There were a few people on bicycles, but I saw no vehicles. Surely people were scared and were taking no chances, hiding in their houses. This second attack of the city was not supposed to happen, and I knew that the carnage from the Tet attack was still on everyone's mind.

Mai came up behind me and I could feel her body press into my back. She put her hands on my waist.

"I don't see taxis."

"No, doesn't look good."

I couldn't hear explosions anymore, nor could I hear any gun fire. Mai then pointed south. "Look, here come MP jeep."

Her eyes were better than mine, but I could now faintly make out the white painted area under the windshield, and then the white bold print of MILITARY POLICE. The jeep was approaching rapidly, and I could see the driver.

"Is that Per?" Mai said.

I squinted and tried to focus as the jeep got closer. Yes, it was Per. I could see his broad face and his ever-present grin. He pulled up on the wrong side of the street and came to a screeching halt.

"Top of the morning, Jimbo!" He looked over at Mai and tipped the brim of his MP helmet.

"How is the most beautiful woman in the world this morning?" Per was in love with Mai too, and always treated her with the greatest of respect.

Mai simply giggled and offered, "Hello, Per. Good to see you."

Per handed me a bag. "All your gear my friend. You'd better throw it on. We're under attack and got to go kill us some VC." Per chuckled.

I still hadn't said anything to him. I opened the bag and saw my MP helmet and web gear, including my .45 pistol. I put the gear on hurriedly, remembering back to the time I slept through a mortar attack at Long Binh.

"Per, what the hell is happening?"

"Well, ain't no big deal so far. From what I've heard there's some fighting going on at the cities edge. They're shooting some rockets into the city right now. People have been killed, mostly civilians from the rockets."

"Rockets? Not mortars?"

"Well, 122s and mortars. They're walking them in and the last bunch hit right downtown. There aren't any reports of fighting inside the city yet, so we need to get on patrol. As a matter of fact, you have to go on patrol, and I'm going to stay here with Mai."

Mai threw Per a kiss." The only kiss you get butterfly."

Per pretended to catch it and slowly opened the palm of his hand and sniffed it, as if sniffing a fragrant perfume.

"Ah, Jimbo, you lucky man. Jump in and let's go to work. Mai I'll be back later tonight."

Mai laughed at Per. "I'll find you a girlfriend today. How about a mamasan with black teeth? You like betel nut, no?"

185

Per took off his helmet and placed it across his heart. "Only you, my love, only you."

I was in the jeep and scuffed Per across the back of his head. "You wanna get us going, junior?"

Mai ran around the front of the jeep to where I was sitting. "You be careful, please?"

"Don't worry, I'll be back later tonight to check on you."

Mai put her arm around my neck and gave me a kiss. Mai looked over at Per. "You keep him out of trouble!" wagging a finger at him.

"Yes, ma'am. But if anything happens you always have me."

Mai had run around the front of the jeep and was now standing next to Per. She grabbed his left ear and tugged on it.

"This is the only kiss you get from me. She kissed Per on the cheek. Now you go, and both be good."

Per had a grin from ear to ear. "Yes, ma'am. Yes, ma'am."

I waved at Mai one more time, as Per stepped on the gas, and drove north toward Tan Son Nhut airbase. I looked over my shoulder to see her standing on the sidewalk with her arms crossed. I waved again and she lifted her arm and waved back. She looked worried.

"Per, what the hell happened?"

"Well, they woke us all up. Didn't matter if you just got in the sack, or not. Everybody mustered for guard mount. They had a roll call too."

Oh, shit, a roll call. I had missed roll call. Instead of being safely tucked away in my room at the hotel I was with Mai. What trouble was I in now?

"Sergeant Stevens called out 'Stewart', and I did my best Yankee impression, 'here'!" Never missed a beat, saved your ass my friend. He never knew the difference. I think everyone was just too damned excited and confused."

"Holy, shit! Thanks man. Whew, that's too close for comfort."

"He teamed everyone up with who we worked with last night, so you lucked out again and got me. I hustled my ass to your room and broke into your locker and got your stuff. Then ran down to the motor pool and got Betsy here and the rest is history."

"You broke into my locker?"

"Well, it wasn't too hard being as you never locked the lock. It was just hanging there."

The gods must be on my side. Every screw up I had been involved in always turned out all right in the end. I'm sure that some of my adventures at Long Binh had resulted in me getting transferred out of the company. Although they were meaningless infractions in the big picture, I'm sure it put me at the top of the list when it came time for the brass to decide who would go, and who would stay. I wind up here in Saigon with Mai and a friend like Per. Luck *was* certainly on my side. Must have happened for a reason.

Per drove north the few blocks toward the air base. I looked left toward the northeast and saw an explosion. I grabbed Per's arm and he pulled to the side of the street. First one plume of clouds, then a few seconds later another, same pattern. They were walking the rounds in. We counted six all told. They didn't care who they hit. Per looked over at me. "I think we'd better get over there."

I slapped Per on the right arm. "Go, let's do it."

Per turned onto Phu Tuyen Street and we sped west. We started seeing civilians leaving their homes, going to work, going to market. Just like the first Tet offensive there were people all over the streets. They were going about their normal business, not knowing how much they put themselves in danger being out like they were. A gun battle could erupt, and they were still getting their ducks off to market. Life went on the in the city, even in the face of war.

We could hear WACO, our MP dispatcher, chattering away. Rockets had hit a residential area, and downtown near Tu Do Street had received several 122mm rockets. These rockets were fired from bamboo tripods and were approximately five feet in length. They packed quite a wallop. They were slow and you could see them flying by overhead. You could also plainly hear the whistling sound they made. I would be sitting on the back of the jeep taking a break at the hospital the next night when one would fly over me, land about 50 yards behind me, and knock me off the jeep. They delivered a lot of shrapnel and shrapnel discriminated against no one, man, woman, or child.

When we arrived downtown it was chaotic. People were trying to help wounded men, women, and children who were cut, and lying bleeding in the rubble left by the explosions.

One older mamasan laid face down in the street, her blouse torn from her body, her head a bloody pulp. Per and I did the best we could to help with the wounded. For this old lady, it would be her last breath. The *My Lai massacre* would make big news in the press, but this indiscriminate killing and maiming of civilians barely got a mention. This was the American press.

During this offensive I couldn't stay at the apartment. We were on duty 14-16 hours a day, depending on the need. I was always able to stop by and make sure that Mai, Dao and Hue were doing okay. I made sergeant while with the 527th. Not bad for a guy with so many "mis-adventures", but these were part of every vets' stories, I'm sure. I would become the driver for LT Frank Ribich, one of the heroes of Tet.

The offensive against Saigon by the VC never amounted to much. They shot rockets into Saigon for 11 straight days, and for 23 out of the 38 days the offensive lasted, causing some civilian carnage, but they never really got any farther than the outskirts of Saigon. It was a bust for them, and the infantry units did a job on them. We mainly dealt with the butchery from the rocket and mortar attacks.

October 1968 rolled around and so did the end of my tour of duty in Vietnam, and my enlistment with the Army. I was getting out. I could either reenlist and stay or go home. I didn't want to re-up but didn't want to leave Saigon. If I reenlisted the Army could send me any place they chose. I wanted to stay in Saigon, not wind up in Korea or Germany. I decided to get out of the Army and work my way back to Saigon.

I told Mai I would return. She didn't believe me. We had an emotional parting. "I will try to get back here as quick as I can."

"Jim, you don't have to lie to me. You get out of the Army and then you find American girlfriend. I understand."

"I promise you. Give me one month, one month. Give me one month to get back here. I'm not staying in America. Can you do that?"

"Okay, one month."

Chapter 21

I was trying to figure out how I would, or could, get back to Saigon. I sat next to the window of the plane looking out at the bright sunlight, and down at the blackened runway. All around me I heard voices of joy and anxious chatter and shouts of the, "Freedom Bird, at last!" I had no idea how I'd get back. Not a clue as to what the process was, or if it was even allowed. After all, there *was* a war going on here.

"We're going to the World now baby!" A black G.I. stood up and waved his cap, giving out a very loud yell.

"Yeehaw! Momma, I'm comin' home!" Others joined the chorus, but I just stared out the portal onto the tarmac.

The stewardesses made their way up and down the aisle trying to calm the jubilation, telling people to sit and buckle up for departure. I could hear the engines humming as the plane turned slowly out onto the main runway ready for takeoff. The hum increased steadily, and I could feel the power building up. The plane inched its way along and then suddenly burst forward. Men began to yell and hoot as if they had been imprisoned and were finally being released. Faster and faster the plane made its way down the runway, and then suddenly you could feel the nose point upward as the plane lifted off the ground. More cheers and jubilation, except for one, me.

The soldier sitting next to me gave me a nudge with his elbow.

"We're gone, baby! We're goin' home! Ain't never comin' back to this place, never. If I never see Vietnam again that will be okay by me. What do ya think?" I turned my head toward him, but didn't smile, or say anything.

I saw men's arms and hands in the air, as if they were on the downward slope of a fast-moving roller coaster. The yelling was constant and hectic. Would it stop, or, would it be like this the entire way home?

189

Looking out the window I could see the buildings and houses surrounding Tan Son Nhut. I looked back toward my apartment and Saigon. I know I could never actually see it, but I squinted hoping to catch a last glance. What had I done? Could I really make it back to Saigon? How would I do it? Was it even allowed?

Where was I going? I didn't know, but I did know that I didn't want to be going. The soldiers all about me were released from their suffering, or loneliness. I was trapped, trapped with no recourse, against my will, with nothing I could do about it. If I could have stopped the plane, I would have. I couldn't. I was absolutely powerless. I was still in the Army until I got to the states.

The passengers continued to whoop it up, but the noise to me was distant, faded in my mind into dead silence. There was nothingness. No one on the plane except me. Me, silence, and a feeling of dread. There was no delight in me. I had said I would come back. Lord knows how, because I surely didn't. Hands were still raised in deafening silence. The plane's engines were silent. A stewardess walked up and down the aisle making sure everyone was buckled up. She had quite a rowdy crowd on her hands. I reclined my seat back, closed my eyes and thought of nothing but the day I would return.

Once the Freedom Bird arrived at Travis Air Force Base we were loaded onto busses and taken to a nearby gymnasium. It was all very casual. A sergeant advised those of us who were getting out of the Army to sit in the bleachers and wait to be called. There would be physicals to take, new uniforms to be fitted, and final pay to be issued.

"Okay guys listen up! You'll be called by alphabetical groups. For example, they may call all of you whose lasts names being with the letters A through E, so you gotta pay attention. Unfortunately, this is gonna take some time. There're snack machines down by the heads and soda machines too. So, if you get hungry, help yourselves. But, listen up for your group to be called." With that he turned and walked away.

At first men sat and chatted about their adventures, and what they thought they were coming home to. How much had things changed in a year? For some, more than a year? Some talked of marriage, and others of jobs that were waiting. But, after a couple hours men began to stretch out on the bleachers and sleep, read books, or drift off by themselves. It would be a monotonous wait. The camaraderie from Vietnam seemed to slip away with the knowledge that it was over, and we were back in the states. You didn't feel like bonding with anymore men, especially since you were going home. It didn't mean you felt any less of them, you were just at an end.

Slowly groups of men were called off to begin their processing out of the Army, or transfers to other duty stations, for those who still had time remaining. We all underwent medical exams and were checked for venereal diseases. It was October, so we were all fitted for winter uniforms. This would include the heavy wool three-quarter length coat and our class A uniform. Mine would be adorned with the name STEWART above my right coat pocket. My sergeant stripes and ribbons, to include my Soldier's Medal, were properly affixed, and last, but not least, our pay records were checked. My last check would be for roughly $500.00. A lot of money because of unused leave and such. That money was a welcome sight. It would pay for a plane ticket back to Saigon.

We had been advised that after being paid we could muster in front of the gymnasium where shuttles would transfer us to the civilian air terminal, so that we could catch our flights home. Those staying in would wait for transfer to their new duty stations.

I walked out of the gym and into the sunlight. I was in a brand-new government issued uniform, adorned with stripes, arm patches, rank and ribbons. I should have felt good about this. I should have felt proud, but I felt out of place. Would people be staring at me once I left the friendly confines of the military base? I had read the papers. I had heard of men who had sacrificed a year or more of their lives for their country, being spat on and ridiculed in public. Our dedication meant nothing to these people. They had an agenda, and stupidly, and purposely, used the American soldiers as fodder. We didn't have time for all the news in Vietnam. We were too busy working. Too busy doing our duty. We only got snippets of the anti-war crowd but were aware that their supposed concern for the soldiers and sailors was just a front for their cause. We didn't like them but had to tolerate them. These people would be the first to run out of alleys that we would run into. We knew we were "baby killers" to them, and we also knew that they had painted the Tet offensive as a great defeat for our troops when, in fact, it was a great defeat for the VC and North Vietnamese troops.

How would I react to these people? Would I lash out? Would I fight back? It hit me that I was scared and was stepping into a new and unfamiliar world. A world that had gone on without me for two years, and for the most part, didn't really care. I wasn't scared of them, but what I might do to them. I didn't want to disgrace my uniform by lowering myself to their level. That's what they would have loved. I wasn't going to do it right now.

I turned and walked back into the gym, walked into the locker room, and opened my duffel bag. I solemnly draped the heavy wool coat on a hanger and hung it on a hook in one of the wall lockers. I took off my uniform and carefully folded it, placed it on top of my shoes in the bottom of the locker, hurriedly put on my civilian clothes, picked up my duffel bag, and jogged back out to the shuttle area. Had a staunch patriot just done a cowardly act? I didn't want to deal with a country that I did not know. I didn't want to deal with shallow minds inside of some people who had done nothing in their lives, but protest and complain.

The cowards who came up and spat on brave soldiers had won the day. I wouldn't confront them, wouldn't fight them. I could only imagine how the press would have treated a soldier in uniform who "interfered" in these freedoms of expression, and speech, by these people. I look back on my actions that day with regret and shame. Never again. My plane trip back to Seattle was uneventful. My time with my brother would not be.

My brother John's face was scarlet. My mother sat in a chair in the corner of her small house with tears running down her cheeks, a hanky to her face.

"What the hell do you think you're doing?"

The veins in his neck were about to burst. His right index finger was an inch from my nose. I thought he was about to hit me. I had always admired my brother's vast talents. He was an outstanding high school athlete, played some minor league baseball, and did nothing while in the military but play baseball, football and basketball

His Jerry Lewis imitations as a teenager kept everyone in stitches, but something had gone wrong. The all-American guy everyone wanted to be around had become an intimidating control freak.

Decisions by anyone else meant nothing to him. It was his way, or the highway, and he was now going to do everything he could to control this situation about Vietnam. He cared nothing about how I felt. It simply didn't matter to him. I looked up at him.

"I'm going back."

"I ought to knock you through the fucking wall for this. Your mom worries for two whole years, and now you're pulling this shit? You're going to put her through this again? What's back there for you, nothing! What a bunch of fucking bullshit!"

No one dared to talk back to him, no one. I continued to sit in my chair staring straight ahead.

Tears must have welled up in my eyes. "Are you gonna cry?"

This was my oldest brother. Brothers were supposed to give brotherly advice, not rip their heart out. They were supposed to protect you. Didn't he know that? My lower lip began to quiver. I was stressed out. I could say nothing. He treated my silence as weakness. He treated everyone in the family the same way.

"Well, what is it? You're not pulling this shit, Jimmy!" He began to pace, his fists clenched as tight as his teeth. I got up and started for the door.

"Oh, leaving? That's it? Just fucking walk out the front door, you fucking sissy!"

My brother always took other people's sadness for what he thought was as a sign of cowardice and weakness. I used to get tears in my eyes because I wanted a big brother. He never knew that people wanted to love him and were hurt when he went into his rage. After two years in Vietnam I was still a sissy.

I walked past my mother who was now blowing her nose into her hanky and walked out into the light mist that was falling. I took a deep breath trying to regain my composure, and then out to the street, turning to look at my mom's house. This was not home. This is just a house in Washington where my mother had moved. This was not where I wanted to be. My brother didn't know it, but his actions had made it so much easier for me to decide. Leaving now would be easier. There would be no tearful goodbyes. There would be no hugs. No one telling me "good luck" or "take care of yourself, have a good trip." It would end in bitterness. But, none of that stuff really mattered now. My brother had made sure of that.

I just wanted the days to go by quickly. My passport would be ready soon and my visa taken care of. I would stay away from my brother and ignore my mom's tears.

Home sweet home.

I could take refuge at my brother Bob's house. He lived in an apartment several blocks from my mother's. I turned and began to walk up the street. "Jimmy!" My mother was at the door.

"You'll need a jacket in that rain. You'll catch a cold!" I waved somberly, put my hands in my pockets, and continued to walk. I would not go back to the house to catch more of my brother's rage. No more guilt, that was it for me.

I had written several letters to Mai and had sent her money. I had no way of knowing if she had gotten any of them. My last few days in Washington would be spent focused on my return to Vietnam. It was November 1968.

I can't explain why I wasn't nervous about returning. Twenty-two years old, no job, and job hunting in Vietnam? I missed Mai. It just seemed so natural for me to do. I'd been gone so long it just seemed right that I was heading off again. The plane trip called for a stop in Hawaii to go through customs. I would meet my first obstacle there.

"Afternoon, sir, may I see your passport please."

I handed the customs agent my passport and placed my luggage on the inspection table in front of me.

"Your plane ticket also, sir."

The agent took it and raised both eyebrows, looked back at me, handing me the ticket across the table.

"Sir, this is a one-way ticket. You need a round trip ticket. You have to show the Vietnamese government that you're leaving after your visa expires."

Roundtrip? I had no idea. I also didn't have the $500.00 extra to buy the return ticket.

"Sir, I don't have enough money to buy a roundtrip ticket."

"Whoa, well what were you planning on doing? You just can't go there and stay. They aren't going to just extend your visa after 30 days."

"Well, I'm returning to get a job and bring my girlfriend back to the states."

"You don't have a job yet?"

"No, sir, I don't." I think the agent could see the worry on my face.

"You mean to tell me you're going back to a war zone and you don't even have a job lined up?

"Yes, sir. I'm going to find one once I get back."

"Well, listen. How much extra money you got?"

"Well, a couple hundred dollars."

"Tell you what. You go to the counter and you buy a one-way ticket to Bangkok. If you don't find a job, you'll have to leave the country when your visa expires. Bangkok is close and it shouldn't cost you much. If you get stuck in Bangkok, just walk into the American Embassy and tell them your dilemma. They won't be happy they've got a stranded American on their hands, but what are they gonna do? Send you to Vietnam?" The agent chuckled.

"Thanks, I appreciate your help."

"Well, I'm guessing you've already done a tour over there. It's the least I could do for you."

I purchased the ticket for $50.00 and was on my way to Viet Nam. All of this thanks to an understanding customs agent.

After a 20-plus hour leapfrog from Hawaii to the Philippines, I was back in Saigon. Vietnamese customs was a breeze. They didn't even look at my plane ticket. After a cursory inspection of my luggage I was out the front terminal and headed for the main gate. As usual, it was hot, but I was completely used to it.

I flagged down a cyclo and within minutes was home. Everything looked the same. Don't know why I thought it would have changed in such a short period of time.

I started my walk down the alley, and as I got halfway Dao walked around the corner. She had her conical hat on and a big straw-like basket. She must have been going out to buy fresh food at the market.

She let out a yelp and dropped the basket.

"Jim!" She put her hands to her cheeks. For a moment she didn't move, and then she turned and began to run back toward the stairs up to the apartments.

"Mai, Mai!" She was shouting in Vietnamese as she ran from me.

I picked up her basket, turned the corner and saw Dao scurrying up the spiral stairs. She stopped momentarily, gave another surprised look down at me, and continued up the stairs.

"Mai, Mai!"

I could see my apartment door open and Dao disappeared inside. I was halfway up the stairs when Mai came around the corner and stood in the doorway. She ran and jumped into my arms.

"You came back!"

"Yes, did you get my mail? Did you get the money I sent?"

She looked surprised. "No, no letters, no money, nothing. I dreamed you would never come back to me."

Mai took me by the hand and walked me into the apartment. "Where's Hue?"

"She is visiting my mother in Phan Rang. Sit down and I'll get some coffee."

Mai looked beautiful. She was shaking but had a wide smile on her face. I was grinning, too. I *was* home at last.

Mai had gone back to work at the bar, pushing Saigon Tea. I didn't want her working there, and she didn't like working there, but until I could find a job, she would push drinks. I had $150.00 on me (a lot of money back then), and it would help with the rent and food. But now I had to concentrate on hitting the streets and finding work.

"Mai, I came back because I want you to come to America with me."

"America? Leave my family? Leave my mother, brothers and sisters?"

"Well, yes, you'll like it. We can get married and start a family. That's why I came back. You want to be with me, right?"

"Yes, but why should I leave? You Americans will always be in Vietnam. You stay here with me. You can live here forever." With that she turned and walked back into the kitchen.

She was right. It seemed we'd always be here in Vietnam. It had already been eight years. Saigon was thriving, we had soundly defeated the enemy during the Tet Offensive, but ill-will *was* brewing back home about the war. The press had portrayed Tet as a defeat, and severe blow to the U.S. troops, instead of looking at how it had decimated the communist troops. I wasn't as optimistic as Mai, but for the time being, she was right. We'd always be here.

I dropped the subject.

There were many American companies and contractors in Vietnam at the time.

They employed thousands of foreign civilian workers. Unfortunately, I didn't know much about job hunting in Nam.

My plans for looking for work were stymied when I fell ill during the middle of the night my first night back in Saigon. A high fever, and the shakes, kept me in bed for one week. Mai didn't go to work during this time but kept me cool with cold packs and medicine that I had no idea what it was. I was in and out of consciousness, never knew what was wrong with me, but survived on whatever traditional medicine Mai had given me.

Vietnamese, especially in the south, practiced sort of very rudimentary medicine that had been handed down through the centuries. Some of the ancient practices would have been scoffed at as voodoo like, but in my state, I was unable to argue with *any* ancient medical practice. I simply succumbed to whatever Mai put in my mouth.

I remember the first time I saw Mai come home one day with what looked to be hickeys all over her neck. I was furious and demanded to know what she had been up to. Mai, always feisty, argued back and finally showed me her back. There were circular black and blue marks all over her back. It had looked like she had been tortured. She had actually been to the doctor. She had gotten the 'hickey' marks when the doctor rubbed the edge of coins hard enough on the skin of her neck to raise deep red welts. The circular marks on her back were from small pre-heated glass cups that would suck out poisons in the system.

One day I saw Mai and Hue sitting on the floor. Hue was plucking Mai's forehead with her thumb and forefinger, pinching the skin tightly. Lines of red welts appeared on her forehead. It was a supposed cure handed down through the years by ancient medicine men. I wasn't happy seeing a pretty face and neck like that all marked up, but I was the visitor to her country, and Mai, stubborn, wouldn't really care if I liked it, or not. It worked for her, bottom line.

I was having no luck finding work. There were possibilities, but they meant leaving Saigon, and that was out of the question. I didn't come all the way back to be sent to some desolate outpost miles away from Saigon, no matter how much it paid.

My visa was about to expire so I made a trip to the American Embassy to see if I could get an extension. I merely told the clerk I was visiting my brother, who was in the military, and my passport was stamped, extending my stay for another two weeks. Simple as that.

Chapter 22

My luck was about to change when I went to the headquarters for the Post Exchange, more commonly known as the PX. This was under AAFES, the Army Air Force Exchange Services. It was almost 1969, troop strength had peaked, and the Exchange was there to support the troops with all the necessities of home. More than the necessities of home. Business was booming. There were close to 150 facilities throughout the country. Large major PXs, such as the ones at Tan Son Nhut, Cholon (more commonly referred to as the Chinese section of Saigon), Long Binh, Danang, in the north, and smaller exchanges, snack bars, and cafeterias smattered throughout the rest of the country. It was a huge money-making adventure. To give you an idea, the reported losses per month, were usually around $100,000.00. To give you an idea that $100,000.00 worth of losses every month would equate to about $750,000.00 today. Now to operate at a profit, you must sell a ton to offset those types of losses. The PXs did. Unfortunately, the sales also stoked the black market.

They had a Security Department headed by an MP Officer, Major Oates. At the time he had one secretary, and two Army sergeants working for him. An Australian and I were the first two civilians hired in country as Security Specialists. The minimum wage back in the states was about $1.50 an hour. I was thrilled with my starting pay of $3.48 an hour, plus $10.00 per diem a day when we had to leave Saigon to conduct investigations and audits. I was also given a grade of GS-7 (Government Service). This gave me an equivalent rank of a 2nd Lieutenant and allowed me access to Officer's Clubs. I was elated.

I was to work out of the Saigon office. My job was to conduct investigations into reported losses, and to also audit facilities for compliance with all the Department of Defense directives governing Post Exchange operations. It was a diverse and challenging job, and I couldn't wait to tell Mai. Success had finally come after almost 30 days of job hunting.

Major Oates had me sit down and spend a week reading through DOD (Department of Defense) and AAFES operational directives. These directives filled two huge three ring binders. I was also given the task of devising an audit checklist so that investigators, such as myself, and those hired in the future, had something to work from. Something consistent to aid us in our investigations and inspections.

Reports would then be generated by the investigator with recommendations to correct deficiencies and forwarded to the Officer-in-Charge of the facility. The Officer-in-Charge would have to submit a report of corrective action to our office indicating compliance within 14 days receipt of the report. All deficiencies, or problems that were noted in the report didn't have to be corrected in their reply, but they had to show that efforts were being made to do so. They would have to keep submitting replies to us until all the problem areas were corrected.

It was a 10 hour a day job, 0800-1800 hours, six days a week, but I wasn't complaining. It was no different than the long hours I put in with the Army, plus I was paid more and didn't have to salute.

It didn't take long for a few other investigators to be hired. Most of them were ex-MPs who, like me had either come back, or stayed on in Saigon after their end of service. A new Saigon regional office was opened near the Saigon Hospital. I would eventually be sent there along with newly hired Bob Morrison, an ex-716th MP (who was decorated for heroism during the Tet Offense of '68), and the newly arrived from the state's supervisor, Ron Halsall. We were assigned a couple of local national girls as secretaries, Hue and Lois, and were open for business.

Our office received all reports of losses from our region, which included the delta areas of My Tho, Can Tho, Vung Tau and areas around Saigon, which were Tay Ninh, Cu Chi, Long Binh, and Bien Hoa. Reported losses were so pervasive we had to limit investigations to all reported losses in excess of $10,000.00 *a single report*....Yes, ten thousand each single incident. Either Bob, or I would then be sent into the field to investigate or conduct audits. Our job involved investigating people who weren't used to being investigated by civilians. Especially 21-year-old civilians. People who had power and authority. I had to learn quickly not to be intimidated by Captains, Majors and Colonels.

We were issued snub nosed .38 revolvers to carry concealed on our persons. We were, more or less, the cops of the post exchange. We were what CID was to the Army. I'd find out what a big mess it was soon enough.

Through an agreement with the Vietnamese government, local nationals had to be hired to drive the supply trucks. Many of them were large flatbed types that would carry pallet after pallet of merchandise. The pallets were strapped with metal bands and seals. The seals were recorded on a packing slip when shipped, and the seal had to be the same when it arrived at the receiving location warehouse to be off loaded. I can't tell you how many seals were reported as missing. A truck would arrive at its destination with no seal, or a different seal number. One particular exchange was notorious for this. Bob and I set up surveillance.

A convoy would leave the main warehouse in Saigon. At the head of the convoy was an MP jeep escort, and at the rear another MP jeep. How could anything be lost in this shipment? During one convoy we were able to shadow them, and to our surprise one flatbed truck, in the middle of this large supply convoy, turned down an alley before we even got out of Saigon. This was out of sight of either the lead or following MP jeep.

Bob and I followed the truck at a safe distance. It stopped deep in the alley where two city police jeeps were parked next to two large unidentifiable deuce and a half truck. The truck driver met a Vietnamese man dressed nattily in civilian attire and was handed an envelope. Several men then began cutting the straps off the pallets and loading the contents into the truck. Armed policemen with automatic rifles stood by.

The supply truck was then left abandoned in the alley.

I turned to Bob. "Well, that explains the missing seals, but has anybody ever reported a flatbed truck missing?"

"Not that I know of." This was not merely petty theft, but theft on a grand scale.

I continued working six days a week, ten hours a day. A lot of hours, even for someone my age. The war was being lost at home in the public's eyes and animosities were building in country. The war was in neutral while men still died. It didn't appear there was any plan on the horizon, or the guts to finish it. Nerves were frayed, drug use was increasing amongst the soldiers, the black market flourished. It seemed like we were just spinning our wheels. Mai still refused to get married. It was difficult to explain to her that things were coming to a head, and a downturn was taking place. Public opinion at home had been changed by the press. The governments' reluctance to pursue a military victory, the mounting death toll was like a dark cloud forming on the horizon.

We got all the press from home. To me it looked like my country had become a bigger battle ground than Vietnam. I never had a problem with protests, per se, but the violent protests I was seeing and hearing about was disturbing to me, and others who were in country.

Although not a soldier anymore I could relate to the frustration they must have felt. Weren't we all sent here for a good purpose, to stop the spread of communism?

Weren't our soldiers the good guys? From what I read I would have to fight a war when I went home. Or, was this just the press continuing to undermine the war effort the way they did following the Tet offensive?

One evening I sullenly reminded Mai why I had come back to Vietnam, to get her. I tried to relate the politics of the war but knew that there was no way to translate my concern over what I saw about the war, and America's future here. Things were falling apart. I had been thinking about returning with her to the states, but to Maryland, not Washington. At my age I needed to think of the future outside of Vietnam because I felt we wouldn't be here much longer. And if it fell apart, we would probably be leaving quick. All of us.

Months dragged by and our security department had grown to almost a dozen investigators. It was all too much. I realized that if I were to return stateside, it would have to be soon. I'd have to think about college and a career. It was time to do that. I continued to pester Mai about leaving, but she'd have none of it. She would not leave her mother, her family.

Mai came to me one day as I walked in the door.

"Jim, I missed two periods. I'm pregnant." She had a smile on her face.

"Pregnant? Wow, that's great." Mai and I embraced each other. Her look was one of jubilation. Mine, full of doubt.

"Mai, we must get married. We must go to American." She pulled away.

"Not now. Don't talk about that now." Mai pulled me down on the bed.

"I was thinking we could go to Maryland. You remember when I showed you on the map? The place where I was a little boy?"

"Jim, you crazy. Just stay here. That's not hard." She didn't understand, and I couldn't explain it. I would just have to force the issue.

Through a friend at work I found a nice apartment on the other side of town on Hai Ba Troung Street. It had a separate kitchen and dining area from the bathroom, and the floor was nicely tiled. There was also a private balcony in the back. Mostly American civilians lived in this complex. The rent was only $50.00 a month. I would talk to her more tomorrow before I went to work.

"I'm *not* leaving Vietnam! Jim, I'm not leaving Troung Minh Ky." Mai paced back and forth in front of me, her arms folded in front of her.

"Mai, I don't understand. It's a nice place. We won't be there long. We'll get married and then we'll go to the states."

"No!" Mai and I shared a common bad trait, stubbornness. But I never realized it was more than stubbornness with her. It meant changing her life dramatically. It meant leaving what was most important to her, culture, family, her mother. Those things never dawned on me at that time. Then the words she had spoken about us always being in Vietnam entered my mind. That's what she thought. Perhaps it was true. I didn't know.

"Mai, Americans are going to start leaving Vietnam."

"How you know this?"

"I just know, I can't explain it to you."

"America will be here a long time, long time."

"Mai, if you don't go, I will go."

Mai stood rigidly defiant. I grabbed my suitcase and began throwing my clothes into it. She said nothing. I packed my bag, zipped it up, and stood ramrod straight in front of her.

"Well?"

She said nothing. I turned and walked to the door and turned around abruptly. "Mai, you must do this." She didn't budge. I turned and walked out.

I went to the apartment at Hai Ba Troung and hurled my bag into the corner of the room, sitting angrily on the edge of the bed. What was wrong with her? How could I make her understand? I couldn't. Who could? The next day at work one of our secretaries told me there was a girl out by the front gate who wanted to see me. I walked down the flight of stairs to see Mai standing next to entrance of the compound. She was dressed in her most beautiful áo dài. I nervously approached her.

"Hi."

"Hi. Jim, you come back home."

"Mai, you come to Hai Ba Troung."

"I can't." We both looked down at the ground. "You must."

"I can't. You don't understand." Mai took off her sunglasses and stared back at me.

"Mai, come to Hai Ba Truong tonight. I will be there at 6:30."

Mai didn't answer but turned and flagged down a passing taxi. She walked quickly without saying a word and got in. I yelled out again as Mai put her sunglasses back on.

"6:30!" I don't know if she heard me or not, but she never looked up at me.

That night I sat on my balcony sipping a beer and waiting. 6:30 came, 7:00, 7:30, nothing. She wasn't coming. I sat until 9:00 passing the time watching the traffic go by, looking up and down Hai Ba Troung Street for a cyclo carrying a girl. 10 o'clock and the cyclo never came. Curfew was now here.

"Stubborn," I stubbornly said out loud.

I went to my bed and laid down with my hands crossed in front of my chest, eyes wide open, watching the fan blades whirl slowly.

"Stubborn!" I was awake for hours.

I went back to work the next day and buried myself in my work. I had been a quick learner, senior go-to-guy on the staff and knew the ropes more than anyone. The next few months would be extremely busy. Hectic was more like it. I would be gone from Saigon quite a bit. I missed Mai, but there was a swelling sense of panic coming over me. She would have to come to me. How could she not? There was no future in Vietnam, was there?

I was sent up to the Tay Ninh Exchange and did an audit of their cash fund. They had reported a cash fund shortage of over $60,000.00. The Officer-in-Charge had no answers. The money was simply missing.

All I could really do was verify that they were, in fact, short this amount of funds.

As is usually the case, nobody knew anything about what might have happened. There were no leads, the money just disappeared. How in the world does this amount of money show up missing other than outright theft? It wasn't a mistake of paperwork, an oversight. It just wasn't there. I could only scratch my head at the blatant grand theft that was going on. My job done and being frustrated I hitched a ride with a convoy and headed back to Saigon. A report would be generated, recommendations made, and reports of corrective action submitted. However, the thefts would just continue to pile up. It seemed like no one paid for their malfeasance. Wheels spun; things went nowhere. No heads seemed to roll.

Hitching a ride in a convoy back to Saigon I had taken my .38 revolver and put it, and the holster, in my attaché case. The shirt I wore that day did not allow me to conceal the gun properly, so in the case it went, placed behind the seat on the passenger side. On the outskirts of Saigon, the convoy slowed to almost a standstill. Young boys sold gasoline and diesel fuel from wine and liquor bottles along the side of the road.

About 10 young boys, ages 9-13 came up to the jeep trying to hawk the gasoline, as well as begging for soap, candy, etcetera. They were all over the driver, pestering him and pulling on his arms. We couldn't have been traveling at any more than two-three mph, and the driver was getting irritated yelling out at the boys to get away from the jeep.

"Di di, go away!" The boys continued persistently, and got quite aggressive, even standing in front of the jeep. I sprang into action and leaned over to the driver, helping to pry the grasping beggar's fingers from his shirt and arms.

"Hey! Go away! Di di mau! go on, git!"

The boys all took off running. The driver looked over at me. "Hey, that was quick. You've got that magic. Man, they split fast."

As quickly as he said that, dread overtook me. I had been had. I didn't even want to look.

"Shit!" I turned to look over my shoulder. The driver looked confused.

"What's up?"

My attaché case was gone. I had fallen for the biggest rip-off in Nam. While the larger group diverted our attention, a thief's hand had stealthily lifted my attaché case. Almost four years in country and these little cowboys got me. They also got my gun.

"Son of a bitch!" I ran my fingers of both hands across my eyebrows. The driver looked in the back of the jeep.

"Ah, shit! Man, that's bullshit. Anything good in it?"

"Well, perhaps my job. Shit! I've been here too long."

"How long you been here?"

"Going on four years."

"Four years! Holy shit man, how the hell you do it? The pay must be good." I swatted a fly off my pant leg. "Yeah, the pay. The pay is good."

I got kidded big time back at the office about my run in with the band of thieves, but, all kidding aside, I would not be issued a new handgun. I had also lost all my investigation notes. I'd just have to try to reconstruct what I had found as best I could, although that wasn't much. Were these investigations and reports doing any good anyway?

It didn't seem that way. Did anybody care? I was a mess. I was stressed out over my job, stressed out over Mai.

I went back to my apartment at night thinking I would see Mai standing outside, or a note would be attached to my door, but it didn't happen. For two days after work I sat on my patio looking up and down the street, still waiting for the sight of a cyclo. It never came. What good was this sitting doing? Go see her. No, that won't change things. She won't leave. She has to come here. I looked down to see my knees shaking.

I didn't remain in Saigon long. Headquarters wanted a team to go up to the Danang Exchange, hundreds of miles to the north. A tip had come in that the place was a bottomless pit, with merchandise just flowing out the front doors. This time the boss, Ron Halsall, Bob Morrison, and I would go. Nobody up there would know us. We took a large C-130 plane. When I arrived, my luggage was not on board. No extra clothes, no toothbrush, no nothing. Great. Something else to bug the heck out of me. The tipster would also be right about the mess in Danang.

After settling into our hotel rooms, we headed out to the PX. Bob and I were able to fill up push carts with anything we could find and stroll leisurely out of the front door. Now, this would commonly be known as shoplifting, something we really didn't monitor, as it was so insignificant in the big picture of things. But this was shoplifting at its most absurd level. Our first haul was over $500 worth of merchandise. We went back for a second trip and walked out with even more. No one watched, security at the door didn't check. The place was an all you could steal buffet. We walked out with merchandise up to it being pointless to even continue. We had the information we wanted. Even though we dryly joked about it, we all shook our heads in wonderment. Would heads roll over this?

Another report would be written, more recommendations made, and more corrective action would be promised. Was anyone doing anything about this? Was anyone being brought to task? Was the Exchange system just living with the losses because of the incredible sales and profits? I stopped asking, and just spun my wheels. Hey, the pay was good.

207

I saw the black market in my MP days, but noticed it even more working for the exchange, and how much all these goods stoked the black market. It was driving me nuts. I didn't realize it was a deeper problem within me, not just my job. I would still sit, look down at me knees, and they'd shake. Stress.

Nobody was awake at the wheel. Nobody cared to be awake at the wheel. The train was crashing. Everyone was out to beat the system, and there was always a way. I had investigated civilian officials who, during the search of their apartments, discovered hundreds of blank, un-issued ration cards. These were supposed to be locked up in some Commanding Officers care someplace. What kind of rationing was this? This man would have sold these unused cards for hundreds, if not thousands of dollars. Would he be arrested? No, he would be fired and sent home. Not a bad chance to take, I guess. It would also be bad press. With the war turning sour, who needed the whistle blown on this?

Of course, the exchange did help the local economy greatly by hiring local nationals, but the collusion involved, and either through apathy or turning the other cheek, nothing was being done to stifle the theft that was rife within the system.

I was continually banging my head against a wall at work. Eat, work, sleep, work, and sleep. The 60-hour weeks were taking their toll on me mentally, and I still looked for that cyclo to come to my door. I broke down, got in a taxi, and went to Mai's apartment.

"You want me to wait here in taxi?"

"Yes, yes, please, just a few minutes and I come right back."

I was very nervous. What if she'd found someone else? No, that just wasn't Mai.

I kept pausing, as I walked through the short alley to the turn that led upstairs to the apartment. At the bottom of the stairway I stopped and stared upward at the closed door to the apartment, took a deep breath, and walked to the door. What was I going to say? I hadn't changed my mind about her leaving with me. Would we just fight over this again? I knocked timidly on the door. There was no answer. I pressed my ear to the door.

Nothing, not a sound from inside. Had she moved? I knocked on Dao's door. No response. I felt panicked and short of breath. There was no one here. My hands began to shake. I was a bucket of nerves.

I walked downstairs and got in the taxi. "We go now?"

"Yes, Hai Ba Troung Street. Hai Ba Troung."

Chapter 23

I was usually in bed before 10 o'clock. I was half asleep when I heard a soft knock on my door. Not sure if I was dreaming, I just laid there. Then the soft knock again, and a soft voice, "Jim?"

I knew it was Mai and scurried to the door in my underwear. I had not seen her in months. She looked the same, always demure, feminine, and beautiful.

"Mai, please come in."

She stepped past me, and I could smell the cigarette smoke in her hair and on her clothes. Obviously, she was working in a bar. She gracefully turned to me and stared at my arms and chest.

"Look how skinny you are. You don't eat?" I could see the surprise on her face. "No, don't eat much. No rice, no shrimp." I had lost almost 30 pounds.

Mai turned serious and gazed straight in my eyes. "You want to see your daughter?"

"My daughter? Yes." My daughter? Had that much time gone by? I felt terrible, embarrassed.

"You don't come back home." Mai looked sad.

"You don't come here." I couldn't believe how stubborn we both had been. There was no need to fight anymore.

Mai you want to take a shower? I'll get you a drink from the kitchen."

"I don't have clean clothes."

"You can put on one of my t-shirts."

Mai turned and walked into the bathroom while I went into the kitchen and took out a can of diet-rite cola. Only one left. I looked down at my arms and felt my chest. I *was* too skinny. I looked in a little mirror hanging above the sink. I looked old, gaunt, my cheeks sunken. I hadn't notice until Mai had said so.

My daughter? I had missed the birth of my daughter. I had worked myself to the bone, stubbornly waiting for Mai to come to me. Had those months gone by that fast? I poured the soda into two glasses and shut the refrigerator door. The shower water was running in the bathroom. I walked into the shower and looked at Mai now lathering her long black hair. She didn't protest, stopping for a moment to look at me.

"Your baby took all my milk." Mai had always had large full breasts, unusual for a Vietnamese woman, but now she looked…well, I guess, normal.

I held out the half full glass and she took a sip from it and placed it on the shelf.

"What's her name?"

Mai didn't answer but put her head under the running water to rinse the soap from her hair, turning again, staring me directly in the eyes.

"Phuong."

I repeated it, "Phuong", but did a horrible job. Mai responded slowly, "Phuong, Phuong."

I repeated it, but no better.

"That's a difficult name to say. What does it mean?"

"I don't know how to say in English. You have a shirt?"

Mai was now outside of the shower drying off. I handed her a brush. She looked in the mirror and began to brush her hair. She looked at her breast again and said, "Your baby took all my milk. You see?"

I handed her the t-shirt, she pulled it over her head. It came down to almost her knees. She began brushing her hair again.

"You come see Phuong tomorrow?"

"We can go now?"

Mai placed the brush on the sink and turned to me, "Curfew."

I didn't know what time it was when Mai knocked on the door, but she was right.

It was past curfew.

"You can stay here?"

"Yes, but you have to be nice. I don't want another baby. I had to wait downstairs for someone with a key to let me in the door. I waited an hour. We could have gone tonight. But now, curfew."

In the morning we got up and took separate cyclos to Truong Minh Ky. It must have been nine o'clock in the morning, or thereabouts. I was feeling embarrassed, but mostly ashamed. The people I had gotten to know surely would not be happy at my presence. I'm sure I upset the entire extended family that was always hanging out at our apartment, eating, watching television, telling stories. I was nervous, but it *was* all my fault.

Mai got out of her cyclo and didn't wait for me but headed down the alley. I wasn't far behind her and saw her disappear through the door as I was approaching the bottom of the stairwell. I could hear the uneasy chatter of Vietnamese.

I took a deep breath, stared down at my shoes, and walked up the stairs to the open door. As I walked in Hue was holding the baby in her arms in the kitchen, patting her gently on the back. Mai was in the middle of the room.

"You sit here." She pointed to the bed. I now had several neighbors standing beside me, all of whom I knew, but I was only able to give an awkward smile of acknowledgement. Dao was standing there with her arms folded and an understanding smile on her face. Everyone else was straight faced. No one acknowledged me. People I had laughed with and shared food with. I couldn't really blame them.

I thought back to the time I had bought a new television and brought into the apartment. It was like a new year's celebration. Everyone came. I felt so good about bringing this little bit of happiness to all of them. Our place became the meeting place for all the girls. We had a television. I had two, three, four girls every night in my apartment, chattering away, sitting on the floor, laughing at their soap operas, drinking iced coffee. I was their hero. Now, times had changed. Family was serious to them.

I sat on the bed with my back to the wall, and my knees up. Mai took Phuong from Hue and carefully placed her between my bent legs. I knew what I looked like as a baby from looking at photo albums my mom kept. Phuong looked just like my baby pictures. She was very light skinned with sandy colored hair. I couldn't help but notice her long slim feet. Mai saw that I was looking at them.

"Those are your feet. She look just like you." Mai sounded angry. She had a right to be.

Phuong gave a silent yawn and stretched. I held her hands for a moment and when I looked up everyone was standing as close to me as they could get. Facial expressions hadn't changed. I was speechless and looked up at Mai.

"Can these people go away?"

Dao heard me and shooed everyone out of the room. "Mai, will you come to America?"

"Jim, I don't leave. My family is here, and I won't leave my family. I can't leave my family. You stay. How come you don't stay."

We had been through all this before.

"Mai, things are changing. I can't stay here forever. Americans won't be here forever. I just know it. Things are not good here. Americans are mad and they want us out. It's all crazy now. You have to come with me to America. I want to leave as soon as I can. You won't leave?"

Mai looked me straight in the eyes. "No," hesitated, "I can't."

I looked down at little Phuong. I then made a decision that would haunt me the rest of my life. I stood up, cradling Phuong, and handed her to Mai.

"Mai, I can't stay. You must come for the sake of the baby." Mai looked considerably upset.

"Ông bà cua chúng ta nói rất đúng, tất cã ngùoi Mỷ nghỉ nhu nhau."

"What are you saying?"

"You Americans are all the same. My ancestors were right."

I could see the hatred in her eyes. How could I blame her? I couldn't. I put my head down, as stubborn as she was, turned and walked out the door. We were both right, we were both wrong. No one could think of hindsight. It didn't exist. There was only the here, and now. We were not even close to the age where hindsight would ever hit us. This would be bad for Phuong.

In July of 1970 I would leave Vietnam for good. I wrote my mom and told her I was leaving Saigon. I did not say I was coming *home*.

There was no fanfare when I left, no party. I went around the office and said my goodbyes to some of the secretaries. I solemnly got on the plane and didn't look back. I didn't have the sense of panic like when I left in October 1968. Then I knew that I had to return. Return for Mai. All I felt was failure. I was too young to know how handle it, too young to know what to really do. It had dawned on me that I had no family to give me their years of wisdom. Dad was dead, mom just wanted her baby home, John would never change, and Bob was just too far away.

Now, I just knew that I had failed. My mind was afloat between two worlds. One that I had known for four years, and the one strange new world that awaited me within the next twenty hours. I was just numb, and out of energy, thoughtless, soulless. I heard no one and said nothing to anyone. I paid no attention, just stared into blank space. I couldn't see Mai, couldn't see Phuong, just pure dark nothing. It was like my bottom had been cut open and my entire soul just dropped to the floor. I hated myself, everything. I thought of the day I had to shoot Duke, and my dad in bed hearing the gunfire.

The plane rumbled down the tarmac, lifted off, and I just closed my eyes. I had run a four-year marathon and felt like I came in dead last. I was no good to anyone. I thought back to October of '68 when I couldn't wait to get back to Saigon. I didn't even get any joy from that thought. It just didn't matter anymore at that moment. Way too much stuff rushing through my mind. Way too much to make any sense of any of it.

Chapter 24

As the plane began its far-off descent towards SeaTac Airport, I could see dark clouds filling the sky ahead. I was groggy, and uncomfortably restless from too little sleep. I began to peer out the window, rubbing my eyes with my knuckles. As the plane broke through the clouds, I could see the vast greenery around Seattle. It was overcast, as usual, and it looked wintry, even though it was early July. Droplets of rain were forming on the window, and large puffs of grayish clouds sped by.

It left me cold. I didn't want to be cold, physically, or mentally. I had felt no better about myself during the entire flight. I was like a grasshopper who had foolishly stepped into a spider's web, unable to shake myself loose. Exhausted, confused over what it was I had done. I could put no meaning behind it all.

Where was the sun? Where were the blue skies? Where was Saigon?

"Ladies and gentlemen, we'll be landing in Seattle in approximately 10 minutes. Make sure your seats are upright and your seatbelts are fastened. The temperature in Seattle is 67 degrees with light rain. We hope you've enjoyed your flight."

Sixty-seven degrees? Cold. I continued to look out at the dreary surroundings, not able to focus on the beautiful greenery that was Seattle. Raising an index finger, I made a line through the moisture that had formed on the window.

The wheels of the plane jolted the plane as they hit the slick runway. I didn't know who would be there to greet me. I knew my mother would be there but was uncertain of other family members. Would those who argued so strongly against me going back to Vietnam two years ago care that I had now returned? Did I care if they cared? No, I didn't. Strangers could have picked me up at the airport. It simply didn't matter. I wanted to be nowhere.

I grabbed my pack from the overhead and got in the slow line of passengers that were departing the plane. There was no feeling of belonging at that moment. No joy, nothing.

I put one foot in front of the other and peered at the back of heads in front of me. What was waiting ahead for me, anything? I deserved nothing. Would what was behind me ever go away? Would I fit in here in this unfamiliar country? Questions with no answers. I was beating myself up.

As I walked up the ramp towards the terminal, I tried looking over the heads in front of me. I spotted my mother off to the side, and saw my sister-in-law, Carol, standing next to her. No one else. I was glad there was no one else. I was simply not in the mood, lost in my own self-pity. Welcome home. I walked toward them expressionless, feigning a slight smile.

My mother was crying tears of joy, and Carol had a big smile on her face. Mom hugged me and I half-heartedly hugged her back while looking over at Carol to offer a weak, tight lipped smile, then a separate hug for her.

Carol had always been one of my favorite people. Never a complainer, always a live, and let live kind of person. She was very nice, and had always treated nana, my mom, with great love and concern. She had been the patient caretaker for my aging mother.

As we walked towards the baggage claim my mother wanted to hold my hand, but I couldn't. I could still hear her telling me, "…but she's Vietnamese."

This was not the time for this flashback, but I couldn't put this thought out of my head. I expressed that I was really tired, even though I had restlessly slept most of the flight from Saigon. This might excuse my silence. I thought of Phuong's feet. Just like mine. Just like mine.

Rain drenched the street as we stepped from the terminal. Water was dripping hurriedly from the parking lot overhang. I tightened my grip on my luggage as the cold, damp air hit me. The rain was falling steadily as the wind blew droplets off passing cars. I shivered slightly, as I had no jacket, and was wearing a short-sleeved shirt.

"Jim, you should have a jacket. Is there one in your luggage you can put on?"

"No, Mom, jackets are not needed in Vietnam. I'll be all right."

I don't even remember saying 'hi' to my mom. Had I even greeted her? I couldn't remember.

"I know, I know, but you should have a jacket on, or you'll catch cold."

I was just a few months shy of my 24th birthday, and here was my mother babying me only a few moments off the plane.

I didn't need this right now. Mai's face flashed before me. She was alone with our child. Eight thousand miles away in a war-torn country, and I'm being babied.

"Mom, I'll be all right." Carol sensed the tension and changed the subject. "Bob is working right now, or he'd be here. The car is really close by, so we'll only be in the drizzle a minute."

My mom and I haggled over who would get in the front seat. I wanted to be in the back, by myself, but she kept insisting I get in the front. I don't know why the front seat held such status, but it was now a bone of contention. I wanted no issue, and hurriedly opened the back door, flung my pack in, and got in the car.

Mom turned to me once in the car. "It's so good to have you home finally. How was your trip?"

"Fine but tiring. Is the weather always like this in July?"

"Well, we get quite a bit of rain. I love it. Keeps everything so green." Mom seemed very happy.

"I'm going to have to get used to this. I haven't been cold in four years."

"I want you to get a jacket when we get home, and I want you to start wearing it. You hear?"

I turned my head and looked out the window. Rain, cold rain, dreary skies, thick dark clouds. It would take us two and a half hours to drive the 90 miles north to Bellingham. The weather never broke, the clouds got thicker and darker. By the time we were at the north end of Seattle the rain was coming down in buckets, pounding the windshield relentlessly. The windshield wipers strained to do their job.

I had put my head back and closed my eyes. I wasn't tired, just couldn't talk. I was in shock. I heard my mother say to Carol, "I bet he's tired. He looks awfully thin."

217

Who were these people? What was I going to do? I had no job. I would not be getting up in the morning to go to work. I had sent some money home, had it put in the bank, so I'd be okay for a while, but what was I going to do with myself? How was I going to get over this hump, this despair and failure that I was feeling? This loneliness. This is the way I felt when I was leaving home and going to basic training. Except, the home I had left yesterday was Saigon.

I knew no one. I had to go through the process now of acquainting myself with everyone again after four years. Nieces and nephews who had grown, brothers and sisters-in-laws who had gotten older, a mother who had gotten her wish for her youngest son to return to her. Would I be a grown man who had returned, or still a teenager in their minds? Who would have changed the most? Them, or me? Would they even notice?

Would I? I was asking myself questions that I didn't even care what the answers were. I needed to get drunk, is what I needed.

As we drove into Bellingham my mother told me we would be having dinner at my brother John's house in the evening. In the meantime, we would go to her small house on Walnut Street, where I could unpack and rest. I was in no mood to see my oldest brother, but I didn't register a complaint.

Bellingham was a small college town, home of Western Washington State College. Moss grew on the north sides of the roofs of the houses from the continual dampness. Mom's house had natural wood floors, and a small potbelly fire stove in the corner of the living room. It was quaint and very neat. My mother had always been an immaculate housekeeper.

"Your room is right here."

My room? This was not my house. I walked in and threw my luggage and backpack on the bed. There was a small wicker chair in the corner, a chest-of-drawers, and a small circular woven rug on the floor. Piled up in the corner were boxes, one on top of the other.

"Those are your things that you ordered and had sent home. I put them over there. Never opened them."

"Oh, I had forgotten about this stuff."

I had purchased a reel-to-reel tape deck, stereo receiver, speakers and a turntable from the Army Air Force Exchange catalog in the Cholon PX. I had sent them home when I was still in the Army. They'd been sitting in the corner almost a couple years.

"If you guys don't mind, I'm going to crash for a while. Where are the pictures that I sent home?"

My mom answered, "They're in a shoe box in the top of the dresser."

Carol smiled and waved goodbye. "Bob is probably home now. We'll see you this evening for dinner. Have a nice rest."

"Okay Carol, see you later." I sat on the bed and took my shoes off. The hardwood floors were cold on my feet.

"Do you need a blanket? There's extra blankets in the closet."

"No, I'll be all right, just need to sleep for a couple hours."

"Here, let me get the blanket for you." Mom started for the closet. "Mom, no blanket please, I'm fine."

"Oh, I know, I know, but let me get it anyway."

"Mom! Please, just give me some time to rest here by myself. I'm fine, I'm not cold. I'm not even taking my clothes off."

My mother went into the closet, took out the blanket, and placed it on the bed. I picked up the blanket, walked back to the closet and put it away.

"You're going to catch cold." I said nothing and sat back on the bed. My mother walked out of the bedroom and shut the door.

I sat with my hands between my legs, bent down, and put the shoes back on my cold feet. Pictures. Where were the pictures?

I walked over and opened the top drawer of the dresser to find the shoe box, leafing through the photos one, by one. There was one of me on convoy with the First Infantry Division. There was a picture of me being decorated for heroism back in '67. Hah! One of John Prahl and me making faces during training at Fort Benning, Georgia. Good old John. Wonder what he did when he left in '67? Ah, my buddy Per mugging for the camera, that big Viking grin on his face. I missed the guys.

I kept looking through all the pictures until I got to the last one. Hmm? No pictures of Mai. I had sent home dozens. I went and opened the door to the bedroom. Mom was in the kitchen busying herself making food.

"Where are the pictures of Mai?" She looked startled.

"Mom, the pictures of Mai? Are they in a separate box or something?" She looked down at the food and continued, "I threw them away."

"You threw them away? Why did you throw them away?"

"That was then. You're home now. I didn't want them around. I just thought it was the best. All that is behind you."

Behind me? I was fuming mad but stunned to silence. How could anyone think Vietnam was suddenly beyond me once I stepped onto American soil? I thought back again to my mother exclaiming, "She's Vietnamese."

I just stood in the doorway not knowing what to do. I wanted to scream. I turned and shut the door and leaned up against it, wide awake in my anger. I had to get out of here, but to where? Saigon? Jesus, I just left, now I want to go back again? What have I done? It might as well have been a million miles away. I went and sat on the edge of the bed, my hands shaking. The ghosts of Vietnam were with me. I sat on the edge of the bed until I was called to go to dinner.

I was still in a bad mood over the pictures. Seeing my brother John and his wife Liz again was stressful for me. John had raised his fist in my face two years ago when I had broken the news that I was returning to Vietnam. He was a man that couldn't control his own life but stepped in and tried to control everyone else's life.

When he saw me, he gave me a big bear hug, and acted as if I had never left. Liz gave me a big kiss on the cheek. She was always sweet with me and just all around nice to everyone.

Bob and Carol showed up, and I was glad. Bob had always been an understanding and caring soul. He was the complete opposite of our older brother.

"Hey, Jimmy, good to see you, good to see you." Bob gave me a big hug. "How was your flight?"

"Long, long. Too much time to think."

There would be the customary small talk of relatives back east, and new babies that were born. I sat quietly eating my meal not responding much, feeling very edgy being around these strangers. It was surreal. Food went into mouths, forks moved up and down, lips moved, and people talked over one another.

There was always tension between my brother Bob and John. John was a conditional person and was rough on Bob having been generous with him, but always placing conditions on his generosity. I could recall how angry he had gotten at my brother after giving him a boat. Bob needed money later, sold the boat, and was angrily accosted by John. How could Bob have sold something that John had given him? Didn't he appreciate it? I had always thought if you gave something to someone it was theirs. If they wanted to give it away, or sell it, it wasn't anyone else's business. The thing just didn't belong to that person anymore. John looked at this as a violation of his kindness.

You had to love and cherish what he gave you…forever.

We had been sitting at the table about 30 minutes and I couldn't take any more of the catching up that my family was giving me. Admittedly, I had more than a couple beers. My brother John was getting sloshed drinking large glasses of white wine. My brother Bob had remained quiet, sipping on his iced tea while eating.

Dessert, apple pie, and ice cream was now being served by Liz. It dawned on me that I hadn't had ice cream in four years. Hadn't had apple pie either. I laughed at the irony of this most amazing American treat.

John looked at me, "What's so funny?"

"Ah, just realized that I haven't had apple pie and ice cream in almost four years."

"Well, whose fault is that?" The room stood still. Nobody was moving, everyone staring straight ahead. I tapped my fork on my plate and didn't respond.

John stared me down. "You mad now?" Jesus, this guy could go off easily.

I said nothing, wiped my fork off, and dug into the scoop of ice cream that was slowly melting down the side of the pie. I closed my eyes and savored the sweetness of vanilla and apple.

"Ummm, Liz, this is good." Everyone started to nervously eat their dessert. John got up and came back with another glass of wine. It was time I spoke.

"How was Vietnam?" John dropped his fork on his dessert plate and wiped his goatee with a napkin. I repeated it.

"How was Vietnam? Bob jerked slightly and gave an opened mouth wince.

I looked around at the faces. Bob looked at me uncomfortably, then down at his food. Carol gave a sensitive smile of understanding. John looked upset. Mom just turned and stared ahead. All that could be heard was the light patter of rain on the picture window in the living room.

"That's over now." Mom said.

"Well, it might be over for you, but it sure isn't over for me. Four years of my life, and I haven't heard one single squeak out of anyone since I got here about how I feel. Does anyone care? Has it crossed anyone's mind that perhaps you should ask me what happened? I didn't leave here yesterday. Four years, and not one of you ask me how was Vietnam? Anybody want to know about Mai, my daughter? Anybody? Anybody want to ask a question about their niece, or grandchild? Does anybody know the little girl's name? You know, this isn't Monday, and I didn't just leave Friday.

Bob looked across at me and shook his head slightly. He wanted me to stop. "Hey, let's go out back. I gotta have a smoke anyways."

He got up from the table and walked to the back door. I sat there momentarily, not sure of what I had just done. Everyone sat silently and fiddled with their food. I looked over at Carol and she gave me and understanding smile. Perhaps I had spoken too soon.

Perhaps the stress and magnitude of the sudden change in my life had overtaken me. Perhaps I should have just shut up. I excused myself from the table and walked out the back door.

Bob was standing in the small enclosed yard smoking a cigarette. "You never did take up smokin', huh?"

"No, never did."

"Hey, man I was going to ask you, honest. I just didn't get the chance. I should have said it right off the bat, but I know how John and mom felt about the whole thing and didn't want to start a mess. I know this must be a culture shock to you right now, having been in the war and all."

"That's okay Bob. I started the mess all by myself. If anyone messed everything up, it was me."

"You wanna go get a beer? Come on, do us both good. Things are probably too hot in there right now."

"Let's get drunk."

"Well, you perhaps, but there are some people who have to go to work in the morning." Bob looked at me and must have seen a look of loss on my face.

"Hey, brother, just kiddin' with you. Let's get out of here. You gotta car? He paused again, taking in my lifeless expression.

"Just kiddin' again, just kiddin'. As the seagull said, let's get the flock out of here." We both walked back in the house. Liz was carrying dishes back into the kitchen and gave me a quick good-natured nudge as I passed her. Bob grabbed his jacket off the coat rack.

"Jimmy and I are making a run out. We'll be back in a few."

John was furious. "Jesus Christ, you just get home, eat our food, and out the door you go? What bullshit!" Mom tried to intercede.

"John!"

"Ah, bullshit, go, go on!" He threw his napkin down and got up from the table and walked to the kitchen.

"Sorry." I said as I walked towards the door.

"Jim, you need to put a coat on, or you'll catch a cold." Bob reassured mom that he had an extra work coat in the trunk, and he would get it for me. I could hear John in the kitchen. With him upset I'm sure he was going to take it out on everyone who stayed behind. That was his usual modus operandi. If he was upset, everyone else would have to be upset right along with him.

Bob opened the passenger side door of his car for me. Now Bob drank about a beer a year. So, this was going to be interesting, but I really appreciated him rescuing me.

Being a college town there were lots of little coffee shops and small quaint bars, with pool tables and dart boards. I chose the bar over the coffee shop. We sat in a dimly lit corner near the juke box. There were only a handful of people in the bar and most were gathered around one of the three pool tables.

My Girl, by The Temptations was playing in the background. "Hey, Jimmy, you guys used to play that song."

"Yeah, I hated it. Man, we must have been asked to play that song three times a night. Over and over, ugh." We both laughed.

"You think you're going to get back into a band?"

"Nah, I haven't forgotten how to play, but man, after being away from it for so long, time has passed me by."

Bob ordered a pitcher of beer. "Well, how was it?"

"How was what?"

"Vietnam, you jackass." I started laughing.

"Ahh. Well, I can't remember. There are so many things going through my head. Honest to god, seems like it was a hundred years ago. How could that be? I was there yesterday. You know I'm really uncomfortable being here."

"Well, we can go to a different bar."

"Bellingham, home, you jackass." Bob started to laugh. He knew what I meant but played the straight man. Some of the pressure was starting to leave me. Bob had broken some of the ice. He never had much to say, but he had a dry sense of humor that I appreciated.

"Nothing feels right. Nothing has felt right since the plane lifted off the runway in Saigon."

"What the hell happened with Mai?"

"Well, she wouldn't leave her family. She said we Americans would be there forever, so why didn't I just stay? She's probably right, too. But it was just in my mind that I just had to leave, but now I wonder why? What was the rush? Now that I've left, I want to go back. Is that screwed up, or what? Christ man, I'm messed up."

"Yeah, that's not making much sense. Sounds like guilt talkin' to me. What about your baby?"

"Guilt? What do you think this gigantic 'G' tattooed into my forehead stands for? Geez, I don't know. I really fucked up. Bob, my mind is spinning with so many mixed images and messages I can't even put thoughts together. I can't make any sense of anything, or myself. I guess I'm taking that out on everyone else right now. Phuong looked just like a Stewart." I took a swig from my beer.

"I feel like a complete failure."

"Well, geez, Jim, you aren't that. You've seen a lot. You've grown up a lot, I'm sure. Things in life happen. You know how naïve you were before you went there? Shit, you'd run out of gas and call me telling me you had car troubles. Car troubles, can you imagine?"

"Four years. You've been gone four years in a war. Hell, I wanted to see the world when I was in the Air Force and got stuck in Bangor, Maine for my entire tour. Can *you* imagine that? Bangor, Maine? You've seen Vietnam, Thailand, Hong Kong, what else? You gave it a shot and you can't beat yourself up over it. Jimmy, you went back and tried. You didn't even have a job lined up when you went back. How crazy was that?"

"Pretty damned responsible of you, if you ask me. You did what a lot of people would not have done. Man, you at least tried. You went back to get her, and she didn't leave. What can you do? Huh?"

"But did I try hard enough? My daughter is there. Mai is still there. You know me. I'll wear this with me the rest of my life if I don't get some help. You know mom threw away all the pictures of Mai. She was sending letters to mom and everything, and just like that, in the trash. Geez, what am I saying? I guess I threw her away too. I threw away my daughter."

"Well, Jimmy, unless you jump on another plane, I think it's done. I mean, I understand it's emotional, and you'll need some time to adjust. You can't adjust in, what, the few hours since you've been home? Don't beat yourself to death over this. I'm gonna say it one more time to try to get it through that thick Stewart head of yours. You went back. You went back to Vi-et-nam. That registering with you? From what I recall everyone was either trying not to go or trying to get home. You went back and tried. Beat yourself to death if you want, but it gets you nothing. I really don't know what to tell you about Mai, and Phuong." Bob refilled my glass.

"Did you kill anybody?" Bob took another swig of his beer. "The way I shoot?" Bob started to laugh.

"Bob, never fired my gun."

"You're shittin' me, right? Geez, all I see on the news is fighting, and people being killed."

"Well, even during the second Tet offensive, never got into a situation where I had to shoot. I can't explain it, can't justify it, it was just my fate. I was lucky."

"Yeah, remember when pop got you your first shotgun? You used up about six shotgun shells trying to knock one little squirrel out of a tree. How far away were you from it? Twenty feet?"

"Yeah, I remember that. Sure, stunted the growth of that tree though. How many tree limbs I kill that day?"

Bob and I both got drunk. It took him two beers and me a couple of pitchers. Bob looked blurry eyed at me.

"You're gonna have a Vietnam vapor trail comin' out your butt following you around. You know that don't you? Bob chuckled at his own humor.

I fiddled with my glass and let out a laugh. "Is it showing already?"

"Smells like diesel fuel, Jimmy." Bob chuckled again, satisfied at his jokes. The beer was getting the best of him.

Bob looked at me solemnly. "I'm glad your home, Jimmy. I know that doesn't give you much solace right now, but time will heal this. Let's get out of here, I gotta go to work in the morning."

As drunk as I probably was, I was the most functional. I drove Bob back to John's house. It was 11 p.m. The porch light was on, and I could see heads through the living room window. Everyone but John was sitting down and talking when we walked in.

"Where you bad boys been?" Liz said with a playful grin.

"Well, getting drunk, actually. Bob is shit faced on two beers, and I'm right behind him after a couple pitchers. I drove because he had become delusional. I've also called the cops on him, and they should be here any minute, so you'd better get him out of here." Bob poked me on the shoulder.

"Carol you should drive this drunkard home and never let him out of the house again. He's a danger to mankind, women, and children everywhere. Me, I'm going for a walk." I gave Bob a hug.

Mom protested, but I assured her I would be all right. Her house was only a few blocks down the street. I asked her to just leave the front door unlocked. I had to pee anyway, and the park across the street looked like the perfect place. I walked out the front door into the cool night.

A sudden sprinkle of rain began to tap at my feet as I crossed the street to the park. The pine trees were as thick as a Vietnam jungle. Not even the streetlights penetrated the thick foliage as I stepped from the sidewalk onto a narrow dirt path that led to the middle of the park. I could vaguely see a merry-go-round and some monkey bars near the center. Sitting on the merry-go-round I leaned back and looked up through a small gap in the trees. I could see one star.

"What have I done? The star twinkled back at me.

"Are you going to haunt me all the days of my life?" I shut my eyes. My head was spinning from the beer.

I got up and walked to a clump of bushes and took a pee, not even looking around. Heck, who was in here this late at night except me, and that one star?

I realized how lonely I was, how sad I was. Self-pity. How could I have self-pity with my child sitting in Vietnam?

I walked back to the merry-go-round and looked up through the gap. The star was gone.

"Hey! Where'd you go? I wanna talk!"

The star had left me as quickly as I had left Vietnam. It was only fair...payback. I walked out of the park and to my mother's house. The front door was unlocked, and the living room light had been left on. The door to my mother's bedroom was shut. I quietly walked into my bedroom, turning off the light, and fell across the bed, hugging the pillow close to my head. Spinning, spinning, spinning, and then sleep.

I could hear light tapping on my door. "Jim."

I thought I had heard a girl's voice. The light tapping continued. "Jim."

I righted myself up onto one arm, and half awake, looked at the bedroom door.

"Jim, its Mai. Can you open the door?"

Then came the pounding. Several times...loud pounding. The door finally splintered, and I saw a large pointed metal bar violently poke through the shattered wooden frame.

I sat up quickly in the bed and looked around. A soft light peered through the window drapes. Looking over, the bedroom door was still closed. It wasn't shattered. I could see light filtering through the window blinds. All was quiet. I had been dreaming. Dripping with sweat, my head fell back onto the pillow. I looked through the drapes of the bedroom window to my left. Out of the window I could see one star…one star. It blinked at me. I closed my eyes and fell asleep.

I woke up with a headache, remembering the dream from last night. I wondered how often it would repeat itself. My mom had breakfast made, but I wasn't hungry.

"You have to eat. You're way to thin."

"Mom, I was a lard butt when I was young, and I plan on staying thin."

"You look sick, you're so thin."

I put on a sweater and headed for the front door. "Where are you going?"

"Jogging."

"You have to eat."

"Please don't make me food. I can feed myself. I have a really funny eating schedule, and only eat when I'm hungry."

"Well, you need to eat. I'll put it back in the refrigerator, and you can have it "Okay, that's fine."

Trying to shake the cobwebs, I started a slow jog. Lightheaded, I was unable to jog 50 yards, stopped, and began dry heaving last night's beer. I'd just take a tour of Bellingham, walking. The dream came back to me. I remembered the one star.

I was a wreck. Coming back from four year where I had a full time job, my military experiences as well as all I had learned about the black market and how the world worked Bellingham was, well, dull, boring, full of hippies who didn't know much except for what their college professors told them. Protests with talking points for this party or that. I filled up a backpack and walked out the door. I was going to hitch hike back to Maryland. This decision was again met with much disdain and crying. Nobody knew what I felt, went through and thought I should just suck it up, get a meaningless job and move "forward." I was not ready for that.

I got a ride all the way to Wisconsin. So much for me enjoying the sights and sounds as I trekked the highways and byways. After Wisconsin it wasn't so easy. A short trip with a hippy made me realize why I never smoked marijuana or did drugs. His car was filthy, half-smoked blunts sat on the middle console, he reeked of the stuff, but I was already in the car and maybe it would get me 20 miles closer, if he didn't drive off the road and kill us both. The conversation was straight out of Woodstock, with "dude" this, "far out" that all the while his speech a bit slurred. But he was a happy fellow, I guess. As we drove along the freeway a pigeon flew in front of the car and smacked hard against the windshield.....BAM!

You would have thought he had killed Jimi Hendrix himself.

"Fuck man! Oh, shit!" as he took his hands off the steering wheel and tried wiping the blood off the other side of the windshield. He grabbed a half-smoked blunt and tried lighting it as his hands shook violently. All the while, "fuck, shit", but no "far out." He was falling apart. I didn't feel so bad about myself at that point. I just wanted o-u-t of this drug mobile before the cops pulled him over for swerving all over the road. Guilt by association I didn't need.

"Hey man, pull over, pull over."

Almost taking out a telephone pole and still in great distress the car came to a stop.

"Fuck man, did you see that? I killed it. Me, I killed it"

"It was a bird, man. Things like that happen."

"No, no man, this was death. Like Vietnam. You know those killers think nothing of this kind of shit. I want just peace! I can't live with this!"

The guy was actually crying. This is the son-of-a-bitch that probably spit on the troops as they got off planes. I gave him the finger as I opened the door and got out.

"Hey, fuck you, hippy." I got a few more uneventful rides. A Volkswagen bug full of college type girls picked me up and I squeezed in between two of them in the back seat. They giggled and seemed to be enjoying themselves immensely. I almost felt like they were going to kidnap me and make me their sex slave. Once in Amish country, nobody would pick me up. I called my friend Chip and he drove out and got me and took me to his place. But nothing changed. Home did not have the home feel. It was still Vietnam for me. I lasted a week and flew back to Washington state.

I was able to get up to Vancouver, B.C. and spend some drinking time with my buddy Per. He was sort of drifting aimlessly too, at the time. He had been out of the Army almost a year. We spent many an hour in the pubs drinking copious amounts of brew. Strangely enough, Per missed Vietnam, and wanted to go back. It was strange how it could take hold of you, and not let go. Other than that, we didn't discuss it much. We drank.

I had taken the money I had saved and bought a new car, a 1970 Mazda R100. I had dreamed of owning an MG Midget, having seen it in some of the magazines I read in Vietnam. British racing green was a must. Unfortunately, the pictures betrayed how small the midget was. I could squeeze myself into it but getting out was going to take an act of congress. I opted for a more conventional, but still compact car, the Mazda.

I got the road trip bug and drove back east to visit Chip again. I was still the 'ramblin' man'. Things were happening fast, but nothing of substance, nothing to settle me down. I had thought I might be able to hook up with a band and get back into music, but I found out that I was too rusty. Times had changed, and I was not ready to take on the changed complexity of the music that had occurred in my four years absence. So, back to Bellingham I went. Bottom line, my music career was over.

I offered Chip a deal. If he'd drive with me back to Washington, I would pay his airfare back to Maryland. He agreed.

"Let's drive it straight on through, nonstop."

"You're on."

Fifty-two nonstop hours later we arrived in Bellingham, smelly, and tired. Chip liked Bellingham so much he decided to move out. He joined Per and I in many a drinking session.

I dated a nice Chinese girl from Western Washington State College, majoring in History. Her folks even owned a Chinese restaurant in town. She was a great girl and we got along fine, but I was having problems. My mother had even revisited the past one day when she asked me.

"Jimmy, you aren't going to marry her, are you?"

"I don't know. Why do you ask?"

"Well, she's Chinese."

I had to get out. I would do anything. I couldn't stand Bellingham. Cold, damp, dreary, rain almost every day. I packed my bags and headed south. South to the warmth of San Diego, California. It was 1973. I just left everything behind. Sort of like Vietnam, but I felt better about this.

Chapter 25

I spent the next 17 years drinking too much. I look back on those years, and even though I had good work, security, I was never happy with myself, and never forgave myself about leaving my daughter. But, living in a fog of self-pity, I never did anything about it. The alcohol probably had as much to do with my lethargy regarding this as anything. Alcohol always made those who weep, weep more. I was never a fall down drunk but drank enough to kill the pain. I did not blame the Vietnam War. I flat out just blamed myself.

I got a job with the Department of Navy as the Security Manager at the Navy Exchange at NAS Miramar, San Diego. Even went down to Puerto Rico to work there for a year. When I returned to the states, I got a job with the San Diego City Schools Police Department as a Community Services Officer. After a couple years there, I went to the police academy during the evening hours, and all-day Saturday, and continued to work as a CSO during the day. My marriage was falling apart. I was 43 years old.

In 1989 I decided to give up the bottle. I could not get through the rigors of the upcoming academy hung over. With my head cleared I also began to search for my daughter. Every government agency that was available was of no help. During this time, I found the love of my life. I first saw Carmen standing next to a copy machine at Valencia Park Elementary School in southeast San Diego. She was beautiful. It was truly love at first sight for me. I just knew that this woman was somehow **sent to me**. I would learn later in life that she **truly was a gift from God**. It was December of 1989. We started talking. She too was in a crumbling marriage.

What did we start talking about? Phuong.

I spent all of 1990 in the police academy, had gotten myself in tiptop shape, and had a new love in my life. I was still searching for

Phuong, but the search was slowed down by my divorce, working full time, and trying to finish the academy. The academy had added Monday night, Wednesday night, and Thursday night to my 40-hour work week. Saturday was an all-day training session.

After the academy I was supposed to be hired as a sworn police officer by the school district, but budget cuts put a hold on that. Knowing I wasn't getting any younger, I applied for, and got hired by the Brawley Police department in the desert of southeastern California. Sixty miles from Yuma, Arizona and about 20 miles north of the border of Mexicali, Mexico. As luck would have it, Carmen's family lived in Mexicali. It was perfect.

Carmen and I were married in 1991 and we were deeply in love. I had never met a woman quite like her. She was so full of faith and love for me. She supported the search for my daughter 100 percent. But, more than that, she loved me unconditionally. She truly gave me renewed spirit.

In 1992 PBS contacted me and did a special on me titled "The Children of the Dust." This is what the Amerasians (half American/half Vietnamese) were called by the Vietnamese. They were shunned by the Vietnamese as nothing but the 'dust of life'. It is estimated that approximately 50,000 children were left behind in Vietnam. I had no idea how Phuong had faired, but I wanted to find her. I had been told that many, if not most, of these children (now adults) had made it out of Vietnam. The only problem is they were spread out all over the world. If she had made it out, I knew there was a chance for me. A chance for us.

The local Brawley newspaper and even the Los Angeles Times did an article on me about my search. With Carmen's full support I continued my hunt for Phuong.

I was sort of a Johnny-come-lately when it came to new fads, and only got my first computer in 1995. With the internet at my hands I began a continuous, daily search of web sites and information available through search engines. It was painstakingly frustrating and slow.

I had located addresses and emails of a several dozen Nguyen Thi Mais. Letters and emails were sent. Other supposedly helpful government agencies were of no use. I struggled along with this for years, losing hope, facing mounting frustration of the complexity of finding a little girl who would now be an adult, married, kids of her own (my grandkids). Plus, who knows where she was living?

I had started drinking again in 1992. In 1995 I decided, again, that I should stop. Carmen was surprised as she told me, "I've never even seen you drunk."

I knew better. In my eyes I was a functional alcoholic. It was after the police department Christmas party of 1995 that I never looked back. I woke up hung over the next day, and it was just crystal clear to me how much of a waste of time and productivity drinking was for me. I did try to rationalize my way out of my decision. What would I drink when we went out for pizza? What would I drink with Mexican food? The answer was simple…anything but beer. My drinking days were over, once and for all. I stopped again, cold turkey, without a second thought.

I had also been blessed with having a friend in my life since 1978 named Mick Hurst. Mick and I had met in 1977 when we both worked for a large retail chain in San Diego. We hit if off instantly when the topic of baseball came up. We could spend hours talking about who was the better hitter, and why we both hated the Yankees.

Later in life Mick became a deacon, and whenever I needed 'counseling' he was always there bringing me back to reality. In 2000 I was baptized by his hands in a large Lutheran Church in Escondido, California. I started drinking again, but this time, only for that evening. Mick and I, along with his wife, and Carmen, each had a small glass of red wine in celebration of my rebirth.

It had to have been the rejuvenation brought on by God coming into my life, along with Carmen, my shining light, that things began to click for me. I started to make some headway in my search.

Through the internet an Amerasian girl out of Baltimore put me in touch with a man from Denmark who worked with the last remaining Amerasians still in Vietnam. I emailed him and he gave me the email of his office in Saigon. I emailed the office and was in contact with his case worker, Nguyen Phuoc. It took a couple days, but Phuoc went to my old address at 195 Troung Minh Ky Street. Ironically after 30 years there were people still living there who remembered 'MP Jim'. It was unbelievable.

Phuoc emailed me and told me that Dao had married an American around 1972 and was now living in Colorado Springs, Colorado. Mai's whereabouts were unknown. Then I read the last part of the email that made me ill. ."..your daughter died of the sick..."

It was impossible! Certainly, he was mistaken. What was 'the sick'? I did not want to believe what I read. I urgently emailed him and wanted to know more, but he didn't know how to explain it in English. I didn't believe it. Surely this was a miscommunication.

He told me that Dao's last name was Koonce. Not a common name. I did a Google search and came up with one hit on the name, Brian Koonce, in Colorado Springs. Finally, I had a name, and a telephone number. This had to be her husband. I nervously dialed the number and waited for several rings. Brian answered the phone. After a brief explanation he asked me, "Do you want to talk to Dao?"

My eyes welled up. I had done it. Through the grace of God, through the support of my beautiful wife, I had done it. Thirty-two years later I almost had my answers.

I heard Brian's faint voice as he handed the phone to Dao. "It's Jim Stewart, from Vietnam."

Dao was excited. "Jim, how are you? How did you find me?" I explained it all to Dao. It *was* like talking to a lost sister. "Dao, is it true? Is my daughter dead?"

There was silence for a moment. "Yes, Jim, she got killed in 1977."

"How?"

"She was at her grandmother's in Phan Rang. She was playing with her best friend. They ran into the street and were both hit by a big truck and killed. They were buried together. I'm sorry to have to tell you this."

Silence.

"Jim? Jim!"

"Yes, I'm here." I was thinking how ironic it was that the only death I witnessed in Vietnam was a young girl run over by an Army truck, and now my daughter.

"Jim, Mai lives in Dallas. She got married and has four kids of her own. She came here in 1991."

"Did she marry an American?"

"No, no, a Vietnamese man."

Dao spent the next several minutes explaining to me how she had left Vietnam in 1973. She had traveled the world with her husband Brian, a career, but now retired soldier. She had even spent time in Germany. Dao told me she would be calling Mai to let her know, and that Mai would call me tomorrow. I told Dao I would be at work, gave her my work hours, and told her I would be talking to her later.

"Jim, I'm so sorry about this. She was a beautiful little girl. Jim?"

"Yes, thank you sister Dao. I'm sorry, too. Talk to you later."

I didn't quite know how I was going to explain my feelings to my wife. I had always hidden my emotions from people, except for the war. Carmen had always been puzzled at how I could strike up a conversation with another man I had passed in a mall that might be wearing a cap with an Army, or Vietnam war type insignia on it. The stranger would always respond in kind, and we would be able to chat for several minutes about where we had been, when we got out, and what we had done. We'd then shake hands, or casually salute, and part ways. It was hard for me to explain it to her. I had heard many say before me, "It's a Nam thing."

Carmen always understood my search for my daughter. She had been a loving and giving wife to me and was the best mom in the world to our two kids, my step kids, Danny and Janine. They had been with me since they were babies, Janine two years old, and Danny not quite five. I had always tried to raise them as my own and was called "dad" by both of them. I never referred to them as my step kids, but as my kids.

Carmen had made herself busy while I spent about an hour on the phone with Brian and Dao.

"Well, how did it go?"

"Well, my daughter *is* dead."

It must have been the look on my face as Carmen came to me and gave me a hug. I was still in shock from everything happening so quickly. I filled Carmen in on all the events told to me by Dao.

"You know, Carmen, all this started to happen so quickly after my baptism."

"Yes, I know, I know. What now?"

"Well, Dao is going to call Mai, and she is going to call me tomorrow at work"

I was conscience of Carmen's feelings. Although she had always been completely supportive of my search for Phuong, I needed to be sensitive to her about Mai. I didn't want her to be jealous.

"I'm just going to talk to her about Phuong. Maybe I can get some pictures of her."

"I understand. It's late, you have to get up at six, so we'd better be off to bed." I can't explain it, but I slept soundly.

I had gone to work a little anxious. This was a woman that I had not talked to for 32 years. Mai had been my first real love. It was hard for me to even fathom that I would be on the telephone with her, and even harder to believe I had actually located her. She would also tell me about Phuong. What was I going to say to her?

My day at work was typical. I was senior patrolman and was kept busy. It was the 0730 to 1530 shift, so there was lots of radio traffic, the school to patrol, and of course, taking calls from the public. The day was going by fast, but in my mind, I still had no idea what I was going to say when I got her call.

"907, station nine."

907 was my badge number and station nine was our dispatch center. This was how all our radio calls went out.

"Station nine, 907." I responded.

"907, you have a long-distance call waiting. Do you want me to take a message, or hold the call?"

This was it. It was around 1700 hrs. (4 p.m.) as I was pulling into the back-parking lot of the police station.

"Station nine, please hold the call, I'm 10-19" (at the station).

I would need a quiet place to talk, so I couldn't go into the squad briefing room. There was just too much foot traffic in and out. I unlocked the side door of the station and entered the hallway. I hurriedly walked past the sergeant's office and up the stairs to the break room, hoping nobody was on break. If so, I'd have to politely

237

plead with them to leave, so that I could talk in private. They'd understand.

Many of the officers knew about my time in Vietnam. They also knew about my daughter. I spent a lot of time answering typical questions from some of the younger officers who were curious about the war. It was a subject I was well versed in, and never got tired of talking about. But now my stomach was just full of knots.

I walked into the break room and saw that the telephone was sitting on the table in the middle of the room with one single red-light flashing. The room was empty. I sat and removed the phone from the receiver.

"Hello."

"Hello." A female voice answered.

For some dumb reason I said hello again. "Don't you know who this is?"

I was speechless. "Hello? Jim, its Mai."

"Mai, how are you?"

"Fine." I now recognized her voice. It hadn't changed after all these years.

"I can't believe I'm talking to you. Were you surprised when Dao called you last night and told you I had called her?"

"Yes, it's been many years. I had wondered what happened to you, if you knew about our daughter."

"Well, I had only found out recently. I had no idea. Mai I'm so sorry. I never thought that this would happen. I'm so sorry about Phuong."

Silence.

"Mai, can you hear me?"

After a slight hesitation, "Yes, I hear you."

"Mai, was she a good girl?"

"Oh, yes. She used to sing a lot. All the other children loved her. She had many friends. My husband used to walk her to school every day. He would hold her hand and walk her. She was very smart, and always smiling."

"Your husband is a good man for doing that. I wish I could thank him. Mai, who did she look like."

"You!" I sensed some anger at me. "You!" her voice rising. "She looked just like you. Her eyes, her feet, everything was just like you."

Suddenly I was at a loss for words. I was drawing a blank. "Mai." What should I say next?

"You make me think back now. I'm very sad having to think about her and that day." I could tell Mai was weeping. I couldn't ask her about the accident. It was too painful. I had hurt her enough.

"Mai, I haven't forgotten. I began searching in 1989, and it took me years to find you."

"How come you never came back to Vietnam?"

I didn't know what to say. Mai had a great question. Why hadn't I gone back.

Vietnam fell to the communist in 1975. I had followed the fall of Saigon in the newspapers. I tried to answer that question in my head before I talked more, but there was no answer. I stumbled for something to say.

"Well, I don't know. I guess after 1975 it was just too dangerous. I know that only a few years ago some of the G.I.s were going back. I don't know, I don't know. I just didn't." I was a little defensive with my answer. But I didn't want to offer any excuses.

"Mai, I came back in 1968 to get you, to bring you to America."

"Jim, you know I was too young. I was 17 when I met you. I didn't know anything, and it was not easy to just leave my family and country."

"Seventeen? I didn't know you were that young. Seventeen? We were both young and made mistakes. It was such a long time ago. Mai, do you forgive me?"

"No."

Her answer stunned me, but I don't know why. How could she forgive a man who abandoned his child? Yes, I was young at the time, and not very wise in the ways of the world, or adulthood, but other men had not shunned their responsibility. But, then again, most *had* walked away from their Amerasian babies. I had tried to find mine.

"No?"

"No, I hate you."

"You hate me?" This is not what I had ever thought I would hear. "Mai, I've never, ever had one bad thought about you, ever."

What did I know? How could I even come to understand what Mai had been through in her life? How difficult was it living under the communist when the American's had made Saigon thrive? How difficult it must have been to see her daughter dead in the street at seven years old. She had every right to hate me, but I still was not expecting her to say it so bluntly. There was uneasy silence on the telephone.

"Mai, I don't know what to say. I can only say I'm sorry. I know that's not enough. I too have lived with this every day since I left Vietnam. I know it doesn't compare with your pain, but I have pain too. My dream had been to meet her, her husband, her family, and my grandchildren. I would ask for forgiveness, and she would give it to me. I just knew that my daughter would forgive me."

907, station nine, you clear for a call?" It was my turn in the rotation to take a call for service.

"Mai, wait a minute." I'm sure she heard the cackle of the police radio over her phone. I had to get one of the other officers to fill in for me. I no sooner thought that when officer Caudill walked around the corner into the break room. He acknowledged me with a nod of his head.

"Hey, Jeff, do me a favor. This is a long-distance call, and I've only got a half hour left on shift. I'd like you, and Officer Torres to get together and take any calls that I might get. If it's an emergency I'll break from this, but I'd really appreciate it."

Jeff must have sensed by the look on my face what was happening. "You okay? Is that the call you've been waiting for?"

I gave him the thumbs up, so he understood.

"No problem I'll get Torres and we'll work it out. I'll tell dispatcher that you're out of the rotation, too." Jeff began to walk toward the door.

"Thanks man." I returned to the silence. I had lost my train of thought and grasped for something to say.

"Mai?"

"Yes."

"I don't know what to say about you hating me. I don't even know what to say about Phuong. It's been a long, long time." There was no answer.

"Mai, do you have any pictures of Phuong?"

"I have a couple. When the communist came, I threw away all the pictures of you, and most of Phuong's. If they caught me with pictures, they would have punished me. It was hard trying to hide Phuong from people. She looked American, and it was very dangerous. I had to go back to Phan Rang to my mother's house. Things weren't too bad there. I hid her for a while, but things got better."

"God, I feel so bad. I always thought I would see her. I always had hope that one day I would see her, that she would be beautiful, and she would not hesitate to forgive me. She'd just be glad to see her father." My voice was choking as I fought to hold back the tears.

"She always asked 'where's my papa'."

I began to cry, fighting back more tears. "Sorry, wait a minute."

I wiped my eyes and blew my nose in a napkin from the table. Mai continued. "I told her one day she would see you. I didn't know when, but that it would happen. She was young and that made her happy. She would get a big smile on her face and everything would be fine."

God, I had let her down so badly. Phuong wanted to see me. Even though she could not remember the time I had held her, she wanted to see her dad. God, this was awful. I felt about as low as a human being could feel.

"Dao told me you didn't leave Vietnam until 1991?"

"Yes, my family and I escaped on a boat, and went to the Philippines. After that we came to the states."

"Mai, do you have any other children? "I have four."

"Four? Lots of babies."

"Jim, you had another baby?"

"What?"

"You had another baby."

"What? I don't understand." I had no idea what she was talking about.

"You had a son. Remember the last night we were together? I got pregnant. After about three months the baby died, and it came out on the floor. It was a boy and he looked just like you. Ask Dao. We picked him up and looked at him. He looked like you." Mai was softly sobbing as she spoke.

I again had no idea what to do or say. What could I do, or say? Two children, both dead. I don't think we spoke for a minute. I envisioned Mai and Dao picking up my son. How old was Mai then? How long would that horror last for someone? Obviously long enough to make her hate me.

"God, Mai, I'm so sorry, I'm so sorry. I had no idea. This was not supposed to end like this."

I thought back to that last night when she had come into my apartment. She had told me I was going to make her pregnant. Why didn't I stop? Why didn't I use my head? Why didn't she hit me, shove me, make me stop? Perhaps because she loved me and missed me.

"Mai, I don't know what to say to you, I don't have any idea. I put you through a lot, and that's not what I wanted to do. I never thought that Phuong would die. Why would that happen? Many fathers never looked for their children. Those children want to find their fathers, and I look for mine, and they're dead. I don't blame you; I hate myself too. I wish you didn't hate me, but I understand why. I just wish you didn't."

Mai's voice softened. "Do you remember everything?" Mai had stopped sobbing. "Do you remember the shrimp and rice I would make you?"

"Yes, it made me fat. I remember you used to get mad at me because I would get mad at you for getting mad at your sister, Hue. You used to yell at her a lot. How is Hue?"

"She's fine. She has three children. She is in Phan Rang with my mother. My mother is getting very old and I might go back and visit her.

"I would like to see where Phuong is buried."

Mai's voice softened. "Are you going back to Vietnam?"

"I would like that, yes. Mai, can we talk tomorrow?"

"Will you call me."

"Yes, I'll call Brian's house. I'll call you tomorrow, okay?"

"Okay."

"Talk to you tomorrow, bye."

"Bye."

I hung up the phone and put my face into my hands. I rubbed my eyes hard with the knuckles of my hands and wondered if it was obvious that I had cried. I just needed to put my sunglasses on, that would do it. It was now 1715 hours; my shift was over. I'd spend the next 15 minutes getting my gear out of my patrol car, and that would be it for the day.

I walked downstairs and around the corner towards the back door, past the briefing room, and saw that the evening shift was already there milling about. Some were writing reports, some just joking around. Jeff saw me and got up and followed me outside.

"Hey, how'd it go?"

"Man, I don't know Jeff, I just don't know. I haven't talked to here in 32 years, and really it was like she was right there with me. Her voice hadn't even changed. Better English," I said jokingly, "but it was a strange, strange feeling. I'll fill you in tomorrow. I have to get my stuff out of my car and then head home. I'm really drained from this. Take care, and thanks."

"Yeah, I'll see you tomorrow. You gotta tell me everything. I'm interested."

"I will, I will, promise."

I went to my patrol car and got in behind the wheel, unlocked the shotgun from the rack. I placed the shotgun across my legs, and just sat in the car wondering if what I had just been through was real or imagined. A son, a daughter, both dead. It was real. Was I paying for my sins?

Chapter 26

It had been two days since I talked to Mai on the phone for the first time. I was still struggling with the news, and the guilt that I was carrying. It just wasn't right. I still did not want to believe that Phuong was dead.

This was *not* the way it was supposed to turn out. I had searched, hadn't I? I did what many vets did not do. I wanted to find her. I was trying to make up for deserting my child, wasn't I? But I was too late. I knew I was being punished. That's what I got. I doubted my baptism, doubted and blamed God, even though I knew that this was not His fault….this was mine.

My daughter was dead because of me. She had been abandoned…by *me*. I had always envisioned seeing Phuong for the first time, perhaps with a husband by her side and children, my grandchildren. She would have a big smile on her face, glad to see her father. She would look like me, but her real beauty would come from Mai. She would run up and give me the biggest hug and would not care why I left. She would only relish that she had found her father, and we would cry, something I've been unable to do in my life. I've always hidden my feelings, those tears of guilt and shame, always internalizing. I would cry out of happiness and relief. I was completely inconsolable.

Carmen had left to go visit her mom in Mexicali, and had taken the kids, leaving me alone with my thoughts. She had been so supportive, and was as sad as I. I had always joked with Carmen, who is fourteen years younger than me, that I always wanted to be like her when I grew up. Such a rock-solid person, a person of tremendous faith and love.

I was sitting at the dining room table drinking a cup of coffee, feeling cheerless, and obviously depressed. I couldn't get Phuong's death off of my mind, and even visualized how it had happened, and how awful it had to have been having myself seen the young girl hit by a truck and killed in Dian back in '67. How awful for Mai and her family to have to pick this gift from God up from the ground. I saw the dead face of the girl killed in Dian. Is that what Phuong looked like in her death? How ironic that I witnessed this death, only to have my own daughter killed in the same way.

I had my chin on my hands, and my eyes were shut. Suddenly I felt movement, a wave of air blow gracefully by me. It was the same feeling you get when you're waist high in the ocean and gentle surf passes above your chest. I sensed I wasn't alone, opened my eyes and placed my hands on the table. It was then I heard a voice...a young girl, clear as day.

"Don't worry papa, everything is okay."

Alert now, I looked around the room. It was her voice. It had to be. She was in the room with me. I stood up, looked right and left. Nothing. My knees weakened and I collapsed back in my chair. I had heard her. My breath shortened. I wasn't dreaming. My daughter had come to me. In my despair she had come. Had she been looking for me too? Was she just waiting for the right time? Or, had she always been there, perhaps pleading with me to change my ways, to look for her, to find out, to find her through God?

She was forgiving me. She had always forgiven me. I had done the most awful, demonstrable thing to her by abandoning her, but here she was. I began to cry, but not out of despair or depression. My daughter had come to be with me...as fresh and as soothing as the current of air that had gently passed by me. I felt peace. I wanted more. I wanted her to appear before me.

"Phuong." It wasn't a question, but a statement. Silence.

I looked down at my dog, Rocky. I saw Duke. Sitting there next to him, tongue out, panting quietly waiting for a command. He looked happy, peaceful, unconcerned, like he was home. He looked down and licked his paw. I looked at Rocky.

"Duke." Softly. He looked up at me.

"Rocky, did you hear that?" He sat up and crooked his head to the side. "Did you hear that, boy?" I wiped the tears from my cheeks. "Did you hear Phuong? She was right here, Rocky. Did you hear her?"

God had not abandoned me. No, He had not. I would never doubt again. I had been led to this point for a reason. Thirty plus years to this point. But, I was finally where I should have always been....home. I was home. These four walls, the smell of the coffee, this roof over my head. ***This*** was home. I missed my wife. If only she could have been here to hear this. Phuong had shown me home. Phuong had brought me peace. I knew she was safe, no more harm, no more tears. She had been there all this time, waiting, waiting for me. She was an angel that I had not believed in before.

How would I explain this to anyone? I knew Carmen and Mick would understand completely. I had always lacked their unfaltering faith, their ability to forgive. Their ability to believe. I would have to share this moment with both of them. I would tell them everything. Why? Because it was real. An angel from Vietnam had spoken to me.

It was so quiet. Had Phuong simply come in the back door, spoken to me, and then left through the front? No that would have been impossible. I would never feel alone again. If I could just see this angel that was with me, her giant white wings gently fluttering, keeping her afloat, and watching down on me.

Had I now a guardian angel? She had been there all this time. An angel waiting for me to become a better person. Waiting for the right time to reveal herself. I thought of my baptism, the faith my wife and friend had in me during my search, finding Mai, and talking to her. Phuong's timing was perfect. She was no child of the dust.

Now, it was all up to me. Would I continue to carry this to my grave, or would I free myself? Forgive myself, finally? Phuong had given me the answer. I had no choice. I had heard Phuong, and I also needed to see Phuong. There was only one answer for me. Each day would be lived as if it was my last. Most people, given that circumstance, would probably party, drink, and do things to meet secret lustful desires. Not me. I would live each day as if the next I would meet my Maker, the Fisher of Men, and Phuong. My angel of Vietnam.

I thought of my dad. Would God have seen fit to have opened his arms to this weary child of his? Of course, he would. Then I would see my dad again too. A healthy strapping dad, pitching me a baseball.

Mom would be by his side, and Duke too. Yes, each day as if it were my last.

I would have lots of help. The ghosts were gone, and an angel was at my side. I would also go back to Maryland one more time.

Dad was buried in a spotless, tree-filled cemetery outside of Newark, just east of the Delaware/Maryland state line. A wrought iron fence surrounded the cemetery, the grounds slopping gently down from the side of the roadway. It was rather small, and it was full of markers and tombstones dotting the landscape. It took me only a few minutes to find his place of rest.

Frank Allison Stewart, Sr.
1914-1964

The headstone should have said more. I think anyone would have wanted more said. How could we leave this world with just a name, and dates on a slab of stone? There was no perceived legacy for anyone to draw from. How could anyone know about him from just a name, a date? There should have been a few words to let people know who Frank Stewart was.

The small sapling that I had remembered from his funeral in 1964 had grown and offered him shade from the hot summer's day sun. A gentle wind had picked up as I stared down at the spot where my father rested.

"Hey, pop. How's the deer hunting in heaven? I nervously chuckled at what I had said.

"Well, I guess there isn't any, huh? Bet you and Duke are having fun though chasing those rabbits. I've been off to war. Yeah, me, can you believe it? I bet you can. Bet you been watching. Been all over and seen a lot. I've done something's I'm not really proud of pop. Wish I had you there to snap that belt of yours at my behind. I needed it. I know you never wanted to hurt me, you just wanted me to learn, that's all. I understand that now. Well, I wish you were still around. I bet we would have been good buddies.

Heck, I'm just like you. That ain't bad, is it?

"I guess you know mom died. Get this, she never dated." I laughed softly. "All those years. Mom wanted her ashes spread up at Mount Baker in Bellingham. She loved it out there. You would have liked it. Lots of good huntin'. She would have come back here, but, you know, it's where you go afterward that counts. Hope you two are together."

A woodpecker landed on dad's tree and began feverishly pecking at the bark. He paused to eye me warily, and then got back to work pecking away.

"Hope you're doin' okay. Pop I never told you, but you're a good man. Want you to know that's what I think. I was too young then to tell you, and a little scared. Oh, there's nothing for you to be ashamed of. You got sick, that's all. Nothing you could do. I'll always remember you as that big hearty fellow who coached me in little league. Pop, watch after Phuong for me, will you? I know you will. She's a good girl. I'm sure you've found one another."

The wind had stopped. A leaf fell from the tree and landed at my feet. The leaves were starting to turn, and soon the cemetery would lose its green foliage to a bright array of fall orange, reds and yellows. The woodpecker stopped his pecking and anxiously looked at me again.

"Pops, gotta go. Hey, I know you loved me. You didn't have to say it. Me too. I want to thank you for being my dad. Keep an eye on me, would ya. Tell little Phuong to do the same?" I gave him a salute, turned and walked to the top of the hill.

As I plan my trip to Saigon I know now that I would not be going home but leaving home. Home wasn't even Elkton, and it surely wasn't Bellingham. Elkton, dear to my heart, was the wonderful paradise that I played in as a kid. Elkton was a place where I suffered through the death of my father.

Vietnam was a place of new experiences and adventure. It was a place where I had been very lucky. A place that taught me great respect for those who gave their all, many to never return. Many, including myself, changed forever. Vietnam was a place where I fell in love for the first time, and where I learned the lessons of commitment by returning, as well as the irresponsibility of my youth that led to tragedy for my daughter. No, home was with Carmen. There was nothing I could do about the past. I couldn't carry it with me anymore.

In fact, if I were to change just one thing in my past, I would not be where I am today. I would not have the gift of Carmen in my life.

Did I come home a man? Perhaps, in some ways, but also a confused and angry person who carried failure with me for many years. Only through God giving me the gift of Carmen, the gift of my friend, and baptism, was I able to start healing.

Through Phuong's own voice I realized that she is safe, that she forgives me for the tragedy of Vietnam. I know now that I *will* **see** the angel that is my daughter, not just hear her. I know that one day she will reach up and take my hand, look up at me and smile.

I've talked to many, many Vietnam Vets. Most of them say their time in Vietnam was the most profound time of their lives. All had different experiences. Most of us, aging as we are, can't remember what we had for breakfast yesterday, but can remember almost every day of our tours over there. It's hard to explain, but Vietnam is stuck to us like glue. That's not necessarily a bad thing.

I was there three months shy of four years. I arrived an inexperienced 19-year-old, a few weeks short of my 20th birthday, and returned home three months shy of my 24th birthday, a success, *and* a failure. Not unlike the story of many men's lives.

I thank the Army and Vietnam for all those experiences, good and bad. I thank all my buddies for putting up with me, and I guess they would ask the same of me today.

Thanks to my spiritual advisor, Mick Hurst.

I beg forgiveness from those that I hurt. For those that I helped, I wish I had done more.

I thank my beautiful wife, Carmen. The absolute love of my life. Solid as a rock, full of faith. Thank you for supporting me in the search for my child, my daughter Phuong. I love you very much.

Thank you, Phuong, for speaking to me…I heard you. We will see each other one day. We'll sit down under a tree with a woodpecker overhead, pecking away. We'll just sit and talk. That will be nice.

There's more to tell here. More that will happen upon my return to Vietnam. Perhaps next time.

Special Thanks

Thank you, Lisa Painter. You inspired me to keep going and your friendship, and input have been immeasurable.

Thank you Phuong Le for calling me "Big Brother", your translations, and reminding me how kind and forgiving the Vietnamese people are.

Deacon Mick Hurst, the man who baptized me. Thanks for putting up with me for all these years. Your friendship has been a great reward of life.

Thanks Doug Dragert, from the "Deuce", for refreshing my fading memory. And my beautiful wife Carmen. Am I glad God brought you into my life? For sure.

Fading memory has caused me to take liberty with some of the names of people, places, and incidents. Some names of people have also been changed.

See my website at <u>www.militarypolice.com</u>